Praise for *Winding Paths to Success*

"From each career episode of the Japanese women protagonists, emerge universal lessons—double down on your core skills, turn disadvantages into advantages, and seize the right opportunities all while never losing empathy for others. Nobuko Kobayashi brilliantly captures the essence of long-term career and life success in *Winding Paths to Success*."

—**Dr. Otto Schulz**, board member of the German
Sustainability Award Foundation

Winding Paths to Success

Winding Paths to Success

Chart a Career in Uncertain Times

Nobuko Kobayashi

WILEY

Registered Office(s)
John Wiley & Sons, Inc., 111 River Street, Hoboken, NJ 07030, USA
John Wiley & Sons Ltd, The Atrium, Southern Gate, Chichester, West Sussex, PO19 8SQ, UK

Editorial Office
The Atrium, Southern Gate, Chichester, West Sussex, PO19 8SQ, UK

For details of our global editorial offices, customer services, and more information about Wiley products visit us at www.wiley.com.

Library of Congress Cataloging-in-Publication Data is Available:

ISBN 9781394157990 (Cloth)
ISBN 9781394158003 (ePDF)
ISBN 9781394158010 (ePub)

Cover Design: Wiley
Cover Image: © Soul Art Workshop/Adobe Stock Photos
Author Photo: Courtesy of Masakatsu Nagayama

SKY10059201_110223

CONTENTS

PROLOGUE

The genesis of this book began with a simple idea a couple of years ago—we are close to the 40th year anniversary of the enactment of the Equal Employment Opportunity Act in 1985, a significant milestone in the history of gender equity at work in Japan, which prohibits discrimination against women by their gender at the workplace. The women who entered the workforce in the years following the enactment are now approaching retirement. Before it was too late, I decided to capture their natural voices to chronicle their individual career journeys, which run parallel to the progress of women's status in Japanese society. The original aim was to reflect on how far we have come and what still needs to be done in leveling the playing field for working women in Japan. This project took shape as a series of articles published on *Japan Times* starting in late 2021 under the title "Women at Work," 12 of which are included in this book.

As I started interviewing these women, all in their 50s and 60s and still professionally active, it dawned on me that their stories carry a larger story beyond that of battling the odds as a gender minority—their stories apply to any ambitious individual building purposeful long-term careers in uncertain times.

Whereas men in their cohort largely followed pre-established paths, say by diligently climbing the ladder of a large corporation with consecutive positions handed down from the previous cohort man-to-man, women have been compelled, or in some cases liberated from, the norm to forge their own trajectories. By necessity, they were resourceful, creative, and agile about how they approached their career. The minority status as professional women compelled them to ask themselves why they worked and how to position themselves in a man's world.

Today, we live in an increasingly uncertain world. The traditional notion of a "good job" has been upended or remains elusive at best. Large corporations no longer dependably provide lifetime employment. Unthinkable when I started my career in the late 1990s, start-ups and professional service firms are popular destinations for top college graduates, who have lost their fear of switching employers several times during their career. The external environment of volatility continues to accelerate, leaving us unsure of what anchor on which we can base our career. The more opportunities and mobility we gain, the more instability and anxiety rises—this is true for both men and women at the start or middle of their career.

These are the reasons why stories of senior Japanese women who successfully navigated the uncertainties and disadvantages are relevant as lessons on how to build a meaningful career today. Their motivation for work professionally, which was not a given when the society expected women to stay at home following marriage or childbirth, is inspiring; their ingenuity to carve a space for themselves in the male-dominated world is insightful. In a world accepting of more diversity in all dimensions, every one of us is a minority in some way, bestowed with its upside as well as its downside.

Three core themes emerge from the 12 life stories. One is the women's sense of purpose—it can be as clear as a near-religious calling in the case of **Mami Kataoka**, director of the Mori Art Museum; she believes in the power of art to change the world. Or it can be more subtle, such as the altruism inherited from her mother in the case of **Ayako Sonoda**, the founder and CEO of Cre-en, a boutique sustainability consulting firm. **Noriko Osumi**, professor and vice president at Tohoku University, finds joy in uncovering topics, in academic research as well as in real life, overlooked by others but that quietly scream for investigation.

Although career purpose is a part of life, it is not necessarily an omnipresent driver—**Yuki Shingu**, CEO of Future Architect, a major IT consulting firm, expresses little regret for jumping off the rails of a promising ascent to answer to a then higher life priority: to be close to her ailing father.

Second is the strategic positioning of oneself. **Miyuki Suzuki**, former president of Cisco Asia Pacific, Japan, and Greater China, fully leveraged her outsider-insider status to transform Cisco Japan, and **Ryoko Nagata**, an independent nonexecutive director and retired executive from Japan Tobacco, deliberately chose the not-so-mainstream—noncigarette—businesses within the conglomerate to ensure freedom.

It is encouraging that Japan, with traditional Japanese companies at its economic core, has evolved over the three so-called lost decades starting from the early 1990s to be more accepting of outside talent such as external hires into senior positions. Two protagonists, **Chikako Matsumoto**, executive officer at Sumitomo Mitsui Trust Bank, and **Masae Yamanaka**, vice president at Panasonic Connect, found homes in blue-chip Japanese companies in the later phases of their careers.

Last, resilience emerges as a key tenet across many women's careers. **Yasuko Gotoh**, a career bureaucrat turned independent nonexecutive director, described her blackout of memories of her 20s and 30s when strong gender bias at work shattered her self-confidence. Gotoh never gave up work, however—her faith in people prevailed and eventually increased awareness of gender equity worked in her favor.

Masami Katakura and **Makiko Nakamori**, female certified
public accountant (CPA) pioneers, have led long careers in
the professional service work of audit, a sector known for its
conservativism. One of them stayed to eventually lead an audit
practice for a Big Four firm in Japan and the other opted to trailblaze
a path as a career independent nonexecutive director. These are
unconventional outcomes for CPAs of their generation, a result of
patiently crafting their own space within the profession.

Resilience enables careers to meander in unexpected ways and
to eventually course-correct—what seems like a detour may end up
accreditive in the long run. In the case of **Yumi Narushima**, head of
the Extracurricular Education Company at Benesse, a mid-career five-
year stint as principal of a private girls' school expanded her horizon
as an educator, consequently benefiting her as she returned to her
mothership of Benesse.

To give context to each woman's story, I have included in each
chapter two supplemental opinion columns, originally published
by *Nikkei Asia*. These writings aim to provide an in-depth analysis
of gender equity at the workplace in Japan. I hope these writings
will help readers understand the cultural background of our
12 protagonists.

The women are diverse not only in their sector but also in their
approaches to life. Some had families, others not. The course of their
careers has been dynamic in their implicit and explicit purpose, which
evokes the 16th-century Parisian motto, *Fluctuat nec mergitur*: "tossed
but not sunk." It is from these real-life tussles that I hope the readers
will take away lessons for their own journey of career building in
these uncertain times.

1 Levity

It is a universal phenomenon that the IT sector is male dominated. Multiply this IT condition with working in Japan—a conservative society that stubbornly favors men in mainstream roles and women in supporting roles—and you can imagine the painful double penalty that a woman in the IT sector suffers in Japan.

Yuki Shingu, CEO of Future Architect, a major domestic IT consulting firm, elegantly overturns this assumption. It certainly helps that Future Architect is a relatively young firm with a progressive culture. Rather than emulating the conventional tech-savvy IT engineer archetype, Shingu has consistently played to her strength—differentiating herself early on through her management skills.

Shingu is also nontraditional in that she abruptly left her job and eventually returned to her employer mid-career. True to her own life priorities rather than the world's expectations, Shingu, at the height of her career, quit to care for an ailing family member. Her decision, and her return prior to her eventual ascent to the CEO role, sent a strong message to employees about the new relationship between them and their employer: your life is yours to design; the company will back you up. Shingu stresses the importance of customizing one's career path through dialogue between the employee and employer.

It is a tale especially refreshing in the Japanese work context. Future Architect, unencumbered by the heavy weight of history—the founder is in his late 60s and still presides as CEO of the group company, Future Corporation—is an anomaly for being thoroughly meritocratic. Meanwhile for most Japanese employers, achievement of gender equity is an ambitious goal. As I argue in my column, "Japan—Almost Silent over #MeToo," the #MeToo movement never caught on at full volume in Japan, not because of a lack of sexual harassment, but rather due to the strong and implicit hierarchy between gender roles that stifles full-on confrontation.

Shingu was chosen for her merit. At the same time, having Shingu at the helm of Future Architect carries weight in the male-heavy tech industry. In my column, "Why Having Women at the Top Is Not Enough," I define *womenwashing*, where businesses appoint a small number of women in visible positions to feign gender equality. This is a tempting "solution" in the face of a large gap between the goal of gender equity and the status quo. But it is worth noting that having women sprinkled at the top is not enough, on its own, to achieve gender equity. The pipeline must be balanced at every level of the organization.

Yuki Shingu, CEO of Future Architect, Inc.

1971: Born into a family running a motorcycle maintenance shop in Nagasaki, Japan

1989: Future System Consulting Corp. founded by Yasufumi Kanemaru as a new type of consulting firm that integrates corporate strategy with IT strategy[1]

1994: Graduated from Nagasaki University with a degree in mathematics

1994: Started her career at City Ascom, a subcontracting systems integrator in Fukuoka

1998: Joined Future System Consulting as an IT consultant

2002: Future System Consulting is listed on the first section of the Tokyo Stock Exchange.[2]

2007: Company name changed from Future System Consulting to Future Architect, Inc.[3]

2012: Left Future to take care of her ailing father full-time

2014: Joined Microsoft Japan as lead of cloud promotion for public sector

2017: Returned to Future as the second female executive officer at Future Architect

2019: Promoted to president and chief executive officer, Future Architect, Inc.

Yuki Shingu Makes a Brilliant Comeback to IT Career After Nursing Care Leave

This article was originally published in the Japan Times *on December 27, 2022, and has been modified for the purpose of this book. The information contained in this article is correct at the time of publishing in the* Japan Times.

Imagine a vibrant 40-year-old woman suddenly forsaking a prestigious full-time job in Tokyo for "family reasons." She is a rising star at a major IT consulting firm. She disappears for the next two years, immersed in nursing her ailing father in Nagasaki, 960 km from Tokyo. Only after her father's passing does she resurface, eventually assuming the top position of the company she had left at the age 47, far earlier than the average age of 58.5 for CEOs of listed companies in Japan.[4]

This story sounds implausible, particularly in the rigid and seniority-based, not to mention gender-biased, Japanese work environment, where one hapless step off the mainstream career ladder—full-time and committed for life—means an irretrievable derailment.

Yuki Shingu, the 51-year-old president since 2019 of Future Architect, a major domestic IT consulting firm, proves otherwise. And according to Yasufumi Kanemaru, 68, chairman of Future Architect and the group CEO and founder of the Tokyo Stock Exchange Prime–listed parent company, Future Corporation, Shingu's journey is "completely normal."

Welcome to the junior varsity team of Japan Inc. This lesser-known ecosystem of local companies in relatively nascent tech fields such as IT consulting is the much younger sibling of the long-time visible elder brothers in established industries ranging from trading companies to heavy machinery.

Within these younger companies, meritocracy, where women are treated no differently than men, and individually tailored work styles are the norm. Their management philosophy, such as found in Future Corporation, and the career path it enables, such as Shingu's, can teach the senior varsity players of Japan Inc., valuable lessons—for employers, that the pursuit of productivity and support of staff members' individual lifestyle are mutually enhancing, and for employees, that taking control of your life and work is important.

Shingu is the eldest of three daughters in a family who ran a local motorcycle maintenance shop for two generations—according to Shingu, "Nagasaki is too hilly for bicycles." She obtained a degree in mathematics from Nagasaki University. Explaining her reasoning for taking a different path, she told me, "we had no salarymen in my family. But before plunging into my family business, I wanted to experience corporate life to learn the ABCs of management."

The bubble economy had just burst before her graduation in 1994, signaling the dawn of "the glacier period" of recruiting, where fresh college graduates struggled to land full-time positions. It proved an extra hard time for women with four-year college degrees— employers preferred to hire women from junior colleges, which offer two years of tertiary education, to be in support roles at the office. Put bluntly, the four-year college women graduates were overeducated and were starting two years too late to be "the flowers of the workplace."

The unfriendly job market forced the young Shingu to be strategic in her choice of sector—IT. There, she could use her math skills to get ahead in programming, and it was a growth industry. As a bonus, IT transcended geography, which she thought might allow her to work anywhere.

Screening for companies with 200 to 300 employees, rather than established giants, made sense to her as the size felt closer to her family business. This targeted approach worked, and she had "many offers," among which she chose a subcontracting systems integrator, a bank subsidiary in Fukuoka, about 100 km from Nagasaki within her native Kyushu.

After three years of on-the-job programming, Shingu decided that she wanted to design the system directly for the client rather than subcontracting—which meant working for a general contractor.

Future System Consulting, the predecessor of Future Corporation, was founded in 1989 by Kanemaru, 35 years old at the time, who cut his system-integrating teeth by building large-scale programs for retail clients such as convenience store chains.

When Shingu applied for a Kyushu-based position with Future System Consulting, it was for a large local project on which "I bet the future of the company," recalled Kanemaru. "The project was the final hurdle before we could go public." They were commissioned to build a core system to be released in 1999 for a large department store with an, at the time, cutting-edge open architecture. Kanemaru himself played the role of project manager and was responsible for hiring staff.

"Kanemaru-san rejected me at first," said Shingu flatly. "I felt sorry for her" is how Kanemaru looked back on rejecting her on the first interview, "because I knew how brutal the project was. And to be honest, I was concerned she could be a drag." Shingu refused to give up, however. "That's when she showed her true colors," said Kanemaru reminiscing. "She called our HR and spoke to the people around me." Appreciating the "challenger spirit" in her, he finally caved in and brought the 26-year-old on.

The decision proved to be fortuitous for both sides. Yes, the work was demanding—"everyone was young (Kanemaru was 44) and worked till 2 a.m. every day." Recalling the work style, which would be condemned by today's work-life-balance standards, Shingu said she "grew so much" in her 20s. For Kanemaru, she was "a cheerleader with an ever-positive attitude."

"I wanted her to be a project leader early," said Kanemaru, which she became by her early 30s. She found her strength in strategizing and orchestrating the team—the role of a general on the battlefield—as opposed to being technically deep or in the trenches. "I played basketball in high school, where we developed a similar division of roles into strategists and technicians," Shingu explained. "We need both roles, of which a combination is important."

As consultants move up the ladder, they start taking on the sales role. Winning large, complex projects is the high road to respect. Kanemaru described Shingu as strongly sales oriented. Her first successful pitch was of her younger self to Future, undeterred by the original rejection. "She has a knack for building close rapport with the top executives," explained Kanemaru. When I pressed him on the difference of sales approach between himself and Shingu, he answered with a metaphor; "if I were a cannon, she would be a machine gun."

While her professional star rose, her family situation in Nagasaki took a darker turn. By the time she turned 40, her father fell sick (he was in his 60s)—it was when her parents started planning for retirement after closing the family motorcycle store. Shingu's mother struggled to care for her husband at home for a few years but increasingly depended on her eldest daughter. Shingu was bouncing back and forth between Tokyo and Nagasaki and was approaching her physical and financial limits. Her father was diagnosed with another serious health condition in 2012, which became the last straw.

"I had done all I wanted to do at Future by then," she recounted. "I had no regrets and some savings." At 40, she quit—"I was never so hung up about my career," she told me. "Whatever happens, I just know I can make do."

I asked Kanemaru if he had tried to convince her to stay. "On the contrary, I found her decision [to quit] quite natural," said Kanemaru. "We encourage all our people to customize their careers. We flexibly customize our company policies based on our employees' needs as well. However, with the remote work environment at the time, there was difficulty in satisfying the customers' needs and we understood that Shingu had to leave the company." Tomoko Sumida, global business strategy vice president for Future Corporation, another long-timer a few years junior to Shingu, was "both surprised and unsurprised" to learn of Shingu's decision. "The news came out of the blue. At the same time, it felt right—Shingu-san favors clear-cut decisions to muddling with the noncommittal options."

For two years, Shingu cared for her father full-time alongside her mother. After he passed away, she felt that she would try something new, rather than returning to the nest. It was 2014 and Satya Nadella had just been named global CEO of Microsoft when Shingu decided to join the company. "I learned a lot from Microsoft, who was determined to catch up in the game of cloud technology," she said, "particularly the growth mindset and clear-cut key performance indicators to align the large, global organization."

Kanemaru thought it was "positive that she experienced [something] outside [Future]." He also confessed to quietly wondering if the job of an account executive could meet her high motivation. Sumida, working closely with Kanemaru, bridged the communication between the two and enabled Shingu's return.

In 2017, Shingu returned to Future as the second female executive officer at the company, after a four-year hiatus from Future—two years in Nagasaki caring for her father and two at Microsoft Japan. "It was great to have her in the leadership," gushed Sumida, "having grown up within Future, Shingu-san represents mainstream—a woman leader with such legitimacy sends a signal of meritocracy and gender equality."

The tap on the shoulder for even higher recognition arrived in 2018. "We organized surprise entertainment at our 30th anniversary event in Hawaii," said Kanemaru, who emphasized that this was not a formal CEO selection process but framed as lighthearted fun for the staff. Eight internal candidates for the next CEO of Future Architect—the then-CEO was an industry hire from outside—gave a speech about their leadership vision, on which ground the staff of 757 members anonymously voted. "First, I wanted the staff to sense the possibility of a leadership change. Second, the vote served to sound out public opinion."

Shingu spoke about diversity, a change mindset, and partnership—the last being something she learned from Microsoft.

"Future is strongly self-reliant. But to achieve a greater change in the world, we must cocreate with clients as well as with competitors," she explained.

The employee vote did not put her on top, Kanemaru recalled. Four years of absence in an industry known for high churn had hurt her visibility. Plus, because Future was proud of its engineering prowess, popular opinion "preferred the techy type." Nevertheless, Shingu was one of the selected candidates to present to the board.

"After the board presentation, I mulled over the final decision," the founder told me. What was the decisive factor to pick Shingu over others? "I could trust her," promptly answered Kanemaru. "I knew she would consistently score 7 out of 10. I also wanted someone with flair—in terms of appearance, communication, positivity—at the top of the company."

Where the staff members gravitated toward the natural extension of Future Architect's persona—a techy CEO—Kanemaru saw a greater potential for complementary traits—less techy and more sales-savvy—in Shingu. However, what Kanemaru underestimated was the impact of a returnee being promoted to CEO. "People were shocked," he said, "and it gave momentum to the hiring program for our returnees dubbed Back-to-Future."

Shingu said that instead of Kanemaru, it was her husband, a former colleague from Future who had left the firm before she did, who pushed her to accept. "He is my mentor," said Shingu.

From Hong Kong, where he was working at the time, Shingu's husband sent her an itemized list of "what good you bring to Future as CEO," confident that she would do well in the role. He embodies the ideal partner of working women in Japan; for example, I gathered from my interview his support of dual surnames for married couples. In Shingu's case, Shingu is her maiden name, which she uses at work. Japanese law stipulates that married couples adopt one surname, which is most of the time the husband's name. Despite the legal stipulation, however, popular sentiment is more liberal, a majority supporting optionality in surname for married couples. (See Figure 1.1.)

Changes Shingu brought to the company as CEO since 2019 are "palpable," confirmed both Kanemaru and Sumida. Shingu instilled transparency by sharing real-time information with the executive officers and reshuffling the divisional leaders—"I wanted to shake up the entrenched organization, introduce fluidity," she said.

"She lifted the mood," Kanemaru attested, "and there are no more inner circles." Inclusive culture is a result of her careful observation. "My strength is to discover the hidden talent," self-analyzed Shingu, "rather than the self-promoters; the quiet and talented workers are the ones I want to highlight."

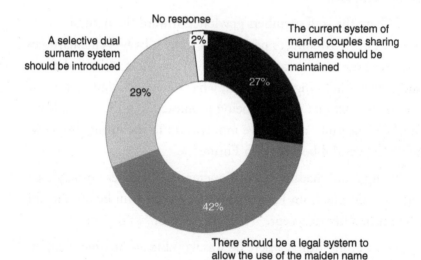

Figure 1.1 Public opinion on a selective dual surname system for married couples, *n* = 2,884 (2021)

Notes: Majority of Japanese support optionality in surname on marriage. Adapted from Cabinet Office (2021). 家族の法制に関する世論調査 (Translation: Public opinion survey on family legislation). https://survey.gov-online.go.jp/r03/r03-kazoku/index.html (accessed 4 June 2023).

Sumida appreciated Shingu's straightforward communication style, consistent with her younger days. "Shingu-san makes on-the-spot decisions with a clear rationale so the rest of us can move on quickly," she observed. For Shingu, priority is clear: "quality of the system and customer satisfaction are our top of mind. And its communication should be simple." And there is a bonus to being a woman leader in a male-dominated company, according to Sumida: "Sometimes it is easier for a female leader [like Shingu] to be straight up with a male colleague than it is for men."

The two years off work spent on family care was not lost on Shingu. The burden of care on the working population is a societal issue in Japan—over 95,000 employees left work due to family care in 2021, of which 75% were women.[5] (See Figure 1.2.)

"I am convinced that there will be more and more cases like mine," she told me. "Employers today must ensure the purpose of work and its enablement." Offering a client-facing professional a back-office track to accommodate certain conditions, for example, may be misaligned to their purpose. To this end, Future Architect offers a discretionary labor system, where a consultant can temporarily scale down both work and compensation to 60% while they, for example, care for young children.

Remote work, an option since its inception, helped Future Architect to weather the COVID-19 storm. The adoption accelerated under Shingu—recruitment under their "location-free" program[6] was deployed full-scale nationwide in February 2022, and as of October 1, 2022, 124 employees, including contractors, work "location-free" from Hokkaido to Kyushu, and are compensated equally as they would be in Tokyo. Some choose to return to their home region while others opt for their new lifestyle.

A woman born to a family running a motorcycle shop in Kyushu ends up leading a technology company of ¥18.9 billion[7] turnover in Tokyo, despite a major interruption in the middle

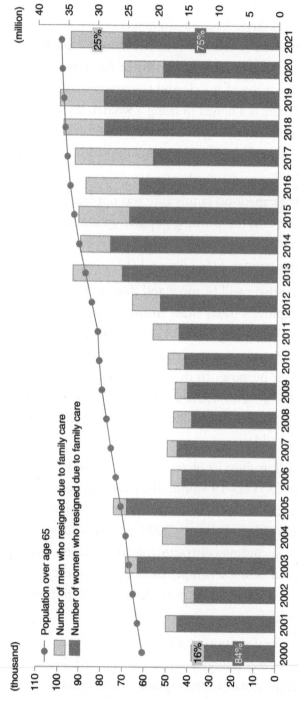

Figure 1.2 Number of people (thousands) who resigned from their job due to family care by gender and population (million) over age 65 in Japan

Notes: Women make up the majority of people resigning from their jobs to take care of their families, suggesting that gender roles are still prevalent.

Created by the author based on: Ministry of Health, Labour, and Welfare. (2022). Survey on Employment Trends. https://www.mhlw.go.jp/toukei/list/9-23-1.html (accessed 3 June 2023); Statistics Bureau of Japan. (2022). Population estimates. https://www.stat.go.jp/data/jinsui/ (accessed 3 June 2023).

of her career. When I marveled at its dramatic turnout, Shingu laughed. "I just carried on, and this is how it ended up, dramatic or not," she shrugged.

Shingu's story is based on a pas-de-deux only possible by juxtaposing two parties: the employer, Future Corporation, and herself. Future Corporation, however eccentric its process or lack thereof may seem with its "let's vote for the next CEO" to the conventional eyes, is progressive in its everyday meritocracy and respecting of the choice, including leaving and returning, made by its employees. Shingu is dedicated and strategic, firmly driving her destiny. Regarding equal engagement between the employer and employees, the junior varsity of Japan Inc., the young emerging tech companies clearly foreshadow the future for their more established counterparts.

Japan—Almost Silent over #MeToo

This column was originally published in Nikkei Asia *on February 23, 2018, and has been modified for the purpose of this book. The information contained in this article is correct at the time of publishing in* Nikkei Asia.

The global movement of #MeToo, the protest movement against sexual harassment, has spread around the world at tsunami speed since the first allegations were leveled against Hollywood producer Harvey Weinstein.[8]

As it has multiplied, #MeToo has developed in different forms in different countries. But where is Japan in #MeToo? The answer is nowhere, really, and that for me is troubling.

It is not as if Japan is some sort of nirvana, free of sexual harassment. But it does appear that Japanese women are extremely cautious about speaking out. And when they do, the public reaction is often very muted, in contrast to the storms generated in the US, in parts of Europe, and even in the emerging world, notably in India.

A few months before the first women complained publicly about Weinstein, Shiori Ito, a young female journalist, went public with claims that she had been raped in a Tokyo hotel room by a senior male television correspondent who had political connections.[9] She alleged the assault happened in May 2015 after a meeting in a sushi restaurant to discuss work opportunities. She felt dizzy, she said, and only recovered consciousness after the attack when she felt pain and realized what had taken place. The police investigated but prosecutors dropped the case, citing a lack of evidence. Last September, Ito filed a civil case against her alleged attacker, who has publicly denied her accusations.

My point in recounting these allegations is to emphasize that they received little publicity. The case has hardly caught the national attention in Japan, even with #MeToo roaring around the globe.

The contrast with other countries is striking. Britain, for example, has followed the US closely in emphasizing the protection of women in ways that at times seemed almost obsessive. However, in France, film star Catherine Deneuve put her name to a letter[10] condemning Anglo-Saxon "puritanism," though she later made clear she utterly opposed sexual "harassment." In India the #MeToo protests focused on the awful tragedy of child abuse, with researchers highlighting a 2007 government study that estimated that more than half of Indian children suffered from some kind of sexual abuse.[11]

It is not as if there is no sexual harassment in Japan. Far from it. The Japan Institute for Labor Policy and Training in 2016 published a survey showing that 29% of women have experienced sexual harassment at work.[12] That is higher than the 22% reported by Pew Research in a 2017 study in the US.[13] For full-time workers only, the figure rises to 35% in Japan.

The relative silence on sexual harassment in Japan, despite its in-your-face prevalence, can be partially attributed to the long-standing Japanese tradition of prioritizing group harmony at the expense of individual suffering.

But there is more—sexual harassment at work comes in many shades. Typically, cases in Western countries involve men with higher status taking advantage of more junior women, who are often climbing up the professional ladder. Women who have leveled accusations against Weinstein, including young actresses at the time of the alleged assaults, fit this pattern. In Japan, the claims voiced by Shiori Ito appear similar.

But in Japan, however, in addition to this "Western" or "global" formula, I observe two other patterns that tend to breed silence.

First, there are still two parallel corporate worlds—the male and the female. Strict gender role division is still a central feature of modern Japanese corporate life. Although the model is certainly not unique to Japan, it has lasted much longer in Japan than in the US or much of Europe.

Men in the workplace can take advantage of women of junior status—even though the women know that they can rarely aspire to promotion as managers. They will mostly remain in support or administrative staff positions. So why do they submit to the unwanted advances of senior males when they cannot hope for corporate advance? The answer is that some women, at least, feel that they can secure an ambitious and successful husband in this way.

There is here a blurred line between consensual relationship and sexual harassment. At what point does a senior male manager's assertive behavior toward a junior woman become harassment? Does it make a difference whether the woman is a subordinate in his department or works elsewhere in the company? At what point can the manager be accused of exploiting his position? To what extent is a woman inhibited from saying no because of corporate rules, which generally demand obedience to superiors?

There is also what I call "low-level" sexual harassment— unwelcome verbal banter. It affects people like me—"career women" who are allegedly on an equal professional footing with men. Almost everywhere, I hear comments from older male colleagues on a woman's appearance or marital status and questions such as "Why do you never wear skirts but pants to work?" Women generally respond with silence rather than claim sexual harassment. But that does not mean they have not taken offense.

Complaining is difficult. I have witnessed—at meetings of senior company executives—how such disturbing comments are casually brushed aside as light-hearted jokes. What can you expect when the leadership is 90% male? But such attitudes exasperate women and no doubt discourage some from seeking promotions.

This combination of gender stereotyping and juvenile joke-making contribute to holding back women's careers. Japan is an advanced economy, but just 13% of corporate managers are female, the lowest ratio among OECD countries.[14] A lack of senior female executives creates a lack of critical mass in challenging harassment.

The long-term answer is clear. Put men and women on an equal footing and harness the power of diversity. Promote equality at work and support family life with, for example, better childcare, so women are freer to advance their careers.

But what can be done in the meantime? Companies need to place a critical mass of women in groups that influence top managers on gender-related issues. These managers must make clear that there is zero tolerance for hurtful or disrespectful comments and behavior. Communication lines must be established so incidents can be anonymously reported and the alleged offenders confronted in private with the accusations.

Rather than talking vaguely about stopping sexual harassment, the government must start defining specific types of unwelcome behavior. If the workplace reforms by the administration of Prime Minister Shinzo Abe intend to make the factory and the office a better place for women, then women and men alike need to feel they are respected at work.

Last, women must realize they have the right and the responsibility to speak up against the inappropriate. Although #MeToo in Japan may never be quite the same sensation as elsewhere, Japanese people need to learn that silence about harassment does not eliminate harassment. Quite the opposite.

Why Having Women at the Top Is Not Enough

This column was originally published in Nikkei Asia *on March 8, 2021, and has been modified for the purpose of this book. The information contained in this article is correct at the time of publishing in* Nikkei Asia.

Greenwashing is an act by a corporation that, sensing the rising tide of environmental, social, and corporate governance, exaggerates—or even fakes—how environmentally progressive it actually is. How to clamp down on the practice has become an important issue to investors.

Equally, as we mark International Women's Day today, we must be wary of *womenwashing*, where businesses hastily put a small number of token women in highly visible positions to feign the semblance of gender equality.

The thought crossed my mind as Seiko Hashimoto, a 56-year-old former Olympian and Olympic minister, accepted the nomination to succeed former prime minister Yoshiro Mori as president of the Tokyo Organizing Committee of the Olympic and Paralympic Games.

To be clear, Hashimoto's appointment—one of two women in Suga's 20-member cabinet—was the right decision. It is also encouraging that half of the selection panel for the position were women. Nonetheless, critics contend that Hashimoto's appointment paid lip service to gender equality following Mori's demise for making sexist remarks, evoking this concept of womenwashing.

This process can happen in business and politics when the reality of gender imbalance collides with an urgent need to appear otherwise. In such cases, a candidate's gender outweighs any assessment of the person's other qualifications. Counterintuitively, this hurts the cause of gender equality in the long run.

First, an appointment made in the interests of womenwashing lacks transparency and can imply that the appointee has not met the same qualifications as others. This can result in resentment from peers, whose lack of support makes the success of her job even more difficult. It is not fair to the woman and is hardly a desired outcome for the organization.

Moreover, such appointments make women appear interchangeable with one another that they are in the role only because they are women. Such a stigma can weigh heavily on the appointee.

Sometimes even the intention behind womenwashing can be malicious. The term *glass cliff* refers to a crisis in which a woman leader is hurled at a monumental challenge. It is a lucky break if she manages to steer clear, and it is also acceptable if she does not. The organization takes consolation from the nod of approval it gets for having been so progressive as to appoint a woman to handle such a high-stakes situation. Throwing a woman from a glass cliff is sexism in disguise.

Just as greenwashing is a by-product of greater awareness for sustainability, so is womenwashing tied to the well-intended push to see greater gender diversity at work. How can we then avoid the trap of womenwashing, without taking a foot off the gas?

The answer lies in the coverage. Rather than obsessing over women at the top, we must work on gender balance across all levels within organizations. In other words, we need to put substance over symbolism. This can be achieved by examining gender balance from two directions: top to bottom and bottom to top.

For top to bottom, succession planning holds the key and brings to mind an anecdote shared by a consultant colleague. One day, a male CEO announced that all his senior executives—at the time 100% male—must have at least one female report to him directly or they would receive no bonus. It did not take long for the stunned leadership group to look at each other and realize that this meant that one of them, too, would have to be replaced by a woman.

Quotas with a penalty can send a powerful message. Contrary to popular belief, a study published in the *American Economic Review* in 2017, written by Timothy Besley, Olle Folke, Torsten Persson, and Johanna Rickne, found that gender quotas for politicians can weed out less competent men and raise overall competence of male politicians.[15]

Concurrently, quotas should be examined progressively with a time coefficient when it comes to bottom to top. In our favor is the grassroots change in gender balance in society at large. In a blue-chip Japanese trading company, the ratio of women in the incoming cohort of college graduates easily exceeds 30% today, a huge uptick compared to the single-digit ratio of 20 years ago.

The bottom to top examination of progressive quota forces management to face the problem known as the *leaky pipe*—for example, mothers dropping out mid-career due to the lack of support for their needs as young parents. Fixing these on-the-ground issues may not be glamorous but does promise greater sustainability compared to one-off womenwashing appointments.

By combining these two views, top to bottom and bottom to top, an employer can design an ambitious yet achievable blueprint to continuously improve on the organization's gender balance at all levels. The benefit of diverse perspectives is not limited to the boardroom. And in the boardroom, if progressive quotas are in place across the organization, the gender of the CEO matters less.

In a country like Japan, there is a wide gap between the reality—dire scarcity and therefore elevated prominence for a few senior-level women—and the desire to halt Japan's slide down the international gender gap rankings. Currently, Japan sits at 121st out of 153 nations, according to the World Economic Forum in 2019.[16] This gap makes womenwashing, diversity for the sake of optics, tempting.

Before appointing a woman to a senior executive role, we must stop and think—what about the rest of the organization? Is our plan holistic and sustainable to truly enhance gender diversity across the board? Sometimes we must slow down to go fast; going back to the drawing board of progressive quotas may be the right path.

References

1. Future Corporation. (2023). Company profile. https://www
   .future.co.jp/en/company_profile/corporate_profile/ (accessed
   15 June 2023).
2. Ibid.
3. Ibid.
4. Teikoku Databank. (2022). 全国「社長年齢」分析調査 2021年
   (Translation: National "Company Presidents' Age" Survey
   analysis 2021). https://www.tdb.co.jp/report/watching/press/
   pdf/p220301.pdf (accessed 15 June 2023).
5. Ministry of Health, Labour, and Welfare. (2022). Survey on
   Employment Trends. https://www.mhlw.go.jp/toukei/itiran/
   roudou/koyou/doukou/22-2/index.html (accessed 15 June 2023).
6. Kyodo News PR Wire. (2022). 働く場所を自分で選ぶ「ロケーションフ
   リー制度」で多様な働き方を推進～地域キャリア採用を積極化 (Translation:
   Promoting diverse work styles through a "location-free system"
   in which employees can choose where they work—proactively
   encouraging regional career recruitment). https://kyodonews
   prwire.jp/release/202202227677 (accessed 15 June 2023).
7. Future Corporation. (2022). Annual securities report (FY21).
   https://global-assets.irdirect.jp/pdf/securities_report/batch/
   S100NPQU.pdf (accessed 15 June 2023).
8. *Washington Post.* (2017). #MeToo: Harvey Weinstein case
   moves thousands to tell their own stories of abuse, break
   silence. https://www.washingtonpost.com/news/morning-mix/
   wp/2017/10/16/me-too-alyssa-milano-urged-assault-victims-
   to-tweet-in-solidarity-the-response-was-massive/ (accessed
   25 June 2023).
9. *New York Times.* (2017). She broke Japan's silence on rape.
   https://www.nytimes.com/2017/12/29/world/asia/japan-rape
   .html (accessed 25 June 2023).
10. *BBC.* (2018). Catherine Deneuve defends men's 'right to hit on'
    women. https://www.bbc.com/news/world-europe-42630108
    (accessed 20 June 2023).

11. Save the Children's Child Rights Resource Centre. (2007). Study on child abuse: India 2007. https://resourcecentre .savethechildren.net/document/study-child-abuse-india-2007/ (accessed 20 June 2023).

12. The Japan Institute for Labor Policy and Training. (2016). 妊娠等を理由とする不利益取扱い及びセクシュアルハラスメントに関する実態調査結果 (Translation: Survey on disadvantageous treatment due to pregnancy, etc., and sexual harassment). https://www.jil.go.jp/ institute/research/2016/150.html (accessed 20 June 2023).

13. Pew Research Center. (2017). 10 things we learned about gender issues in the U.S. in 2017. https://www.pewresearch.org/short-reads/2017/12/28/10-things-we-learned-about-gender-issues-in-the-u-s-in-2017/ (accessed 20 June 2023).

14. OECD.Stat. (2017). Employment: Share of female managers. https://stats.oecd.org/index.aspx?queryid=96330 (accessed 20 June 2023).

15. Besley, T., Folke, O., Persson, T., and Rickne, J. (2017). Gender quotas and the crisis of the mediocre man: Theory and evidence from Sweden. *American Economic Review*, *107*(8), 2204–2242.

16. World Economic Forum. (2019). Global gender gap report 2020. https://www.weforum.org/reports/gender-gap-2020-report-100-years-pay-equality (accessed 16 June 2023).

2 Independence

Japan in 2023 may be behind in gender equity at work compared to other mature economies, but starting a professional career as a Japanese woman today in the mid-2020s versus the mid-1980s when the Equal Employment Opportunity Act was enacted is a night-and-day difference in women's status. When Makiko Nakamori entered the workforce in 1987, the women who opted for a lifelong career were an extreme minority.

Is the minority status always a hindrance to a career? Nakamori proves otherwise by highlighting a natural gift associated with minority status: independence. A trained certified public accountant (CPA), she established her career spanning over three and a half decades as an independent, nonexecutive auditor and board member. Never swayed by the majority or the loudest voice in the room, she can stand firm to her principles and speak on behalf of the minority shareholders.

Eventually time caught up with Nakamori, who quietly pioneered the professional career of independent board membership. Corporate governance reform, which started about 2013, encouraged companies to increase the number of nonexecutive directors on the board, which opened more doors for Nakamori.

However, it will be a failure of the company and Japan's corporate governance reform at large when "women on the board" is a mere box to check. We must focus on substance over optics, as I argue in my

column, "Gender Diversity in Japan Inc. Must Blast Past Tokenism."
As a career independent director, Nakamori preaches to the management with a spine. To defeat tokenism, matchmaking between the
company and the director requires care; the director must have courage to stick to her guns and management must be willing to listen.

Meanwhile, being independent never means being disconnected.
Nakamori has networked well throughout her career, soliciting mentors as well as coaching the younger generation. Her network has
enabled her to broaden her reach for companies and cross-pollinate
her learnings.

Women tend to network differently than men—often being shy
to use their network to solve their own problems yet altruistic and
open to helping others in their network. As explored in my column,
"Women Must Learn to Harness the Power of Networking," this
is a behavior we must unlearn; give and take makes the network
fortify itself. Without an organization to back her up, this is exactly
how Nakamori advanced her career, which has been marked by
independence—by leveraging her personal network through two-
way streets.

Makiko Nakamori, Head of Nakamori CPA Offices, External Board Member to M&A Capital Partners, LIFULL, and Itochu Corporation

1963: Born in Osaka, Japan

1987: Graduated from Kyoto University with a degree in management

1987: Started her career at Nippon Telegraph and Telephone (NTT) Corporation

1991: Joined Arthur Andersen (Inoue Saito Eiwa Audit Corporation—currently KPMG AZSA)

1996: Registered as a certified public accountant

1997: Established her own accounting firm Nakamori CPA Offices

2000: Appointed as an external audit and supervisory board member of Oracle Corporation Japan (until 2008)

2006: Appointed as external auditor of istyle Inc. (until 2019)

2008: Appointed as external director of Oracle Corporation Japan (until 2011)

2010: Appointed as external auditor of Global-Dining, Inc. (until 2014)

2011: Appointed as external auditor of LOCONDO, Inc. (until 2017)

2011: Appointed as external audit and supervisory board member of M&A Capital Partners Co., Ltd.

2013: Appointed as external director for Itochu Techno-Solutions Corporation (CTC) (until 2019)

2013: Appointed as external audit and supervisory board member of NEXT Co., Ltd. (currently LIFULL Co., Ltd.)

(continued)

2015: Appointed as external auditor of TeamSpirit Inc. (until 2021)

2019: Appointed as one of four independent nonexecutive directors of Itochu Corporation

Makiko Nakamori Approaches Corporate Governance with Resolve

This article was originally published in the Japan Times *on November 10, 2022, and has been modified for the purpose of this book. The information contained in this article is correct at the time of publishing in the* Japan Times.

In the early 1980s, then high schooler Makiko Nakamori found herself in a small Idaho town with a population of 400, selected as a participant in one of the prestigious AFS Intercultural Programs which have sent Japanese high school students on exchanges abroad since 1954. Having grown up entirely in Japan until then, "the one year spent in Idaho was a turning point," Nakamori told me, who liked speaking English.

The American culture forced her to vocalize her opinions—in Japan, she would hold her tongue "in fear of saying the obvious," recounted the 59-year-old. Meanwhile, she also experienced being an ethnic minority amid a predominantly white population for the first time in her life. Considering equity for minorities and the importance of self-assertion were etched into her teenage mind as guiding principles with which she later formed her successful career.

When in 1987, Nakamori joined the then freshly privatized Nippon Telegraph and Telephone Corporation (NTT) after graduating from Kyoto University with a management degree, she only vaguely aspired to do "something new." However, Nakamori was quickly disillusioned with the stifling bureaucracy at NTT reminiscent of its public origin, and she opted to "reset" her career after three years.

The Equal Employment Opportunity Act had been enacted only a few years earlier. Back then, it was still common for young women—and it was always the women—to retire after marriage. The custom even had the honorary term of *kotobuki taisha* or "auspicious farewell," as opposed to the ominous-sounding *teinen taishoku*, "age-based retirement." For women, working after school was considered an interim period during which they meet their future husbands.

When Nakamori married an NTT coworker at 26 and retired, at least optically following the tradition, she quickly found that the conventional path was not for her. "My life as a housewife lasted only three to four months at best," laughed Nakamori, who decided to sit for the CPA exam with her husband's moral support. This landed her in the accounting firm Arthur Andersen, which in Japan later became part of KPMG AZSA. She stayed with the firm for six years until she founded her own firm.

Nakamori's story is that of a woman who shaped her career in the early days of the professional service industry in Japan at the cusp of the 21st century. Striking out on her own early, Nakamori pioneered the uncharted path of a truly independent knowledge professional. In hindsight the independent nonexecutive director (INED) role, given its emphasis on objectivity, was a natural destination. As her reservoir of skill and experience expanded, so did her role correspondingly expand, creating a virtuous cycle.

The mother of two daughters is soft-spoken with an easygoing smile. At the start of our interview, which took place at her accounting office, she was deeply apologetic that she made me wait a few minutes. During our conversation, she seemed as curious about me, her interviewer, as I was about her.

My three other interviews with individuals close to her, however, consistently confirmed the steely resolve beneath the velvet surface. "She would be unafraid to point out what is right rather than to read the room (and follow the crowd)," summarized Yuji Takayasu, a former colleague of Nakamori's from Arthur Andersen.

Nakamori worked for five years at Arthur Andersen, a period which she described as intense but fun—"the fast-growing, untidy company gave me a lot of authority, so I learned to time manage through delegation." However, her father, an independent accountant himself, first encouraged her to go solo.

Encouraged by her ex-colleagues, she set up her own firm, Nakamori CPA Offices, in 1997 at the age of 34. "It felt like stepping out from a large ship into a tiny boat, setting out into the vast ocean all alone," recalled Nakamori in an essay published in 2011, "but at the same time, it was exhilarating to earn the fee directly for your work."

When one of her clients from Arthur Andersen, Oracle Corporation Japan, the Japanese subsidiary of Oracle Corporation, prepared to list on the Tokyo Stock Exchange, Nakamori was asked to be the nonexecutive auditor on the board—she "knew the company's numbers very well from working with finance for the initial public offering (IPO) preparation," she recounted. The appointment proved to be the cornerstone of her career development as an INED.

"She was stubborn," is how Shigeru Nosaka, Oracle Corporation Japan's chief financial officer at the time, described Nakamori. "She was determined to protect the independence and the interest of minority shareholders for Oracle Corporation Japan, whose super majority was owned by the listed US parent," Nosaka explained. "She had the resolve to be the vanguard of the rules of the capital market."

At the time, the scarcity of women on the board also propelled Nakamori to pick up issues that "would have been brushed aside by male board members," recalled Nosaka. Nakamori and another female INED at the time, a lawyer, doubled down on addressing the root cause of the sexual harassment incidents that came up to the board.

Although it was decades before the #MeToo movement, leaving the sexual harassment issues unaddressed "would ultimately undermine healthy management," insisted Nakamori. As a result of their urging, the company started taking trailblazing actions including establishing a hotline with a third-party law firm to ensure the anonymity of whistleblowers. Nosaka acknowledged that much improvement came as result of the initiative.

After working with Oracle Corporation Japan before and after its public listing in 1999, Nakamori's reputation solidified as an INED with a knack for advising for IPOs. As she sought to reconcile the direction from Oracle Corporation and the management independence of Oracle Japan Corporation, Nakamori would always be attuned to protecting the independence of the company, recalled Nosaka.

Her hallmark was balanced and objective viewpoints supported by hard skills. In the context of start-ups, Nakamori provided recommendations on pre- and post-IPO capital structures to balance the interests of the company, the venture capitalist, and the general shareholders.

By the mid-2010s, the timing was right for Nakamori to ride the wave of heightened attention for the women INEDs. One of the notable marks that womenomics, the former Prime Minister Shinzo Abe administration's push to promote women into senior positions in corporate Japan, left was to increase the presence of female directors on corporate boards. (See Figure 2.1.)

Having been on the boards for Oracle Corporation Japan and a number of start-ups by the early 2010s, Nakamori was ready when Itochu Techno-Solutions Corporation, known as CTC, knocked on the door in 2013. Nakamori said that CTC opened her eyes to "the virtues of Japanese companies including lifetime employment as a management selection mechanism."

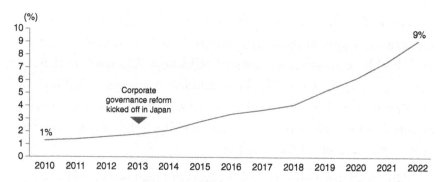

Figure 2.1   Proportion of women in boards and corporate officer roles in Japanese listed companies (%)

Notes: Women's representation on boards increased dramatically as a result from corporate governance reform starting about 2013.

The roles include directors, auditors, and corporate officers.

Created by the author based on: Gender Equality Bureau Cabinet Office. (2023). 上場企業の女性役員数の推移 (Translation: The number of female directors in listed companies). https://www.gender.go.jp/research/weekly_data/05.html (accessed 9 May 2023); Gender Equality Bureau Cabinet Office. (2020). White paper on gender equality 2020. https://www.gender.go.jp/about_danjo/whitepaper/r02/zentai/html/honpen/b1_s02_02.html (accessed 9 May 2023); Financial Services Agency (2022). 日本のコーポレートガバナンス－過去・現在・未来 (Translation: Japan's corporate governance: The past, current, and future). https://www.ifra.jp/pdf/2021/1/121_web.pdf (accessed 28 June 2023).

"While Oracle Corporation Japan is built on the assumed fluidity of talent, CTC nurtures in-house talent," she observed, with these different approaches "you end up with different organizations—being monitored by the company from the first year of your career, your reputation stays with you forever. Self-discipline is the currency of Japanese companies."

Her performance at CTC did not go unnoticed by the parent company. In 2019, Nakamori was appointed as one of four INEDs serving on the board of Itochu Corporation, one of the six major trading conglomerates in Japan. What Nakamori simply explained to me as "a referral by CTC" was, in fact, the consummation of her many years of INED experience.

When I asked Nakamori how she chooses which board to join, she explained that it depends on the openness of the management to take advice from INEDs. "I would look for CEOs free from *idée fixe*," said Nakamori. As Takayasu pointed out, "many companies check the box by having INEDs but in reality are not looking for their input." Nakamori "would either be there to fix things, or she wouldn't join at all," observed Nosaka.

Nakamori's assertiveness at the right moment, a consequence of her time in Idaho, resonates with her INED experience. "When CEOs listen to and leverage INEDs' perspectives, they grow as leaders," her observations tell her; "therefore, you can judge whether companies can transform by their CEO's attitude."

The appraisal goes both ways. Takeshi Hanai, a former top executive at Mizuho Group who has served on the board of IT start-up LIFULL Co., Ltd. (previously NEXT Co., Ltd), with Nakamori from 2013, is a mentor figure and helps her navigate the relationship. Hanai also noted that some large companies' secretariats might be bent on the visibility value of INEDs over their substance regardless of the intention of their CEO—an indirect headwind that Nakamori, not the household name of a celebrity executive, sensed even after being onboarded. When it happens, "I advise her not to worry," said Hanai, "as long as she is legitimately elected at their annual shareholder general meeting."

Undaunted by the criticism, Nakamori keeps updating her perspective by balancing multiple lines of work—40% of her time is still spent on long-term clients with her accounting office. Within the remaining 60%, she rotates the portfolio of companies where she serves as INED on the board—M&A Capital Partners, LIFULL, and Itochu Corporation for now.

"Six to 10 years is a good time frame to spend on a board," she reflected. "Longer than that, both sides get too cozy." She is particularly mindful of cross-pollinating large companies with start-ups in her portfolio because she "wants to sharpen the eye for comparison."

Balancing acts are the constant of Nakamori's life. After having her first daughter in 2000 and second in 2005, she always sought to balance her career and motherhood. "I threw money at the problems," she told me, meaning she maximized the use of babysitters and preschools—her parents were in Osaka and were largely unavailable for on-site help.

Still, she agrees that the back-up system for working mothers is insufficient in Japan. She recounts a client who walked away, concerned that her pregnancy meant deterioration of service. "I didn't want to be seen as incompetent just because I was pregnant," she told me, "even though my husband chipped in, I nearly drove myself insane trying to solve everything by myself."

Looking back, she realizes how psychologically isolated she was. "For women, it is important not to interrupt your career," she advised in her 2011 essay, "but never look for perfection, and accept help from others."

We have come a long way on normalizing the presence of women on corporate boards, particularly INEDs. According to ProNed, a corporate governance advisory and executive search firm, three out of four prime-listed companies on the Tokyo Stock Exchange had one or more women on the board as of July 2022. The total of 1,985 women occupied 11.9% of total board seats.[1]

"Female INEDs are at crossroads," observed Hanai, who has served the last decade on the board of notable public companies, including ASICS, a major sporting goods company. Due to the sheer lack of senior professional women with top management experience at large corporations, "companies initially tapped into lawyers, accountants, and professors."

Hanai thinks that "now that the box is checked, their substance comes under scrutiny. One trick pony of accounting or legal knowledge alone no longer cuts it." Nosaka echoed, "While executive directors tend to represent their own silos, INEDs add value by bringing in a horizontal perspective."

Nakamori wrote in her 2011 essay that soon after embarking on her INED career, she realized the importance of retaining the global view unencumbered by the details. A trained consultant, she combines her accounting skills with knowledge in peripheral domains— finance, tax, legal, internal and corporate governance—to broaden her recommendations.

What makes her stand out as an INED, however, is beyond these hard skills. Her spine to protect the rules of the market provides the objectivity that management dearly needs. And her calculated outspokenness is a breath of fresh air in a culture where the ability to read the room is prized above all.

Many years have passed since Nakamori spent a year of adolescence in a small town in Idaho in the 1980s, where—yanked out of the comfort zone of Japan—she lived the discomfort of being a minority and appreciated the power of assertiveness. The seed for what she is today was planted then.

Gender Diversity in Japan Inc. Must Blast Past Tokenism

This column was originally published in Nikkei Asia *on October 29, 2019, and has been modified for the purpose of this book. The information contained in this article is correct at the time of publishing in* Nikkei Asia.

For the first time, more than 10% of board members at TOPIX 100 companies are women.[2] Reaching 10.5% as of July 2019, this represents an increase of 2.5% from the previous year. Although a step in the right direction, it would be delusional for Japan Inc. to start congratulating itself.

First, this figure pales in comparison to the UK FTSE 350 and US S&P 500 companies, where more than 30%[3] and 27%[4] of board members are women, respectively. The OECD average is 22%.[5]

Second, and more important, 10% isn't sufficient for enabling a productive board discussion based on different perspectives, which is part of what female directors bring. Fifteen TOPIX 100 boards are still left without any women,[6] and for those with even some gender diversity, the average is 1.2 women among every 10 board members.

Unfortunately, 1 woman out of 10 makes for a lonely voice in the boardroom and seems like a mere tokenism. Complacency can seep in as companies feel they have checked the box for another governance requirement.

Having two women on a board can be awkward, lending to stereotyping and typecasting as rivals or, at best, contrasts. But 3 women in a group of 10, at last, normalizes women in leadership. This is the minimum goal each individual company should aim to reach: 30%.

Under Japan's traditional lifetime employment system, companies often operate as patriarchal tribes, each equipped with unique habits and languages. With nearly all employees homegrown, there has been little sense of a need for diversity.

Although homogeneity may have been serviceable in the postwar economic catch-up era, Japan Inc. faces a very different reality today. The world is changing fast. Businesses lose out without constant self-assessment and innovation.

Only a meaningful minority can raise a red flag against group-think. If innovation is defined as new combinations of knowledge, the more diverse the group, the better its chances of coming up with innovative ideas.

Homogenous tribes can only innovate so far. This is a sobering fact that Japanese businesses are waking up to after 30 years of stagnation, as they're overtaken by more diverse and vibrant competitors such as those from the US.

Of course, having more women on boards is but one dimension of gender diversity. The 30% goal needs to be mirrored at all levels and in all divisions in order to be meaningful. Indeed, progress is being made as the workforce gender balance is starting to look healthier at the entry level. The gap between boys and girls going to university—a ticket to a full-time career—is closing each year across Japan. Nevertheless, in 2018 the gap was still at 6.8%.[7]

Tokyo, which has the most headquarters of large corporations in Japan, is a natural place for ambitious women to gravitate. In fact, more women than men have migrated to Tokyo since 2009—14,000 more in 2018.[8] Traditionally less prominent in rural family life, women tend to be less tied to their hometowns, thus freer to move on graduation in search of career opportunities.

Recently, this exodus of young women to Tokyo[9] has even been viewed by some as a demographic threat, as urban-dwelling women tend to get married later and therefore have fewer babies. At the same time, there is a surplus of men in the countryside unable to find partners.

Although this is existentially problematic on a national level, it is good news for the Tokyo offices scouting for talented, career-minded women.

So far, the best examples in Japan of an improved gender mix have been multinational corporations, which have a global mandate to promote local women as a matter of principle. It is not a coincidence that 6 out of 10 "Great Place to Work" awards, in the large-office division, went to multinationals this year.[10]

If the countryside is seeing a brain drain of young female graduates to Tokyo, then so are Japanese businesses, with women opting to instead work for multinationals.

Japanese companies, because of their tribal nature, tend to benchmark among themselves, assuming that *gaishi-kei*—foreign companies—are different. But in terms of giving women the right environment to thrive, it's time for them to learn from foreign practices.

It's unrealistic to expect to hit a 30% gender diversity board target overnight. But through a company-wide commitment, with leaders devising a plan to get there—and being held accountable—progress can be made. Accountability means that compensation and promotions must be tied to the realization of that plan.

Anecdotally, I have seen signs for optimism firsthand. I have a female friend who sits on multiple boards of large Japanese companies, and who reflects positively on the evolution of boardroom conversation. According to her, it used to be that you were expected to speak strictly in line with the corporate Japan, in other words, read the room. Now she feels "freer to be different."

This is encouraging. But 10% is still just not enough to touch the threshold for change. We cannot afford to be complacent. If Japan Inc. is serious about increasing diversity and hence competitiveness, it is time for it to act boldly.

Women Must Learn to Harness the Power of Networking

This column was originally published in Nikkei Asia *on July 16, 2022, and has been modified for the purpose of this book. The information contained in this article is correct at the time of publishing in* Nikkei Asia.

Gender parity in the workforce is backsliding globally, according to the Global Gender Gap Report 2022 published by the World Economic Forum this week, which concludes that at the current pace, it will take 132 years to close the gap.[11] Before we sigh in despair, there are immediate actions that women can collectively take to boost our societal position by changing the way we network.

It was the late US Secretary of State Madeleine Albright who declared during a campaign rally for Hillary Clinton in 2016 that "there is a special place in hell for women who don't help each other."[12]

With that clarion call still ringing loudly in our ears, professional women worldwide, including myself, are trying to stick together.

Most of us belong to a couple of women's networks set up by our employers or wider corporate associations that have become cradles of mutual support. There are also private networks of women based on friendship, shared alma maters, or hobbies, such as gospel singing, which led to the formation of one women's network that I know of.

So, although there is no shortage of networks to support professional women, there is a difference in the way women approach these networks compared with men.

As Ginka Toegel, a professor at Swiss business school IMD who specializes in leadership development for female executives, told me recently, men "get their work done" through their networks, while women only activate theirs to "help others," preferring to find solutions to their problems on their own.

Men do not hesitate to use their networks to help win a promotion or find the right mentor, explained Toegel, citing one man who contacted her out of the blue, mentioning an encounter he had with Toegel at an event eight years previously.

Reaching that far into the past is something a woman would never do, chuckled Toegel, but in this case, the man's persistence paid off. She ended up accepting his offer to work on his project. Most men play this game of giving and receiving favors with loose acquaintances, whom sociologists label as weak ties, intuitively, whereas women tend to recoil at the idea, finding such actions too calculating.

This, argues Toegel, is learned behavior that undermines the power of female networks to advance the ambitions of individual women and prevents too many from realizing their full potential.

Minority networks can be effective tools for consolidating power. Whether it be the civil rights movement in the US or the LGBTQ community advocating for same-sex marriage, history shows us that a consolidated minority can successfully disrupt the status quo. In this vein, the #MeToo movement showed how people linked by a common cause helped surface the unheard voices of female victims of sexual harassment.

But when it comes to advancing women in the modern workplace, successfully overcoming the unconscious bias that is holding so many women back remains elusive. Laboriously, we chip away at this using grassroots actions without claiming the breakthroughs, such as the high-profile wins in lawsuits brought during #MeToo.

As a result, many women's networks end up as little more than feel-good, self-help groups that overeducate its members and occasionally commiserate among themselves.

Undoubtedly, a community that allows women to let their hair down has its positive aspects. Mingling with other professional women who know what it is like to soldier on alone is especially comforting. But should women expect warm and fuzzy feelings from these networks and nothing else?

The truth is that women are leaving many of the benefits of networking on the table. Men, however, unabashedly regard their networks as tools that can help them achieve their goals.

The minority status of women in the working world explains why they are shy to leverage their looser acquaintances. Self-reliance is our second nature. "They don't want to bother others," Toegel rationalized, "as women over-censor themselves before asking."

One senior female executive in the UK told me a few years ago that when fellow women colleagues declined offers to join a corporate board, they typically failed to suggest other qualified women in their stead.

The fear of potentially bothering others, thinking that "they must be as busy as I am," especially people outside their closest circle of friends, often proves more powerful than the desire to help advance other women.

This is a pattern we must unlearn. Not only should women support fellow women they know well but also they should consider how promoting loose acquaintances can increase the worth of the network itself. Cashing in favors will ultimately help to serve the collective purpose of advancing women in the workplace.

Although clubs such as the 126-year-old Paris Automobile Club still deny women membership,[13] male networks are evolving. "Men are opening their networks to women," observed Toegel, "because more women are in positions of power and thus can be useful to include in their networks."

Still, in the new mixed-gender networks, women who are oblivious to the rules of the game may end up being exploited. To benefit from and give back to these networks, women must be able to activate weak ties the same way men do.

In my experience, female leaders tend to put the collective priority before their own interests, a case of "us before me." As such, few of us professional women may need to be reminded by leaders, such as Madeleine Albright, of the need to help each other. A sure way of providing better help, however, would be to rethink the way we approach networking.

References

1. *Nikkei*. (2022). 女性取締役の登用広がる　プライム企業、4 社に 3 社 (Translation: Promotions of female directors are increasing—3 of 4 companies among prime-listed companies). https://www.nikkei .com/article/DGXZQOCD125860S2A810C2000000/ (accessed 15 June 2023).

2. *Nikkei*. (2019). 女性役員比率、2 ケタに (Translation: Percentage of female executives becomes double-digit). https://www.nikkei .com/article/DGKKZO50718930X01C19A0TJ2000/ (accessed 16 June 2023).

3. Cranfield University. (2019). The female FTSE board report 2019. https://www.cranfield.ac.uk/som/research-centres/ gender-leadership-and-inclusion-centre/female-ftse-board-report (accessed 16 June 2023).

4. Spencer Stuart. (2019). 2019 U.S. Spencer Stuart Board Index. https://www.spencerstuart.com/-/media/2019/ssbi-2019/us_ board_index_2019.pdf (accessed 25 June 2023).

5. OECD.Stat. (2017). Employment: Female share of seats on boards of the largest publicly listed companies. https://stats .oecd.org/index.aspx?queryid=54753 (accessed 16 June 2023).

6. *Nikkei*. (2019). 女性役員比率、2 ケタに (Translation: Percentage of female executives becomes double-digit).

7. Gender Equality Bureau Cabinet Office. (2018). 2018 white paper on gender equality. https://www.gender.go.jp/about_ danjo/whitepaper/h30/gaiyou/html/honpen/b1_s05.html (accessed 16 June 2023).

8. *Nikkei*. (2019). 進む少子化と「女性の都市志向」　東京への流入鮮 明 (Translation: Declining birthrate and "women's urban orientation"—Clear increase in influx to Tokyo). https://www .nikkei.com/article/DGXMZO46046110T10C19A6I00000/ (accessed 16 June 2023).

9. *Nikkei Asia.* (2019). Japan's countryside empties as young women set out for Tokyo. https://asia.nikkei.com/Economy/ Japan-s-countryside-empties-as-young-women-set-out-for-Tokyo (accessed 16 June 2023).

10. Great Place To Work Institute Japan. (2019). 日本における「働きがいのある会社」ランキング 145社 (Translation: "Great Place to Work" ranking in Japan out of 145 companies). https://hatarakigai .info/ranking/japan/2019.html#main (accessed 16 June 2023).

11. World Economic Forum. (2022). Global gender gap report 2022. https://www.weforum.org/reports/global-gender-gap-report-2022 (accessed 16 June 2023).

12. *Politico.* (2016). Albright: "There's a special place in hell for women who don't help each other." https://www.politico.com/ video/2016/02/albright-theres-a-special-place-in-hell-for-women-who-dont-help-each-other-042709 (accessed 16 June 2023).

13. *Bloomberg.* (2021). Paris's 126-year-old auto club still says "non" to women members. https://www.bloomberg.com/news/ features/2021-12-17/paris-s-126-year-old-auto-club-still-says-non-to-women-members (accessed 16 June 2023).

3 Purpose

Two broad mental approaches exist when you start building a career; one is purpose-driven—you already know what you need to accomplish—and the other is process-driven—you figure out the meaning of your work on the fly. Although many of us belong to the latter category and feebly attempt to answer the ultimate question through years of trials and errors, there are an enviable few who fall into the former—Mami Kataoka is one of them.

Her father instilled a sense of purpose in her that she was on this earth to achieve something. Young Kataoka marveled at the power of art to change society by speaking to people's hearts and resolved to dedicate her life to this end. With such a calling, she never felt compelled to compare her work with other people, only to measure against the yardstick of her own satisfaction. She regards the fame and status, certainly associated with her role as director of the Mori Art Museum, only as tools to achieve a larger good.

Diversity is a keyword that touches her career on many dimensions. First, the international art world itself is changing, pivoting from its male-dominant and Western-centric viewpoint to include more diverse perspectives. That Kataoka is one of the few women directors of a major museum around the world today is a testimony of both progress and work unfinished. Then, through her curation and directorship, Kataoka consciously lifts formerly lesser known Asian artists, including those who are Japanese and female, into the mainstream. Finally, she taps into diverse voices, coworking with younger curators, to produce her exhibitions.

But diversity is a conundrum. It necessitates labeling by gender, race, and sexual orientation, but it is important to penetrate the identity label haze and reach at the essence of the individual. Labeling is but a tool of convenience.

Therefore, we must tread the terrain of diversity with care. On the one hand, my column "Every Day Is International Men's Day in Japan" argues that Japan must face its misogyny and put up a fight to eradicate it. At the same time, there is a danger that such a movement may divide society and trigger backlash, as I analyze in my other column, "Companies Must Face Up to the Downsides of Workplace Diversity." The corporate world has certainly not yet cracked the code of diversity and neither has the art world.

Mami Kataoka, Director of the Mori Art Museum

1965: Born in Nagoya, Japan

1985–1986: Awarded a scholarship to study in the US

1988: Graduated from Aichi University of Education with a degree in arts

1997: Appointed as chief curator of the Tokyo Opera City Art Gallery

2003: The Mori Art Museum opened at Roppongi Hills Mori Tower

2003: Joined the Mori Art Museum as a curator

2007–2009: Appointed as the first international curator at the Hayward Gallery in London

2009: Appointed as chief curator of the Mori Art Museum

2009: Curated "Ai Weiwei: According to What?", a major survey show of a contemporary artist from China[1]

2012: Appointed as co-artistic director for the 9th Gwangju Biennale

2012: Curated a first major solo exhibition of Makoto Aida, a Japanese artist known for his provocative style[2]

2014: Curated the mid-career survey exhibition of Lee Mingwei, who is known for his participatory artworks[3]

2018: Appointed as artistic director for the 21st Biennale of Sydney, the first Asian director

2019: Curated the first major survey of Chiharu Shiota, recording over 666,000 visitors, the second highest in the Mori Art Museum's history[4]

2019: Appointed as the first non-European president of the International Committee for Museums and Collections of Modern Art (CIMAM) (until 2022)

(continued)

2020: Appointed as director of the Mori Art Museum

2022: Appointed as artistic director for the Aichi Triennale 2022

2023: Appointed as inaugural director of the National Center for Art Research

Mami Kataoka Believes in the Power of Art to Change the World

This article was originally published in the Japan Times *on September 20, 2022, and has been modified for the purpose of this book. The information contained in this article is correct at the time of publishing in the* Japan Times.

The Mori Art Museum, which will celebrate its 20th anniversary in 2023, has never been your grandfather's contemporary art museum. Not only is it internationally recognized for its generous coverage of a wide range of contemporary art but also a visit to the museum is an experience in and of itself.

First, you can't simply strut into the museum directly from the street. You must be elevated to the 53rd floor of the futuristic complex of Roppongi Hills Mori Tower, with a dedicated escalator feeding straight into the museum, much like a sacred promenade rising up to a shrine. Inside, the atmosphere is young—the target audience is in their 40s or below—and comfortable to urbanites. It is open until 10 p.m., except for Tuesdays, and the audio guide is provided through a web application. Suhanya Raffel, museum director of M+, the museum of visual culture in Hong Kong, and a board member of the International Committee for Museums and Collections of Modern Art (CIMAM), called the Mori "the most interesting art museum in Japan" in a recent phone interview.

On a scorching August day, I enjoyed the museum's exhibition "Listen to the Sound of the Earth Turning: Our Wellbeing Since the Pandemic" featuring 16 artists, including Wolfgang Laib and

Masatoshi Naito.[5] By chance I ran into Mami Kataoka at the exit, who was greeting visitors from overseas. Accessorized with her large signature earrings, she was dressed in a colorful, flowing garment and comfortable flat sandals. The director had the air of a relaxed host welcoming a friend to her house; the Mori Art Museum is her baby and home—a place she has dedicated her past two decades of career building and curating.

Mami Kataoka, who joined the Mori Art Museum in 2003, is currently its director since 2020. She recounts that her career has been led by a higher calling. "Through art, I want to create a society where we respect individuals, irrespective of their identity and associated biases," she told me in an interview. Her drive is purely internal— "so what if I run a museum?" she asked with mild bewilderment. "Fame and status never interested me. I simply try to deliver my best vis-à-vis the task which happens to be in front of me."

And the diligence has paid off. "Mami uses her deep knowledge in the most productive way," admired Raffel. During Kataoka's tenure, lesser known Asian artists, including Japanese and female artists, benefitted from Mori's advocacy springboard. And her own success coincided with the global shift to recognize women leaders in the art world. Kataoka's accomplishments as director of the Mori Art Museum and CIMAM president (2020–2022) are the product of a marriage among her unwavering drive, inclusive leadership style, and fortuitous timing of the world's evolution synchronizing with her core beliefs.

"I spent my first 20 years of life in a church," recounted Kataoka, who grew up near Nagoya with her father, an Anglican priest. Although no one in the family was an artist, she knew early on that she would "go see the world." The family often hosted visiting Anglican priests and guests from around the world—borders meant little for Kataoka, who, in her childhood, mingled with this global community of clergy as family friends.

Her priest father instilled a moral compass on life within Kataoka. "He taught me what it means to live—I am here to do something," she said. "Through art, I want to offer alternative value systems to people. It is not a medical or societal reform, but a mindset reform."

Influenced by her mother, who liked paintings and children's literature, Kataoka chose to study art at Aichi University of Education. Contemporary art presented itself as her vocation in New York, when a government scholarship sent her to study in the US in 1985–1986 as a student. "I've never imagined becoming an artist myself," she said, "but, in New York, I witnessed how art could work to pivot the perspectives on existing authorities, change the value set. I wanted to study more."

After setting her target on contemporary art, Kataoka cut her teeth as chief curator at the Tokyo Opera City Art Gallery, a position she took on in 1997 during her early 30s. Her mission was to introduce cutting-edge art into Japan. It was a fight against an "art lag" of two years at the time, which put the Japanese art scene on the hind leg. "I knew exactly what I needed to do," recounted Kataoka. "I contacted and invited artists around the world and curated the exhibitions that I wanted to go and see myself."

David Elliott, a renowned British curator and writer and CIMAM president from 1998 to 2004, was an advisor to the Tokyo Opera City Art Gallery from 1998 to 2001. "She was one of the youngest, brightest curators," he recalled in a phone interview. "She did her research well and was ambitious to take up emerging figures. She seized the moment, and this made a strong impact in Japanese art world." "We ran two exhibitions a year," said Kataoka, "I was working all the time."

Her next big break came when the newly opening Mori Art Museum invited her to join as a curator in 2003 to work under Elliott, the museum's first director. The opportunities are "like peaches floating down the river," Kataoka said referring to a Japanese folk tale, in which an elderly peasant couple catches a giant peach in a creek. Inside the peach is the baby boy, Momo-taro, who grows into a valiant hero under the couple's care. "Opportunities arrive, you catch them, and then you just do your best. The key is never to compare with other people. It is about measuring the outcome against your own satisfaction."

The Mori Art Museum was founded by the late Minoru Mori, former chairman and CEO of the real estate developer Mori Building Company, whose portfolio contains Roppongi Hills. With Elliott as its inaugural non-Japanese director, the museum began as a high-stake experiment. "You need large, attractive, surprising exhibitions to attract a wide audience," explained Elliott. "On the other hand, you must also create space for young emerging artists. Mami made sure that this aspect of our work ran well."

This approach can be risky, as was the case for Tsuyoshi Ozawa, a Japanese artist, born in 1965, famous for his "vegetable weapon" photograph series in which young women pose with imaginary armaments assembled from vegetables[6]—"these works were important because they skillfully and laconically expressed underlying tensions between genders and generations in Japanese society," described Elliott. The museum ran Ozawa's solo show in 2004, which turned out to be a big success with highly reputed catalogs—Elliott attributes the success to Kataoka.

After Elliott's departure to direct the Museum of Modern Art in Istanbul in 2006 and during her tenure as chief curator from 2009, Kataoka deftly combined established artists with the emerging generation—such as Ai Weiwei, Makoto Aida, Lee Mingwei, and Chiharu Shiota.

"Mami lifts and provides leverage for the emerging artists," explained Raffel. "By her amazing installation, Chiharu Shiota is much more well known. Mami refined the expression of Shiota's rather dark view of the world. The result was breathtaking." Shiota's exhibition took place just before the onset of the pandemic and recorded more than 666,000 visitors to the Mori Art Museum, the second highest amount in its history.[7]

"Museum curation must be attuned to the role of art in changing times," discussed Kataoka, "in the 60s, art played a big role in the civil rights movement, feminism, and student activism. We are again in a pivotal moment where the existing value system is being questioned—think #MeToo, #BlackLivesMatter. Art history itself is being rewritten from different perspectives." Finding voices of emerging and underrecognized artists to represent diverse points of view is her way of contributing to the new narrative. As she put it to me, "I would like to make a change from within, without fighting."

Despite Kataoka's pacifist approach, because it confronts life's uncomfortable and often unsightly reality, contemporary art inevitably invites controversy. Such was the case with the Aichi Triennale 2019 arts festival, "After 'Freedom of Expression?'", where a section of the exhibit was shut down due to protest over a depiction of Korean "comfort women" who suffered under Japan's military brothel system before and during World War II. The incident led to national and international press questioning Japan's approach to freedom of expression.

Kataoka, who took on the role of artistic director for Aichi Triennale 2022, kept the lights on at the festival, which had been under attack. The post-pandemic title is "Still Alive," with obvious double entendre, focusing on diversity, life and death, time, healing, and caring for others. The theme takes a cue from the cosmopolitan conceptual artist On Kawara (1932–2014), who has sent an annual telegram saying "I'm still alive" to his friends around the world since 1970. "I want to show 100 ways of 'still alive' through the Triennale," Kataoka told me. "Mami revived the Triennale which was on the brink of being closed," applauded Raffel.

Her resilience also manifests itself in other leadership roles. Immediately after assuming the role of president at CIMAM in 2020, Kataoka faced forced museum closures around the world due to pandemic lockdowns. Acting swiftly, in May 2020, she and her board members launched the Rapid Response webinar series for the CIMAM community, free of charge for its members, to disseminate tool kits for museums' sustainability.[8] "It was pragmatic: how to exhibit without artists being present or dos and don'ts for the museum website, for example," recalled Raffel. "Starting with China, Japan, and Singapore, we shared best practice exhibitions voted on by CIMAM members."

It is fortuitous for Japan to have Kataoka as the first non-European and first Japanese president of CIMAM; her international visibility can only benefit Japan. And if promoting different perspectives through art is her life's mission, refocusing on views slipping below the art radar is her most natural project. "Japan's position in art is quickly deteriorating in Asia, surpassed by Hong Kong and Singapore," Kataoka told me. "While traditional Japanese beauty continues to be appreciated, the country is losing power to push its contemporary art out."

In this vein, Chiharu Shiota's solo exhibition, curated by Kataoka, which has been touring around Asia Pacific, is one of the few examples of Japan-originated productions. Under her leadership, acknowledged Kataoka, the Mori Art Museum is progressive in this sense. "After all, arising opportunities should be used to help improve the status quo of the world," she affirmed. "They are not really ends in themselves. I just want to change the world for the better."

Japan's Presence in the Global Art Scene

Japan's presence in the global art market is weak given the size of its economy—and it was especially affected negatively by the burst of the economic bubble in the early 1990s. Although

(continued)

Japan is one of the top countries in the world in terms of economy size, its contribution to the global art market was just 1% in 2022, according to a report by Art Basel and UBS.[9] In addition to the US and China, which have larger economies than Japan, countries such as France, Germany, and Switzerland also recorded greater art sales than Japan.

From the perspective of contemporary art, it is only recently that the Japanese government started to support and promote contemporary art in Japan. For example, the Agency for Cultural Affairs launched the Art Platform Japan project in 2018 to promote initiatives to increase visibility of Japanese contemporary artists globally.[10] This involved initiatives such as digitalizing and translating important literature, holding workshops for networking, and launching a website to improve the accessibility of information on the Japanese contemporary art scene. Kataoka chaired the steering committee for the project and oversaw its delivery.

Nevertheless, Japanese contemporary artists have been celebrated globally, such as Takashi Murakami,[11] known for his style of combining traditional Japanese art and pop culture, and Yayoi Kusama,[12] known for her extensive use of polka dots in her works that are based on her experience of hallucinations.

An important aspect for artists to become recognized internationally is to work together with curators to promote their works globally. A successful example is Chiharu Shiota's solo exhibition titled "The Soul Trembles," which was curated by Kataoka, starting in 2019 at the Mori Art Museum in Tokyo. The exhibition went on to tour countries in the Asia Pacific such as Korea, China, Australia, and Indonesia.[13]

Raffel doesn't hide her joy that Kataoka is the first non-European, and female president for CIMAM. The art world, despite its progressiveness, is far from gender equal. "It is a male-dominated world all around and art is no different," Kataoka flatly told me. "Museums had been boys' clubs." Art history has evolved from white men, with more than 87% of 18 major US museum collections by male artists, according to Artnet.[14] Ironically, the bottom of the pyramid is predominantly female—women make up 68% of art-related university students in Japan.[15] However, women make up only 25% of art museum directors.[16] (See Figures 3.1 and 3.2.) The structure is mirrored in the world of museums. "We have a big reservoir of female talent in curators where men are a minority," explained Elliott.

It is changing from the top, argued Raffel, who analyzed that since the 60 years of CIMAM, membership has shifted from predominantly Euro-centric and male to the current 70% female construct. "We are a part of the shift," Raffel proudly explained,

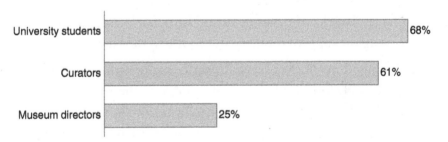

Figure 3.1   Proportion of women in the art industry in Japan, 2021 (%)

Notes: Contrast in gender makeup reverses from female-heavy art students and curators to leadership positions such as museum directors.
Created by the author based on: Ministry of Education, Culture, Sports, Science, and Technology. (2023). 社会教育調査 (Translation: Social Education Survey). https://www.mext.go.jp/b_menu/toukei/chousa02/shakai/index.htm (accessed 3 June 2023); Ministry of Education, Culture, Sports, Science, and Technology. (2023). Statistical abstract. https://www.mext.go.jp/b_menu/toukei/002/002b/koumoku.html (accessed 3 June 2023).

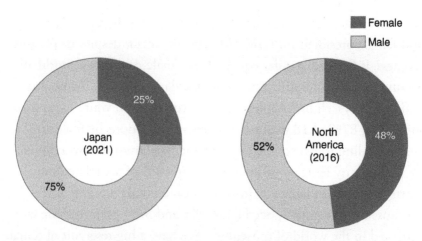

Figure 3.2   Proportion of female art museum directors (%)

Notes: Executive positions in art remain male-dominated in Japan.
Created by the author based on: Association of Art Museum Directors. (2017).
The ongoing gender gap in art museum directorships. https://aamd.org/sites/
default/files/document/AAMD%20NCAR%20Gender%20Gap%202017.pdf
(accessed 3 June 2023); Ministry of Education, Culture, Sports, Science, and
Technology. (2023).社会教育調査 (Translation: Social Education Survey).

pointing to Kataoka, the president, and herself, a board member, "and
artists bring the topic of diversity and equity to the table."

Although Kataoka agrees that diversity, along with sustainability,
is an irreversible force in the physical world as in the art world, her
thoughts reach beyond the dichotomy of gender—"while fixing
the existing inequality, we must try and see the essence of a person,
penetrating the haze of identity labels," she said. "Gender is but a
spectrum. My bosses were always men who wholeheartedly supported me. At the same time, it is categorically untrue that all men
are more brilliant than women." Based on her journey, Kataoka's
career advice is fiercely self-reliant: "do your homework 120% for
yourself, and your outlook will unfold itself. But never expect from
others." The pragmatist in her adds, "You cannot always expect others
to change their views. If you are stuck, I'd recommend switching your
environment to where they appreciate you."

Perhaps her strongest conviction in the power of diversity manifests itself in her on-the-ground workstyle. She admits the fear that "the richer your experiences are, the narrower your strike zone gets." To continue to innovate, she urges younger staff members to voice their opinions in the execution of the Mori Art Museum; it helps Mori connect with their targeted younger demographic, whose "definition of cool is different" from that of older generations.

"Good ideas are age-free," she told me. "I know I grew professionally because my bosses gave me space." In preparing the recent exhibition at the Mori Art Museum, "Listen to the Sound of Earth Turning: Our Wellbeing Since the Pandemic," she collaborated as a three-person team with two other junior curators. "We worked as equals," she explained. "It only makes sense to co-curate as you benefit from multiple perspectives."

Kataoka's enthusiasm for on-the-ground diversity is obvious to Raffel. "In a CIMAM board meeting, all of us are full of opinions," Raffel explained. Many of the 15 CIMAM board members are directors of renowned museums from all over the world, such as Latin America and Berlin.[17] "Everyone talking in a hybrid annual conference," Raffel said, "and Mami quickly texted me on the side, 'isn't it wonderful? I love my colleagues.' She was seeing a moment of pleasure in this diversity."

Every Day Is International Men's Day in Japan

This column was originally published in Nikkei Asia *on March 6, 2020, and has been modified for the purpose of this book. The information contained in this article is correct at the time of publishing in* Nikkei Asia.

International Women's Day on March 8 is about building a gender-equal world. In Japan, however, it is a sad reminder that the other 364 days belong to men.

Despite Prime Minister Shinzo Abe's womenomics, a set of policies to promote women's participation in the workplace now in its seventh year, Japanese society remains stubbornly patriarchal.

Asked whether they recognize any improvement in gender equality in their workplace, 55% of 2,000 working women responded negatively in a 2019 Nikkei survey.[18] According to the World Economic Forum's gender gap index released at the end of 2019, Japan slipped to 121st out of 153 countries, dropping 11 places from 2018.[19]

Clearly, the government's top-down directive, with its feel-good slogan "toward a society in which all women shine,"[20] has had limited effect. To fix the gender gap in Japan, we must face this inconvenient truth and work from the ground up with zero tolerance for disrespect against women.

One of Japan's quirky inventions to deal with the scourge of misogyny in public space is the women-only carriage. Normally limited to rush hours, women-only cars in mainline or subway trains are prominently marked by their large stickers on the windows—pink, obviously.

At a glance, women-only cars may seem like the shallow result of marketing tactics targeting one gender, just like ladies' day at the cinema on Wednesdays. In truth, they are a product of the constant sexual harassment that women, including students, are subject to in crowded trains by groping men who are total strangers. The first such car appeared as early as 1912. More than 100 years later, they are a common sight.

Sociologist Masako Makino points out in her 2019 book *What Is the Crime of Molesting?*[21] that a surge in false charges since the early 2000s twisted the rationale for women-only cars: they now protect innocent men from women wrongly accusing them, rather than women from intrusive men.

In either case, it is a tool to, literally, compartmentalize women, making them a foreign object and therefore second-class citizens in the men's world.

Incidents of harassment, and the resulting women-only cars, are permanent fixtures in Japan because of society's predisposition to objectify women. Not too long ago, men's groping on trains was regarded as lighthearted fun that should never be taken seriously, even by the victims.

Although Japan does not have a monopoly on the normalization of misconduct, its society's homogeneity spreads such behavior and suppresses dissenting views. The fact that many male commuters, often fathers and husbands themselves, casually fondle women points to the banality of their false sense of entitlement.

Naturally, male superiority infects the workplace. Too often women are subject to lewd comments from their male colleagues about their body or how they dress. Often disguised as compliments, the remarks may be, just like groping in the train, defended as light-hearted. But they are in fact a manifestation of male psychological dominance.

If Japan has been relatively muted on the #MeToo movement, it is because the fight here is less about calling out the powerful Hollywood predator types who weaponize sex. Rather, it is against the silent nod of the society that permits everyday acts of misogyny.

The #KuToo movement, a Japanese take on #MeToo that protests mandatory wearing of high heels in certain workplaces, may appear frivolous, but it is in fact a fight against grassroots sexism.

Government policies will not be enough to change this mindset. We need to fight sexism from the ground up. As basic as it may seem, we must denounce wrongdoing by spelling out what is wrong. Just as turning a blind eye to a broken windowpane leads to more serious crimes down the road, giving everyday "small" harassment a pass leads to the overall gender inequality.

Makino approves of the ingenuity of the phrase "Groping in the train is a crime" introduced in 1994 and still often seen on posters in stations. It confronted the prevailing and unsaid notion that it was casual fun. Stating the obvious was necessary.

Taking a lesson from the trains, employers must set clear, zero-tolerance guidelines against petty sexual harassment. The organization will only learn that the company is serious about gender equality after management follows with punishment for behavior against the guidelines.

For most men and women who work in Japan, sexism is still in the air. Unfortunately, there is no convenient barometer, like a measure of toxic particles, to gauge the level of grassroots sexism. Neither is the act of calling out each petty incident as externally laudable as having one more woman director on the board.

But one organization at a time, the male-centric gender hierarchy must be challenged and corrected. Without the ground-up effort, International Women's Day will always bypass Japan.

Companies Must Face Up to the Downsides of Workplace Diversity

This column was originally published in Nikkei Asia *on June 30, 2023, and has been modified for the purpose of this book. The information contained in this article is correct at the time of publishing in* Nikkei Asia.

By now, diversity squarely holds a place at the highest levels of the management agenda of many large companies.

Workplace diversity, of course, comes in many shades, including gender, nationality, sexual orientation, and academic background.

Despite cheerleading by management, diversity can undeniably prompt discomfort in many organizations. Glossing over this inconvenient truth is not only shortsighted but also counterproductive. Businesses must assess the potential repercussions of diversity initiatives and consciously instill countermeasures to mitigate them.

To understand how diversity and discomfort are joined at the hip, it is helpful to consider the obverse: homogeneity ensures comfort. Although homogeneity can be expressed across a gamut of attributes, it recently manifested itself in a simple form for me at an in-person, cross-regional management meeting.

During a coffee break there, someone noticed that as many as 7 of the 18 attendees happened to be wearing almost the same outfit of a crisp white shirt paired with dark gray pants.

Laughter broke out, and group selfies were taken. The rest of us, including a few women and some men in blue shirts who "didn't get the memo," looked on with tolerant smiles while feeling slightly excluded.

Homogeneity can create a strong sense of camaraderie. There is a reason why militaries around the world mandate uniforms. By extension, we naturally gravitate toward those who resemble ourselves and shun outsiders who do not.

Diversity in any dimension inherently introduces dissonance and uneasiness, spoiling a sense of unity and belonging. In fact, calling out a new dimension of diversity can introduce a new dissonance that was absent before. For example, one may be better off not to publicly proclaim belonging to certain minority groups in some cultures. Acknowledging this dark side of diversity is helpful when we discuss the different frames within which we promote diversity.

A well-analyzed, pro-diversity narrative is based on social equity. The starting point is that we all deserve an equal opportunity to advance in the workplace, regardless of our personal attributes. To this end, diversity initiatives encourage us to update our policies and societal norms.

Due to differences in immigration policies and historical context, different places are at different stages of dealing with diversity. For example, Australia, a nation built on immigration and a multicultural society, is now engaged in much more advanced dialogue about equal opportunities at work than homogeneous Japan.

Regardless of contextual differences surrounding diversity in a nation, awkwardness inevitably arises when discussion of diversity forces us to draw clear dividing lines.

This is because diversity inevitably compartmentalizes us into distinct and subtly opposing groups to link a structural minority problem to a structural solution. Such categorization can breed an "us versus them" mentality. For example, more seats for women directors on a board will mean fewer seats for men.

Even though group labeling is an inescapable step in designing diversity policies, management must pay attention to their potential impact on those outside the anointed "diverse" group.

On the shop floor, for example, in the shadow of working parents of small children who receive special paid leave perks, childless employees may feel underappreciated and that they are shouldering an extra load, even as some may be caretakers for aging parents.

The empowerment of one group can disempower another to a degree. It is, therefore, management's responsibility to deliberately equalize the effect. The worst outcome would be a prevailing sense of zero-sum, where any sense of unity is lost.

There is also a sexier version of the power-of-diversity narrative, which holds that workplace diversity is a net positive for business. The notion is that a diverse set of viewpoints provides an antidote to placid groupthink and encourages innovation.

This has been the case at some Japanese companies, which although traditionally known for lifetime employment have started to successfully capture a diversity of backgrounds by welcoming mid-career hires from different industries or non-Japanese companies. In the best cases, those equipped with a different frame of mind can transform unproductive company practices that have long remained unquestioned.

But here as well, we must be cognizant of potential dissonance from introducing new blood into a homogeneous organization. Businesses must carefully calibrate the speed and scale of such injections.

"Powerful medicine is best taken with moderation," cautioned the CEO of a blue-chip Japanese company who strategically appointed an external hire to a key management position a few years ago.

Although the recruit made a significant impact by introducing modern and scientific discipline to the company's sales approach, friction with the incumbent sales team was unavoidable.

"In the beginning, I heavily intervened to mend fences," admitted the CEO. After several years, the outside hire and the team reached mutual understanding. Although the team reached new heights of productivity, it took compromises from both sides.

Simply put, diversity takes work. Although mature economies, including Japan, largely agree on the virtues of diversity, be it the creation of a more equitable society or improved business competitiveness, the notion contains a paradox because diversity is naturally divisive and that flies in the face of unity and inclusion.

Confusion arises when our differences are simultaneously celebrated and ironed over. Such an inherent dissonance is complex and often so unsavory that it is tempting to sweep it under the rug while glorifying diversity.

Interestingly, the business terminology for diversity keeps evolving: from *diversity* alone to *diversity and inclusion* and more recently to *diversity, equity, and inclusion*. Perhaps the sheer proliferation of these terms suggests that, deep down, we remain unconvinced that we have nailed down a solution on how to handle workplace diversity.

And it is likely that we never will. Because it is human nature to seek comfort in homogeneity, our countermeasures against the dark side of diversity will always be less than perfect.

There is no simple solution. To keep pushing, however, management must not shy away from complexity. We must try and make ourselves comfortable as best we can with the discomfort that diversity inevitably brings.

References

1. Mori Art Museum. (2009). Ai Weiwei: According to what? https://www.mori.art.museum/english/contents/aiweiwei/index.html (accessed 15 June 2023).

2. Mori Art Museum. (2012). Aida Makoto: Monument for nothing. https://www.mori.art.museum/english/contents/aidamakoto_main/about/index.html (accessed 19 June 2023).

3. Mori Art Museum. (2014). Lee Mingwei and his relations. https://www.mori.art.museum/english/contents/lee_mingwei/about/index.html (accessed 19 June 2023).

4. Mori Art Museum. (2019). Shiota Chiharu: The soul trembles. https://www.mori.art.museum/en/exhibitions/shiotachiharu/index.html (accessed 15 June 2023).

5. Mori Art Museum. (2022). Listen to the sound of the earth turning: Our wellbeing since the pandemic. https://www.mori.art.museum/en/exhibitions/earth/ (accessed 15 June 2023).

6. Tsuyoshi Ozawa Art Works. (2023). Vegetable weapon. https://www.ozawatsuyoshi.net/selected-works/vegetable-weapon/ (accessed 15 June 2023).

7. *The Asahi Shimbun Company*. (2019). 森美術館で歴代 2 位の入場者 塩田千春展、反響の秘密はどこに (Translation: The second highest number of visitors ever at the Mori Art Museum: What is the secret behind the success of the Chiharu Shiota exhibition?). https://globe.asahi.com/article/12891790 (accessed 16 June 2023).

8. CIMAM. (2020). Join CIMAM and take part in our rapid response webinars. https://www.cimam.org/news-archive/join-cimam-and-take-part-our-rapid-response-webinars/ (accessed 16 June 2023).

9. Art Basel, UBS. (2023). The art market 2023. https://theartmarket.artbasel.com/global-market (accessed 19 June 2023).

10. Agency for Cultural Affairs. (2022). Art platform Japan. https://www.bunka.go.jp/seisaku/bunka_gyosei/artplatform/index.html (accessed 19 June 2023).

11. Artnet. (2023). Takashi Murakami. https://www.artnet.com/artists/takashi-murakami/ (accessed 19 June 2023).

12. Artnet. (2023). Yayoi Kusama. https://www.artnet.com/artists/yayoi-kusama/ (accessed 19 June 2023).

13. Mori Art Museum. (2019). Shiota Chiharu.

14. *Artnet News*. (2019). An estimated 85 percent of artists represented in US museum collections are white, a new study claims. https://news.artnet.com/market/new-study-shows-us-art-museums-grappling-with-diversity-1467256 (accessed 15 June 2023).

15. Ministry of Education, Culture, Sports, Science, and Technology (2023). Statistical abstract. https://www.mext.go.jp/b_menu/toukei/002/002b/koumoku.html (accessed 3 June 2023).

16. Ministry of Education, Culture, Sports, Science, and Technology. (2023). 社会教育調査 (Translation: Social Education Survey). https://www.mext.go.jp/b_menu/toukei/chousa02/shakai/index.htm (accessed 3 June 2023).

17. CIMAM. (2020). Board members 2020–2022. https://cimam.org/general-information/former-board-members/board-members-2020–22/ (accessed 16 June 2023).

18. *Nikkei*. (2020). 「離職したい」は約 6 割　仕事と育児に奔走する働く女性の胸の内 (Translation: About 60% of working women want to leave the workforce—The dilemmas of working women managing work and childcare). https://vdata.nikkei.com/newsgraphics/womencareer2019-2/ (accessed 25 June 2023).

19. World Economic Forum. (2019). Global gender gap report 2020. https://www.weforum.org/reports/gender-gap-2020-report-100-years-pay-equality/ (accessed 16 June 2023).

20. Ministry of Foreign Affairs of Japan. (2023). Women's issues. https://www.mofa.go.jp/fp/pc/page23e_000181.html (accessed 16 June 2023).

21. Makino, Masako. (2019). 痴漢とはなにか: 被害と冤罪をめぐる社会学 (Translation: *What is the crime of molesting?*). Japan: etc. books.

4 Altruism

A sense of calling can take many forms. While Kataoka found her life purpose in challenging the world through art, it took the form of service to others in the case of Ayako Sonoda, the CEO of Cre-en. Being useful to others was the life approach demonstrated by her mother, Fumiko Sonoda, another successful entrepreneur.

Building on the altruistic mindset inherited from her mother, Ayako Sonoda had her own awakenings in early adulthood that strengthened her conviction—a health crisis at the age of 25 and her survivor's guilt from the Great Hanshin Earthquake in 1995. In their spirit of serving others, the mother and daughter alike put no hard boundaries between work and life—the mother would often invite troubled neighbors to a home-cooked dinner and the daughter launched a charity fund in 2017 with her inheritance.

While Ayako Sonoda's professional thesis evolved to address environmental sustainability—Cre-en, the firm she founded in 1988 specializes in sustainability consulting—she always stayed close to her initial proposition: empowerment of women in Japan through side projects and board directorship.

The challenge we face today about empowerment of women is fundamentally different from Fumiko Sonoda's era—the tangible playing field for men and women, from both legal and policy perspectives, is much more level set. What remains lopsided is the intangible playing field, the workplace customs unwelcoming to women and the unwritten societal norms that penalize working women, especially mothers.

Companies can take initiatives to tackle these biases, as I discuss in my column, "Let's Get Real About Female Equality in Corporate Japan." Moreover, my other column, "Rolling with the Punches Hurts Japanese Women," points out that women must remember that they too can be an agent for change to correct the uneven playing field.

The hurdle is in our own hearts—being our own agents requires an unlearning of a lifelong habit for Japanese women, who are taught to always prioritize on others' needs before their own. What the Sonoda mother and daughter pair teaches us is the importance of altruism, distinct from self-sacrifice at all costs.

Ayako Sonoda, CEO of Cre-en Inc.

1963: Born in Kobe, Japan, where her mother, Fumiko Sonoda, ran a small snack store

1986: Graduated from Konan University with a degree in sociology

1987: Joined Recruit as a college graduate

1988: Founded Cre-en Inc. in Osaka as a marketing company focused on women

2000: The sustainability report produced for Matsushita Electric (now Panasonic) won an award from the Ministry of the Environment

2001: Cre-en produced sustainability reports for 17 companies, including Osaka Gas and Suntory

2003: Appointed as Head of Secretariat, Sustainability Forum Japan

2004: Cre-en expanded CSR consulting to full-scale

2004: Appointed as director, Japan Sustainability Investment Forum

2015: Appointed as external director of BIPROGY (until 2023)

2017: Established Mirai RITA Foundation

2020: Cumulatively, Cre-en has created reports for more than 800 companies (includes overlap or same-company reports)

2022: Appointed as outside director of Lotte Co., Ltd.

2023: Appointed as director, Sustainability Forum Japan

2023: Appointed as outside director of Mitsubishi Estate Co., Ltd.

Ayako Sonoda Inherits Altruism and Entrepreneurism Passed from Her Mother

This article was originally published in the Japan Times *on June 14, 2022, and has been modified for the purpose of this book. The information contained in this article is correct at the time of publishing in the* Japan Times.

Ayako Sonoda, 59, is CEO of Cre-en (shorthand for "createur-entrepreneur"), a boutique sustainability consulting firm she founded more than three decades ago. She credits her late mother, Fumiko Sonoda, for blessing her with entrepreneurism and altruism. This is a tale of a mother and a daughter, their stories resonating as time traverses.

The mother, Fumiko Sonoda (1928–2014), pioneered women's financial and social independence in the post-WWII time.

Although Fumiko grew up in an affluent family in Kobe, the family's financial fortune declined after her architect father's premature death. Fumiko decided to support her family by starting a small business—a dare for a 22-year-old woman in the chaotic world of post-war Japan.

Young and single—though she later happily married at age 35 to Sonoda's father—Fumiko opened a small snack store near Koshien baseball stadium, Japan's oldest stadium and home to the famed national high-school baseball tournament.

Through the 1950s and 1960s, her store became an early prototype of the Japanese convenience store, made famous by the Seven-Eleven franchise in the 1970s, selling everything from cigarettes and stamps to children's swimming floats. "Whatever her customers needed, big or small, my mother made sure to deliver," Sonoda wrote in her 2015 tribute[1] for her deceased mother.

Fumiko's desire to serve others reached well beyond the merchandise assortment. "My mother had a knack to detecting anyone carrying a worry inside," observed Sonoda. "From neighborhood schoolteachers to local policemen to neighbors, she would invite any of them to a home-cooked dinner and chat. Our dinner table was busy."

"Always be useful to others" was Fumiko's mantra. Fumiko lived during the backdrop of war and the post-war chaos from which a new Japan sought to emerge. Although crisis bred entrepreneurism in the absence of more stable career options, young women starting a business were out of the norm. But Fumiko thrived unburdened of prejudices, with her unwavering moral compass set on a philosophy of service to others. In a final letter to her family, Fumiko Sonoda declared about her 85 years of life, "Regrets, I have none."

For Fumiko's daughter, Ayako Sonoda, the trigger for entrepreneurism was not financial destitution but a health crisis at the age of 25. After graduating college, Sonoda joined Recruit, today a global empire of HR services with market capitalization of ¥9 trillion, which then was a rising venture newly founded in 1960 as a matching platform between employers and job seekers. However, during her time there Sonoda was hospitalized for 20 days due to overwork and stress. "The sudden shut-down [due to illness] made me reassess my life's purpose," reflected Sonoda, "and I thought of my mother's philosophy—to do good for the others."

After some soul-searching, Sonoda opted out of a career at Recruit to pursue a career with a more direct impact on society as an entrepreneur, following her mother's path.

Sonoda set her eyes on empowering women. "Because of societal constraints, I saw many women unable to maximize their potential," Sonoda told me over a phone interview. What she witnessed in the working world in the late 1980s, even in the wake of the Equal Employment Opportunity Act enacted in 1985, was an uneven playing field. "In general, promotion came very slowly for women. Even with equal credentials in education [to men], women were constantly relegated to assistant roles, and treated as entertainers at client dinners—bonuses were denied when we turned down [such roles]," she said. Such gender-based division of roles persists today in the form of regular and nonregular employees, where 35% of the former and 68% of the latter are occupied by women as of 2023. (See Figure 4.1.)

When Sonoda founded Cre-en in 1988 in her native Osaka, she started with seven or eight employees who were all female acquaintances. She instilled a flexible working model to accommodate their life priorities. Female founders are rare today and were even rarer 30 years ago. (See Figure 4.2.) Unable to get a bank loan or other funding, Sonoda financed the start-up with her own limited savings.

Cre-en initially focused on marketing, promotion, and product development for women. "We promoted how to cut and eat avocado on behalf of a fruit importer, for example, when the fruit had just started to appear on store shelves in Japan," recalled Sonoda.

Over time the business tilted toward content planning and editing for media targeting women, such as *Salida*, a free newspaper advertising job opportunities for women.

Sonoda was 31 in 1995 when she had her second reckoning in life, which changed the direction of her then 7-year-old venture; she witnessed the Great Hanshin Earthquake, which killed 6,434 people.

"I thought hard about why I exist," Sonoda told me. Because of the earthquake "I suffered from survivor's guilt. I had to do something meaningful with my time on earth." After the 1992 Earth Summit in Rio de Janeiro, Sonoda had begun experimenting with mixing environmental issues into Cre-en's priorities. By experiencing the earthquake, which shattered life as she knew it, she became convinced that environmentalism was the answer for her existence.

Content editing for the media, Cre-en's core business at the time, no longer suited Sonoda's life priorities because it indirectly

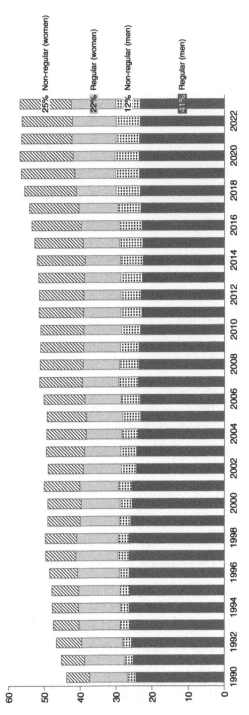

Figure 4.1 Number of regular and nonregular employees by gender (millions of people)

Notes: Although more women participate in the workforce than before, half of them today are employed in nonregular positions, which offer little prospect of promotion.

The data until 2001 is for the month of February. The data from 2002 onward are averages of the months January to March. Adapted from Statistics Bureau of Japan (2023). Labour Force Survey. https://www.stat.go.jp/data/roudou/index2.html#kekka (accessed 9 May 2023).

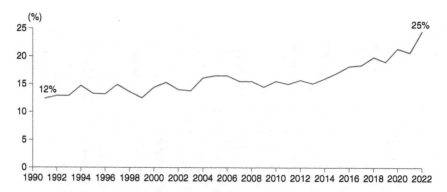

Figure 4.2   Proportion of female entrepreneurs in Japan (%)

Notes: One reason why women are less likely to start new businesses than men are the gendered expectations in society.

The subjects of the survey are companies who received loans from the Japan Finance Corporation Micro Business and Individual Unit from April to September of the previous year and had started the business within a year before receiving the loan. The 2022 survey had 1,122 respondent companies.

Adapted from Japan Finance Corporation (2022). Survey on Business Start-ups in Japan (FY2022). https://www.jfc.go.jp/n/findings/pdf/kaigyo_221130_1.pdf (accessed 9 May 2023).

encouraged mass consumerism, the exact opposite of pursuing sustainability. Even if the avocado is exotic, is it worth consuming the energy required to import it into Japan? The old and new directions were not totally devoid of commonality, however. "The experience of content creation for media built our organizational muscles to produce sustainability reports down the road," she said, looking back.

She pursued the new direction with vigor, leveraging the internet, which was becoming a mainstream accessible platform. With NEC System Technologies, an NEC group company that has since been integrated into NEC Solution Innovators, Cre-en started an online magazine, *Ecology Symphony*, in 1997. It consisted of updates on sustainability from corporate initiatives to subject expert interviews.

After 2000, the business world started catching up with Cre-en. With the credential from a sustainability report in 2000 on a blue-chip name, Matsushita Electric, now Panasonic, they gained momentum to work with more—17 companies signed up in 2001 including Osaka Gas and Suntory.[2]

Today, Cre-en provides end-to-end sustainability consulting services, from articulating company visions to communicating the full spectrum of sustainability-related disclosures. Cumulatively, Cre-en has helped more than 800 companies (including overlap or same-company reports) to create sustainability-related reports— sustainability reports, CSR reports, and integrated reports.[3] With more than ¥600 million in sales[4] and close to 40 staff members, Cre-en is recognized as one of the long-established independent boutique sustainability consulting firms in Japan.

Even as Cre-en became increasingly known as a sustainability consulting house, Sonoda never forgot the venture's genesis—to empower women in Japan—which is aligned with the United Nations fifth Sustainable Development Goal (SDG), gender equality. "I am convinced that for Japan to transform its future for the better, gender diversity is the right pressure point," she wrote to me in an email.

The progress of gender equality over the past three decades in Japan has been slow. Sonoda blames the male-driven operating model, which is glued together by unconscious bias. "It is unfair to expect so much from women without changing the system," she told me, "when they realize how rigged the game is, who can blame women for opting out of working for Japanese companies or the government?" The outcome from differential treatment by gender is clearly illustrated by Japan's gender wage gap, which stands at 22% in 2021, more pronounced than the rest of mature economies. (See Figure 4.3.)

Sonoda has two projects through which she pushes for change. The first is her position as a nonexecutive board member at BIPROGY, a ¥300 billion market cap IT service provider—an industry known to be male-dominated. Over her six years of directorship,

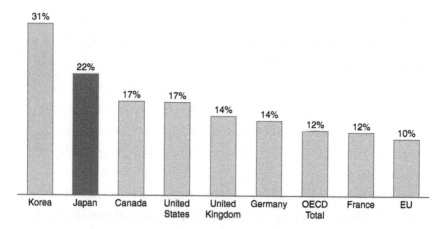

Figure 4.3   Gender wage gap by country (%)

Notes: The gender wage gap in Japan remains higher than other developed countries in the Western region due to vertical and horizontal segregations.

The gender wage gap is calculated by the difference between median earnings of men and women relative to median earnings of men. Data refer to full-time employees and are from 2022 or the latest year available.

Adapted from OECD. (2023). Gender wage gap (indicator). https://data.oecd.org/earnwage/gender-wage-gap.htm (accessed 6 August 2023).

she has pushed for gender diversity across the ranks. Currently, out of 14 board members, 4 are women and another is a foreign-registered man. They mark a significant increase in diversity from Sonoda being the only woman on the board six years ago when she first joined.[5]

Moreover, BIPROGY now sets a target of 18% for the proportion of women in managerial positions. When women back out of a promotion opportunity with the predictable line "I need to discuss this with my family," the company no longer backs down—the drill for this occurrence is for managers to assure the women on the spot of a complete support system. Sonoda believes that a critical mass of incremental, on-the-ground breakthroughs, such as this assurance of support, can overcome the ingrained unconscious bias.

The other project takes place in Toyooka, a city in Hyogo Prefecture with a population of 77,000 facing the Sea of Japan.[6] It has become common knowledge that the precipitous population decline in rural Japan—for example 1% per annum over the last decade in Toyooka City[7]—is due to the loss of the youth population. Young women especially are moving to urban areas with more gender-equal opportunities. The suspected culprit is the more pronounced paternalistic culture in rural regions.

In this context, since 2021, Toyooka City embarked on its Gender Gap Elimination project, for which Cre-en is contracted to assist with strategy formulation.[8] The project focuses on visualizing the invisible—for example, six episodes of manga comics depicting unconscious bias have been posted in the city paper and home page.[9] The city also set quantitative targets to be achieved by fiscal year 2025, such as 30% female leadership participation in the local community organization, an increase from 12% in fiscal year 2019.[10]

Sonoda's entrepreneurial successes, and those of her mother, convince Sonoda that, when women are empowered, the sky is the limit for their achievements. She wants to enable that experience for all women, not only the privileged few with higher education in the big cities. This altruism, in addition to entrepreneurism, seems to run in her blood.

"She is not in it for herself," was what I consistently heard from both of Sonoda's unofficial mentee entrepreneurs—Keiichi Yoshino, founder of Dari-K, an environmentally conscious chocolate producer recently acquired by confectionary giant Lotte, and Dr. Wong Lai Yong, Sonoda's fellow founder of Center for Sustainability and Innovation at Shizenkan University—when I recently spoke to them over video call. "She genuinely wants to do good for the world," Yoshino concluded.

As a young social entrepreneur himself, Yoshino appreciates the generosity of Sonoda in her mentorship. The two met in 2015 through a program hosted by the Institute for Strategic Leadership (ISL), a well-known Japanese NPO focused on leadership education.

Four mentors, all alumni of ISL, were assigned to mentor him on his fledging chocolate business for half a year. Although he appreciated the advice from all the mentors, Sonoda is the only one with whom he still connects after the program's conclusion, meeting semi-regularly for information exchange. "The updates she has are remarkable, truly on the global forefront of sustainability," said Yoshino.

Mother-daughter altruism took a concrete form in the Mirai RITA trust, which Sonoda started using her inheritance from her parents.[11] In 2020, she founded a charity organization to fund social programs such as those aiding single mothers. "Most social entrepreneurs divide their work [in sustainability] and their wallet," said Yoshino, "but not Sonoda-san."

Despite the near-famine wartime hardship, Sonoda recalls that Fumiko, her mother, was always positive and open-minded. Like her mother, Sonoda is an upbeat optimist despite the struggles she endured as a female entrepreneur and her frustration with the glacial pace of gender equality progress in Japan.

But Sonoda and her mother's optimism was never utopian as it counterbalanced their nihilism. "Every day, I imagine I could die tomorrow," Sonoda said, noting her survivor's guilt from the Hanshin earthquake. Likewise, her mother had seen many deaths due to the war. "Because our personal tomorrow is so fragile, we focus on the larger goal for humanity today"—the Sonodas did not dwell on past or present misfortune.

Our sustainable future must be powered equally by women as by men, Sonoda believes. "Women, in general, are more future-oriented as consumers," Sonoda said. "Women can creatively partner with others."

Now, especially, she is hopeful, she said, because Generation Z, roughly those born after the late 1990s, is markedly different from older generations in their concept of gender equality. Sonoda also mentors high school girls, and she sees the change in front of her. "These high school girls complain about advertisements for hair removal salons; their value system is surely changing," she marveled. "Generation Z men and women think that whoever is better at it should do the house chore," she said. "It is time we updated our value system to be aligned with theirs."

"There were times I was envious of the other kids with stay-at-home mothers. But now I am grateful I learned how to take care of myself early on. My mother was my role model as an independent, working woman, fully connected to and embracing the outside world," Sonoda writes in her memoir.

Obviously, she learned far more than how to take care of herself from her mother; she learned a way of living independently yet in service to others. In other words, the mother taught her daughter how to live without regrets, as if each day were her last day on earth.

Let's Get Real About Female Equality in Corporate Japan

This column was originally published in Nikkei Asia *on January 22, 2018, and has been modified for the purpose of this book. The information contained in this article is correct at the time of publishing in* Nikkei Asia.

About 150 years after it opened up to the rest of the world, Japan is one of the globe's most developed, prosperous, and democratic countries. But in some ways it remains a place apart, especially when it comes to the role of women in leadership posts.

Japan ranks a dismal 114 out of 144 countries, according to Gender Gap Index published by World Economic Forum last year, behind India and only one place ahead of Ethiopia.[12]

According to a 2017 Japanese government report, women account for only 13% of managerial positions against 43% in the US and 32% in France.[13] At listed companies, it is even worse—women hold just 3.4% of executive positions[14] against 17% in the US[15] and 30% in France.[16] That makes the Cabinet Office target of 10% by 2020 sound hollow.

At first glance, this is perplexing given that the Equal Employment Opportunity Act was enacted more than 30 years ago. Women already accounted for 30% of college graduates in 1992, when the education ministry first provided gender-based data. By 2016, the figure was 46%.[17] So there is no shortage of young female talent. Moreover, the overall female employment rate—the percentage of women of working age actually in jobs—has climbed to 66%,[18] above the 58.4% average of Organization for Economic Cooperation and Development (OECD) countries,[19] although it is worth mentioning that the Japanese figures include many part-time workers.

The real problem lies with the continuing male dominance of full-time, better-paid managerial posts.

It is therefore no surprise that the government of Prime Minister Shinzo Abe puts female empowerment high on its agenda: it seems a good way to combat Japan's chronic labor shortage. It could also support innovation as theory says that diversity promotes fresh perspectives. The government is now boosting social infrastructure for child rearing, including a recent ¥2 trillion package to increase childcare for working parents and provide free preschool education.[20]

Not Feeling Welcome

Although social support is no doubt necessary, will this really solve the problem? I am afraid that the root cause runs deeper. Here is a dirty secret. The basic reason why women do not aspire to corporate leadership is that they do not feel welcome. Women see through the thin veneer of propaganda when in reality the incumbent power feels little pressure to change. When 62% of first section-listed companies do not have any women on the board or in corporate officer roles[21] the message is that women are a token. Just to check the box. It is indeed quite lonely out there. As a woman business consultant, I have witnessed a case where women in sales positions had to form an underground network to share leads as they often felt excluded from lead flow monopolized by male colleagues.

What then can we do to get serious about diversity in Japan? In other words, how can we avoid the two-faced approach of hoisting ambitious targets while averting our eyes from the real issues?

First, the target itself. Although the Cabinet Office sets the blanket goal of 10% women in executive positions for public companies by 2020, currently being only at 3.4%, the goal loses its credibility. Is it not time to have each individual company set its own target, then hold it accountable? One proponent of this methodology, Germany, records 29% women in managerial positions as opposed to 13% in Japan, according to the Gender Equality Bureau Cabinet Office of Japan.[22]

Globalization has propelled large Japanese corporations to develop substantial businesses outside Japan. Hitachi, for example, generates half its revenue from overseas. These companies are no longer "Japanese" in the traditional sense; they are multinationals of Japanese origin. The more international the nature of business, the bolder a target we should expect. We then can expect a trickle-down effect from these top companies to more locally oriented enterprises.

Second, let us take a really imaginative approach to bringing mid-career women or female staff members who have taken breaks back into their career tracks. This is vital to catapult gender diversity. The labor ministry estimates 60% of women leave work around the time of the birth of the first child.[23] Dentsu, an advertising agency, estimates 3.6 million housewives are out there looking to rejoin the workforce, more than half of the total 6.6 million housewives.[24]

Although there are programs to help these jobseekers, they pale in comparison with the budget for childcare support, which only addresses younger women mostly in their late 20s or 30s. Moreover, companies that are visibly behind this return-to-work movement are usually non-Japanese, such as Microsoft, the American software giant, which offers a "return-ship" program in Japan, and JPMorgan, the US bank, which supports "mom internships." This is an area where the government could really set some fires blazing with assertive policies.

Broader Yardstick

Of course, once back, women need the right environment to flourish. This is only possible if companies shed some of their traditional yardsticks to measure suitability for promotion. If this is judged only by favoring the right degree (say a male-dominated discipline such as engineering), the number of loyal years' service, and the volume of political capital an individual has accumulated with peers, women returnees have little chance of success. Rather, the yardstick should be broadened to include an ability to bring in fresh perspectives, for example, or to demonstrate genuine empathy for clients and employees. One mid-sized company attests that only after a working mother was promoted in leadership did they start offering flexible work hours to employees, which resulted in a jump in retention rate. The key is not to judge women with a men's yardstick but to judge both in the same fair way.

Gender-neutral encouragement at every stage of a career cannot be overemphasized. The glimmer of hope is that where women are evaluated on the right criteria, they lead successful careers, even in Japan. The Cabinet Office reports that in natural science, women scholars already occupy 28% of researcher posts,[25] close enough to the government's 30% target by 2020. This shows that where professional success has a direct correlation with talent and zeal, and is easily tested, women are on equal footing to men. It is in business, where the correlations are murky, that we need to change our mindset.

I am more optimistic for younger generations. The unnecessary distinction of boys and girls at school is breaking down. Today Japanese school kids may choose whatever color they like for their school backpack. When I grew up in the early 1980s it was 100% black for boys and red for girls. Nobody questioned it. These signs subtly signal that we are different and cast us in gender roles. Something is not right when women at work must form a secret sorority group to support each other with sales leads.

Unfortunately, we do not have the luxury of time to wait for Generation Z to reach adulthood to close the gender gap in Japanese management. With the pressures of globalization, a shrinking population, and record domestic labor shortages, now is the time to get serious. Or never.

Rolling with the Punches Hurts Japanese Women

This column was originally published in Nikkei Asia *on April 1, 2022, and has been modified for the purpose of this book. The information contained in this article is correct at the time of publishing in* Nikkei Asia.

A friend of mine—call her Shiho—has a history of relationship woes. Trying to be an understanding partner, Shiho always gave her boyfriends a generous benefit of the doubt until she had had enough.

After seeing a therapist, Shiho realized that she had been "too understanding" in her relationships with men. Excessive backward bending, which as an adult might relate to a petulant child, signaled that she could be walked over and have her feelings disregarded. This is not a recipe for an equal and sustainable relationship.

In my opinion, Shiho's problems with men can be extrapolated. Women being too benevolent is a persistent root cause of the excruciatingly slow advancement of gender equity in Japan.

Structurally, at least, when it comes to education, political participation, and employment, Japan seems to be a nation built to promote gender equity. Yet, according to a survey conducted by Teikoku Databank in 2021, women occupy a mere 8.1% of the Japanese company president positions.[26]

According to the Organization for Economic Cooperation and Development, Japanese married women spend more than five times longer performing unpaid duties at home compared with their male partners.[27] Married women in the West, by contrast, spend only twice as long as their partners performing housework. It is impossible to imagine Japanese women acting resolutely, as was the case in Iceland in 1975 when 90% of the women refused to work, cook, or look after children for a day.[28]

Accentuated gender roles within Japan's high-context culture explain why Japanese women tend to conform. From childhood,

Japanese girls are taught to be vigilant regarding the needs of others before tending to their own. Although high emotional intelligence is a virtue, an excess thereof could suppress the legitimate defense of one's own needs and wants.

Then there is the maternity myth obstinate through its generational echo effect that a child's development depends on how much hands-on affection is bestowed by the mother. The bar is high in Japan. I know one working mother whose nursery insisted that she hand-stitch her child's name on their nap blanket.

The problem with sticking to such accentuated gender roles is that it misses the fact that being a stay-at-home mother in Japan today is a luxury. With a labor participation rate as high as 53% in 2019,[29] women have a lot on their plate. Yet instead of complaining, most women respond by sleeping less and compromising their salary.

This not only hurts women but affects the economy as well by limiting women's career potential. According to a 2020 survey by the Ministry of Health, Labor, and Welfare, 52% of the women are working in irregular positions[30] with limited responsibility or possibility of promotion, citing the difficulty balancing work and family as the primary reason.

Demanding employers make small concessions—flexible work policies or fairer appraisals that do not penalize women for not attending after-work dinners—does nothing to solve the larger problem of advancing gender equity.

Japanese society must acknowledge the scale of psychological abuse when it comes to its women. Resistance to gender equity is less about policy and has more to do with overwhelming mentality.

Vocal role models, men or women, must snap women out of this pattern of behavior. For example, even with the most generous paternity leave provisions in the OECD, in 2020, only 12.7% of the men made use of them.[31] In Japan, fathers are outsiders when it comes to parenting, adding to the pressure on women. There are signs of change, but they are scarce.

Societal expectations reinforced by education nudge women toward certain decisions. "It would just go down smoother on all fronts if women took longer parental leave or reduced their work hours," one colleague with three small children told me.

But instead of accepting the status quo, I would encourage women to consider the long-term impact on their careers. In the spirit of an equal partnership, which should be the foundation of a modern couple, women must be able to discuss all options before bending backward.

Shaking off being too pliant, which has become second nature, is hard. But it can be done. I am encouraged by an anecdote I heard from a Slovenian senior diplomat. In her junior days at the embassy in New York City, the ambassador expected her to pick up phone calls, never her male peer. One day, she had had enough and politely requested the ambassador to ask her male peer to take calls as well, perhaps not the most pleasant request, but she was proud of it.

In a relationship, one party being too understanding can be toxic. Similarly, women being too generous is unhealthy in society. They are overly compliant with the cards of societal expectations stacked against them, and the society is numb to this status quo. It represents the emotional hurdle that Japan must recognize and overcome to move the needle on gender equity. As with the courage of the young Slovenian diplomat, we must act to find a solution.

References

1. JKSK Empowering Women Empowering Society. (2015). 母は、昭和のアントレプレナー (起業家) (Translation: My mother was an entrepreneur of the Showa era). https://jksk.jp/w100-018/ (accessed 15 June 2023).
2. Cre-en Inc. (2023). Company history. https://www.cre-en.jp/company/chronology/ (accessed 15 June 2023).
3. Women's Empowerment Principles. (2020). Leaders in action: Ayako Sonoda. https://www.weps.org/sites/default/files/2020-12/LEADERS_IN_ACTION_Ayako_Sonoda.pdf (accessed 15 June 2023).
4. Cre-en Inc. (2023). Financial information. https://www.cre-en.jp/SDGs/economy/ir/ (accessed 15 June 2023).
5. Nihon Unisys (Currently BIPROGY). (2015). Annual report 2015. https://pr.biprogy.com/invest-j/ir/pdf/ir2015.pdf (accessed 15 June 2023).
6. Toyooka City. (2022). 豊岡市の概要 (Translation: Overview of Toyooka City). https://www.city.toyooka.lg.jp/shisei/shinoshokai/1004513/1002323.html (accessed 15 June 2023).
7. Statistics Bureau of Japan. (2020). National census. https://www.stat.go.jp/data/kokusei/2020/index.html (accessed 15 June 2023).
8. Toyooka City. (2020). 豊岡市ジェンダーギャップ解消戦略会議 (Translation: Toyooka City gender gap elimination strategy meeting). https://www.city.toyooka.lg.jp/kurashi/1007000/1008845/1019237/1012169/index.html (accessed 16 June 2023).
9. Toyooka City. (2021). マンガで考えよう!ジェンダーギャップ (Translation: Think with manga! Gender gap). https://www.city.toyooka.lg.jp/kurashi/1007000/1008845/1019240/1016830.html (accessed 16 June 2023).

10. Toyooka City. (2021). 豊岡市ジェンダーギャップ解消戦略 (Translation: Toyooka City gender gap elimination strategy). https://www.city .toyooka.lg.jp/_res/projects/default_project/_page_/001/016/ 732/gg0401.pdf (accessed 15 June 2023).

11. Mirai RITA Foundation. (2023). About Mirai RITA. https:// mirairita.org/about.html (accessed 15 June 2023).

12. World Economic Forum. (2017). The global gender gap report 2017. https://www.weforum.org/reports/the-global-gender-gap-report-2017 (accessed 20 June 2023).

13. Gender Equality Bureau Cabinet Office. (2017). 2017 white paper on gender equality. https://www.gender.go.jp/about_ danjo/whitepaper/h29/zentai/html/zuhyo/zuhyo01-02-14.html (accessed 20 June 2023).

14. Gender Equality Bureau Cabinet Office. (2017). 2017 white paper on gender equality. https://www.gender.go.jp/about_ danjo/whitepaper/h29/zentai/html/zuhyo/zuhyo01-02-13.html (accessed 20 June 2023).

15. McKinsey & Company. (2022). Women in the workplace. https://www.mckinsey.com/featured-insights/diversity-and-inclusion/women-in-the-workplace (accessed 25 June 2023).

16. European Women on Boards. (2016). Gender diversity on European boards. https://www.votre-administrateur.com/ wp-content/uploads/2017/02/EWoB-Gender-Diversity-On-European-Boards.pdf (accessed 25 June 2023).

17. Ministry of Education, Culture, Sports, Science, and Technology. (2016). Basic School Survey. https://www.mext.go.jp/b_menu/ toukei/chousa01/kihon/1267995.htm (accessed 20 June 2023).

18. Gender Equality Bureau Cabinet Office. (2017). 2017 white paper on gender equality. https://www.gender.go.jp/about_ danjo/whitepaper/h29/zentai/html/zuhyo/zuhyo01-00-01.html (accessed 29 June 2023).

19. OECD.Stat. (2015). Employment: Employment/population ratio, by sex and age group. https://stats.oecd.org/index .aspx?queryid=103872 (accessed 29 June 2023).

20. Ministry of Health, Labour, and Welfare. (2018). 2018年度 (平成 30 年度) 予算案の概要 (Translation: 2018 Summary of the draft budget). https://www.mhlw.go.jp/wp/yosan/ yosan/18syokanyosan/dl/gaiyo-09.pdf (accessed 25 June 2023).

21. Gender Equality Bureau Cabinet Office. (2022). 女性役員がいない プライム市場上場企業数 (Translation: Prime-listed companies that do not have female executives). https://www.gender.go.jp/research/ weekly_data/06.html (accessed 29 June 2023).

22. Gender Equality Bureau Cabinet Office. (2017).

23. Ministry of Health, Labour, and Welfare. (2016). Annual population and social security surveys (the National Fertility Survey). https://www.mhlw.go.jp/toukei/list/118-1.html (accessed 20 June 2023).

24. Dentsu. (2013). 電通総研が「主婦の再就業による直接効果と経済波及効果」を試算 (Translation: Dentsu Institute estimates "direct effect and economic ripple effect of re-employment of housewives"). https://www.dentsu.co.jp/news/release/pdf-cms/ 2013091-0725.pdf (accessed 20 June 2023).

25. Gender Equality Bureau Cabinet Office. (2017). 2017 white paper on gender equality. https://www.gender.go.jp/about_ danjo/whitepaper/h29/zentai/html/zuhyo/zuhyo01-05-10.html (accessed 20 June 2023).

26. Teikoku Databank. (2021). 全国「女性社長」分析調査 (Translation: National "Women Presidents" Survey and analysis). https:// www.tdb.co.jp/report/watching/press/p210702.html (accessed 16 June 2023).

27. OECD.Stat (2023). Employment: Time spent in paid and unpaid work, by sex. https://stats.oecd.org/index.aspx?queryid=54757 (accessed 16 June 2023).

28. *BBC.* (2015). The day Iceland's women went on strike. https://www.bbc.com/news/magazine-34602822 (accessed 16 June 2023).

29. Statistics Bureau of Japan. (2022). Statistical handbook of Japan 2022. https://www.stat.go.jp/english/data/handbook/c0117.html#c12 (accessed 16 June 2023).

30. Statistics Bureau of Japan. (2022). Labour Force Survey. https://www.stat.go.jp/english/data/roudou/index.html (accessed 16 June 2023).

31. Ministry of Health Labour and Welfare. (2021). Basic Survey of Gender Equality in Employment Management. https://www.mhlw.go.jp/toukei/list/71-23.html (accessed 16 June 2023).

5 Conviction

When we find ourselves a minority, we can choose one of two ways to cope: one is to assimilate; fake it 'til you make it and are accepted as part of the majority. The other is to turn your outsiderness into an advantage.

The latter was the intuitive choice of Miyuki Suzuki, the recently retired former president of Cisco Asia Pacific, Japan, and Greater China, currently sitting on the boards of multiple prominent multinational firms as a nonexecutive board member. Her minority status as a Japanese-raised-overseas grew even starker on landing in the working world of Japan in her 40s.

When Suzuki assumed the role of president at Cisco Japan, she was markedly different from her colleagues in the male-dominated tech industry in two ways; not only was she a woman of senior rank but also she was Western-educated with a history degree from the University of Oxford. Suzuki leveraged these attributes to transform Cisco Japan, instilling a Western management style of empowerment and personification of the power of diversity.

The results, not the optics of diversity, undergirded her leadership. Under Suzuki's reign, Cisco Japan achieved an unprecedented pace of growth, sustained by a virtuous cycle of local performance and increased global attention from Cisco headquarters.

Suzuki knows how to swim successfully in a man's world without losing grace. She has practical tips for women so they will be taken seriously—speaking firmly in a low voice, taking the front and center seat in meetings. Fortunately, as I observe in my column, "Meetings with Women That 'Take Too Long' Are a Good Thing," women are increasingly comfortable voicing their views in professional settings. Meanwhile, my other column, "Kawaii Culture Hurts Japanese Women in Business," analyzes that the Japanese culture, which values women who are young, cute, and soft, puts a brake on this momentum. Women must realize that society has made them complicit.

There is a power in numbers. But the complacency bred out of the static dominance of incumbents has its weakness. Suzuki's success in Japan demonstrates that being an astute outsider with fresh perspectives can positively shock the system and bring results.

Miyuki Suzuki, Former President of Cisco Asia Pacific, Japan, and Greater China (APJC)

1960: Born in Tokyo, Japan

1965: Left Japan at the age of five with her parents and was raised overseas in Australia and the UK

1982: Graduated from the University of Oxford with a degree in history

1982: Started her career at Reuters in London, with assignments to the Middle East, Canada, and various countries in the Asia Pacific region

1997: Promoted to managing director, Southeast Asia, at Reuters

2002: Returned to Japan as the executive vice president, consumer business of Japan Telecom

2004: Appointed as CEO of LexisNexis, Asia Pacific

2007: Appointed as president and later as vice chairman of KVH, an IT services company (now part of Colt Group)

2011: Appointed as president and CEO of Jetstar Japan to build the newly formed low-cost carrier venture

2015: Appointed as president of Cisco Systems G.K. (Japan entity)

2018: Promoted to president of Cisco Asia Pacific, Japan and Greater China (APJC) and relocated to Singapore

2019: Appointed as nonexecutive director at MetLife Japan KK

2021: Retired from Cisco Systems

2021: Appointed as nonexecutive director at JERA

2021: Appointed as nonexecutive director of Western Digital Corporation

2022: Appointed as nonexecutive director of Twilio

Miyuki Suzuki Drives Change as Outsider from Within

This article was originally published in the Japan Times *on April 7, 2022, and has been modified for the purpose of this book. The information contained in this article is correct at the time of publishing in the* Japan Times.

Miyuki Suzuki, 61, who retired from Cisco in 2021, is a high-profile executive. Active as a nonexecutive director, she sits on the boards of the Fortune 500 data storage solutions company Western Digital, the insurance company MetLife Japan, as well as that of JERA, a ¥3 trillion Japanese energy company formed by an alliance between two major energy incumbents.

Contrary to any preconceived notion of a woman in power, Suzuki is petite and soft-spoken. One winter afternoon in the sunny Westin hotel lobby in Tokyo, Suzuki perched delicately on the sofa dressed in a trim fuchsia jacket over a black dress, complete with a pearl necklace. She chose her words with care. The Japanese term *Yamato Nadeshiko*, whose dainty floral image highlights the traditional gracefulness of Japanese women, floated into my mind.

How did Suzuki get here? Fully bilingual, her career success is built on the intermingling of experiences in her background— Japanese by birth and Western by education. This background helped her maximize her strengths in the right environment. She took a boldly different approach, honed over years of experience, to management in Japan. This paid off handsomely—for her global employer, for her local colleagues, and for herself.

"My father had no ambition that I'd carve out a career," recounted Suzuki. There was no hint of bitterness; he was from a different era. Sometimes a lack of expectation from others can be a blessing in life.

Suzuki was raised from the age of five overseas in Australia and the UK by her Japanese parents—her expatriate father worked for a large Japanese trading company, one of the most coveted positions by elite businessmen in the boom era of the 1970s and 1980s. Had she been a boy, she is certain that she would have been sent back to Japan in her teenage years to follow her father's footsteps: enter a prestigious Japanese university and join a trading company—most likely her father's.

Instead, escaping the gravitational pull toward Tokyo, Suzuki graduated from the University of Oxford with a degree in history, a path more common to the international elite. Although the proportion of female students was not on par with men at the time at Oxford, Suzuki was likely surrounded by more fellow female students than she would have been at a top Japanese university such as the University of Tokyo. (See Figure 5.1.)

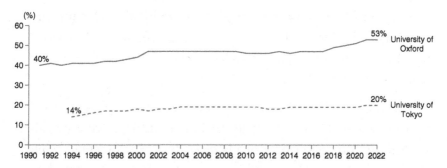

Figure 5.1   Proportion of female undergraduates at the University of Tokyo and the University of Oxford (%)

Note: Despite recent efforts to enroll more women, University of Tokyo continues to lag Western peers in gender equity of its student body.
Created by the author based on: University of Tokyo. (2023). Enrollment. https:// www.u-tokyo.ac.jp/ja/students/edu-data/e08_02_01.html (accessed 9 May 2023); University of Tokyo. (2023); UTokyo outline. https://www.u-tokyo.ac.jp/ja/about/ overview/book_archive.html (accessed 30 May 2023); University of Oxford. (2023). Student statistics. https://public.tableau.com/views/UniversityofOxford-StudentStatistics/DetailTable?:embed=y&:display_count=yes&:showTabs=y&:s howVizHome=no (accessed 9 May 2023); University of Oxford. (2023). Oxford University *Gazette*. https://gazette.web.ox.ac.uk/statistical-information-university-oxford (accessed 30 May 2023).

Out of university, Suzuki joined Reuters in 1982, where she remained for 15 years. She described one of her achievements at Reuters as enabling their capability to deliver data not just in single-byte but also double-byte to reach a broader, multi-language customer base. Her numerous international postings allowed her to experience cultures in the Asia Pacific, including Singapore; Hong Kong; Auckland, New Zealand; and Tokyo, Japan, as well as other assignments in the Middle East and Canada. Her last position was managing director, Southeast Asia. Following Reuters and roles at a couple of start-ups, she landed back in Japan in 2002 with Japan Telecom as the executive vice president, consumer business. Thus began the next chapter of her life: running businesses in Japan—mostly for multinationals. Until retirement in 2021, she worked as president Asia Pacific, Japan, and China (APJC) at Cisco, and held three regional CEO positions for Japan in multinational companies including LexisNexis, Jetstar Airways, and Cisco. Suzuki has had a rich, diverse career over four decades across multiple industries and spanning the globe.

Comparing a hypothetical life against an actual one may be a fruitless exercise. However, a male version of Suzuki, having steadily climbed the corporate ladder of a large trading conglomerate, would have been among the many of his generation who sacrificed his best years for one Japanese company. The male Suzuki would most likely have remained deeply steeped in one industry until he reached upper management in his 60s—a fate that is never guaranteed because it involves decades of outmaneuvering other elite Japanese men.

In comparison, the female Suzuki was able to exert a great deal of control and autonomy over her career and enjoy a variety of industries. Curiosity drove her. Clear-headedness helped her. She honed her distinctive leadership style as she navigated a varied professional landscape, from an e-commerce start-up to a Japanese telecommunication company, back to a budget airline start-up, and then to a large multinational.

How did she decide on each career move? "In most cases, I was not looking for a change," she said earnestly. When the right opportunities knocked on the door, however, she got excited about the possibility of "creating a new, meaningful solution." In retrospect, Suzuki broadly categorized her career chapters into three buckets: turnaround, start-up, and localizing global value propositions for multinationals.

Her first turnaround experience was with Japan Telecom, where she led their consumer business from 2002 to turn that business around from "a source of financial hemorrhaging" back to profit. The turnaround exercise proved to be a turning point for her leadership style.

"I was very individualistic until I was about 40," reflected Suzuki. When she found herself up against a wall, trying to come up with drastic measures to revive the consumer business of a telecommunication infrastructure company, "a penny dropped for me," she said. "I am never the smartest person in the room."

The idea echoes what many modern management textbooks preach. Instead of outsmarting their own team, leaders must recognize specific talent within individuals, create the right team, and motivate them with a compelling vision. However, for a high achiever, taking their hands off the wheel is daunting—it requires relinquishing one's ego. But only then can the team's collective performance exceed the leader's limits.

With this revelation in mind, Suzuki gathered 30 employees with the highest potential from her division, divided them into three cross-functional teams, and asked them to think creatively to resurrect the failing consumer business. No idea was stupid. Three leaders who reported directly to her sifted through the concepts and put the best ideas back into the business for implementation. As a result, restructuring measures were taken, such as selling its consumer asymmetric digital subscriber line assets to a competitor and leasing the assets back from them to service end customers.

Agility—wasting no time between ideation and execution—is a signature of entrepreneurism, and no wonder. With the advent of the boom in internet transactions in the 1990s, Suzuki set up the Asia Pacific operations for a European e-commerce start-up, then built an e-payments venture based in Singapore. Her penchant for entrepreneurialism drew her to the challenge of building a business from scratch with Jetstar Japan, a low-cost carrier joint venture launched by the Qantas Group, partnering with Japan Airlines, where she served as president and CEO in the first half of the 2010s.

Irving Tan, formerly Cisco's chairperson, Asia Pacific, Japan, and China (APJC), recalled changing his Haneda Airport–departing flight to meet Suzuki at Narita airport while she was with Jetstar to interview her for the position of president at Cisco Japan. After her predecessor left, Tan, then president APJC, temporarily filled in for the role.

"We had a really good chat," he recalled. "All the other short-listed candidates were male with more ICT [information and communication technology] experience on their résumés. But I liked her diversity of experience and entrepreneurial spirit. We needed that more than a competent multinational manager type." Tan was so convinced of the fit that he told Cisco's global CEO at the time, John Chambers, that "if it doesn't work out, you can fire me."

Tan needed a new, preferably Japanese, leader to double-down on the transformation he had ignited in Japan. Underlying the change was a cultural reboot, an attempt to make it as open as the rest of Cisco and to weaken the hierarchical culture that tends to develop under conventional Japanese leadership.

In fact, Cisco's frustrations at the time mirrored those of many multinationals who operated in Japan. Despite the overall Japanese market being one-third the size of the US market, multinational business operations in Japan tended to struggle in the face of strong local competition. Sales were stagnant, and local management often offered excuses, but no solutions. In Japan, the global culture of a firm often fails to permeate beyond the veneer of politeness. Therefore, the ideal regional CEO for Japan must meet three requirements: deliver performance, offer a clear analysis of the market, and be an agent for cultural change.

These mandates fit Suzuki's strengths perfectly—the regional CEO being Japanese by birth was an easier pill to swallow for the local staff members. Behind her identity as a Japanese, however, Suzuki was equipped with a global mindset and a Western management philosophy. This combination made it possible to turn around both performance and culture. Finally, the global headquarters had someone who made sense in Japan.

Performance-wise, Suzuki more than met expectations in the three years she led Cisco Japan. Growth boomed into the double digits, whereas before her arrival, Cisco Japan had grown below the level of GDP. Japan became the best performing region within the Asia Pacific under her watch. At the heart of her strategy was clear-eyed realism—"Cisco is a huge global player but is relatively small in Japan." She quickly realized that being US-centric in the way it serviced customers, for example, routing helpdesk inquiries to the US in English, would not be enough in Japan.

Suzuki recounted introducing an unconventional strategy to ride on the backs of local giants such as NTT and Ricoh. For example, she is proud of integrating Cisco's ICT, such as its Wi-Fi and cyber-security, into Ricoh's multifunction printers, which catered to small and medium enterprise (SME) customers. The Ricoh strategy bridged access to local SMEs which had been out of Cisco Japan's reach, while Ricoh provided sales coverage, maintenance, and support.

Empowerment, a relatively novel concept to many Japanese but one Suzuki had practiced at Japan Telecom, boosted the sense of ownership on the ground. "She took [Cisco Japan] to places I had never expected," Tan said. Replicating her success at Japan Telecom, she challenged intergenerational teams of five to seven people to come up with ideas to reinvigorate the business—"a master-stroke," in Tan's words. The flattened hierarchy created a culture of psychological safety. Cisco Japan was ranked first in Great Place To Work's table in 2018 in the large business (more than 1,000 employees) division for the first time.

Michiko Kamata, managing director of APJC Small Business Growth Office, was already a seasoned marketing director at Cisco Japan when Suzuki took the helm from Tan. After many years at the same company and ready for a career change, "I was not in the mood to impress [Suzuki]," she recalled.

In a one-on-one meeting in Suzuki's early days, Kamata candidly shared with her a laundry list of issues she thought were wrong with the company. Kamata cared little if it was a politically unwise move. To her surprise, Suzuki sincerely thanked her for her candidness. "It opened my eyes," said Kamata, "that you can be a leader with little regard for politics."

Indeed, Suzuki turned out to be radically different from the Japanese leaders Kamata was accustomed to. Suzuki firmly said no to weekend golf and late-night drinking to prioritize time with her family—her British husband is fully supportive of her career. Socializing outside business hours is a cultural norm in Japan, especially in the male-dominated ICT sector. Was there grumbling from the old guard? "She drew a clear line in the sand and divided the roles," explained Kamata. Within the realm of global compliance codes, entertainment is fine for the sales executives who believe in its merit. However, Suzuki focused on setting Japan on a growth path with better alignment with the global Cisco organization.

"The level of global attention bestowed on Japan saw a sea change," recounted Kamata. On arrival, Suzuki steadfastly scheduled quarterly business reviews with corporate headquarters, including global visits, which she deftly handled bolstered by her negotiation skills in native English.

For Cisco, Japan was back on the map. As a result, Suzuki secured more global funding. Kamata pointed out that Suzuki made sure to invite the local middle executives, including Kamata herself, to the global meetings to enhance their visibility. Witnessing the uplift of Japan's status, "the grumbling old guards soon quieted," attested Kamata.

When Tan was promoted to the global chief operating officer position at Cisco in 2018, Suzuki succeeded him in the president APJC role and relocated to Singapore amid the complicated and increasingly strained relationship between the US and China. Although the role was less operational and more managerial than her last one, Tan commended her ability to connect with different cultures. "Asia is so complex because of the different levels of maturity." Suzuki ably managed both her APJC team as well as dealings with global management.

Kamata, who eventually followed Suzuki's trajectory from Japan to APJC by being assigned to a regional role in November 2021, emphasized that Suzuki's appointment opened a path for North Asian and female leaders. Often, leadership at Asia Pacific operations in multinational companies is heavily weighted toward native English speakers such as Australians, Indians, and Singaporeans, and Cisco at the time was no exception. "There is now a strong expectation from global to sustain the leadership pipeline (after Suzuki) from North Asia—that is, China, Korea and Japan," said Kamata. Correspondingly, she noted an encouraging mindset shift with the younger generation in Japan—"women started raising their hands to work in Singapore" where the APJC headquarter is located.

Is her success an exception because of her overseas upbringing, or can it be replicated by average working women who are born, raised, and educated in Japan? Suzuki believes that women in Japan can do better for themselves. But there is unlearning to do. "Women are taught to demean themselves," she observed. When considering senior positions "men feel entitled, whereas women must be forced to apply. Japanese women particularly have this glass-half-empty attitude."

On the positive side, she recognizes that women have an advantage; "women tend to speak [better] English, which is such a weapon." The key is to market yourself. She urges women to be vocal about their ambitions. Physical tricks help, too—"women naturally choose to sit in the back of the room. I was taught early on to take one of the center seats." Speaking with precision and in a low voice is also effective.

When it comes to Japanese companies, they also "miss a huge number of practical things," said Suzuki. If you are serious about promoting competent talent, regardless of gender or background, she argued that companies must take risks—go outside of the comfort zone for recruiting and mandate having at least one female candidate for every major leadership role.

In her eyes, womenomics, one of former Prime Minister Shinzo Abe's policies, "didn't have bite" due to a lack of accountability tracking. Companies must set diversity targets, drive metrics, and tie these to management bonuses. Undoubtedly, there would be temporary discomfort, but only through "positive discrimination," she concluded, can corporate Japan beat the diversity lull it has fallen into.

Given her management experience, ex-CEO seniority, and language skills, it is not hard to imagine how highly sought after she is in the current environment where companies and investors double-down on the diversity of the board. "I won't be coy about it," said Suzuki. "You can take it one of two ways. One is to resent tokenism and the other is to ride on it." The realist in her chooses the latter approach, embracing the chance to prove she can add value.

Suzuki's career chronicle is a tale of a nail sticking out so smartly that it avoids getting hammered down, even in the conformity-based society that defines Japan. For ambitious women, this is increasingly a reasonable approach. Japan is changing—mounting frustration with stagnation and increased labor fluidity tip the scale in favor of a new approach to addressing problems. Although an Oxford education is optional, knowing and cultivating your strengths is critical for women to carve out a personal niche. Suzuki's trajectory shows that the right opportunity will come along if you have core strengths, and there is no shame in taking the opportunity. Nowadays, such a fluid career approach is less eyebrow-raising in Japan.

"I used to say, don't mess with Miyuki," Tan jokingly said. "Behind the gentle demeanor, she has a spine of steel." I am reminded of my Yamato Nadeshiko impressions of her. Although it is true that Yamato Nadeshiko implies a traditional gracefulness, it also suggests a mental strength beneath the elegant exterior. Japan can certainly benefit from having more Yamato Nadeshiko in the center of the society. If Suzuki is a "reverse import," Japan Inc. must encourage many native Nadeshiko in the pipeline to step up. Not because they are women, but because they are good.

Meetings with Women That "Take Too Long" Are a Good Thing

This column was originally published in Nikkei Asia *on February 13, 2021, and has been modified for the purpose of this book. The information contained in this article is correct at the time of publishing in* Nikkei Asia.

A domestic and international furor erupted last week when the Tokyo Olympic and Paralympic organizing committee president and former Prime Minister Yoshiro Mori made the comment that board meetings with a lot of women "take too much time."[1]

Although he may have meant the comment as a joke, many found his flippant tone offensive. Amid the mounting public outcry of indignation, he stepped down nine days later. But peering into his subconscious, did he voice a sentiment shared silently by many men of the baby boomer generation? And perhaps a sentiment held even by younger men, who are frustrated because they believe they are powerless to act against the rising power of minorities, in this case, women.

Counterintuitively, this signals a hopeful message: that nonconforming women and other minorities can, and should, challenge the groupthink of the majority that has suppressed innovation and breakthroughs in Japan for too long.

Mori's message implies two underlying and fundamentally inappropriate assertions: that women in important meetings are merely ornamental and that all important meetings should be brief. Analyzing the reasons behind these views can teach us a valuable lesson on how to maximize the power of diversity.

On the first point, we are, albeit, at a frustratingly slow pace making a dent in the number of women in executive positions. Women's representation is progressing beyond the token phase. In fact, Mori's observation was in response to a Japan Olympic Committee initiative to increase the ratio of female directors of the board to 40%, in line with the Corporate Governance Code of Japan.[2]

But checking the percentage box is not enough. Disproportionately, women occupying board seats are external nonexecutive directors, whereas the ratio is reversed when it comes to men. Even in the C-suite, women are often covering corporate function responsibilities such as human resources or legal affairs and are much less visible when it comes to frontline positions such as sales. For women to have a real seat at the table, we need to keep working on the representation of women on all fronts. Only then do we prove ourselves to be anything more than ornamental.

Then comes the question of meeting brevity. There is a cultural context as to why Mori should think that a short meeting is a successful meeting. In the context of Japan's highly conformist business and political environment, open confrontation is uncomfortable. In its place, Japan has perfected the art of *nemawashi*, a technical term literally meaning the preplanned groundwork to eventually uplift a tree root.

Nemawashi requires that an idea be informally vetted by the inner circle of key stakeholders before the final decision. On the upside, it makes the formal meeting extremely efficient. On the downside, the backroom dealing excludes outsiders and hinders transparency. Because the decision-making meeting is merely a rubber stamp, it is too late for anyone outside the inner circle to offer a fresh perspective, however insightful the perspective may be.

Nemawashi can be a useful tool to build consensus within a small circle during uneventful times. But when conjuring a big, bold move in a volatile world, openly debating key issues as a group makes sense. If the debate takes place in the open beyond the confines of nemawashi, there is a high chance that women, because of their minority status within the organization, will be able to bring a radically different perspective. The meeting may tailspin, but their views could challenge the tunnel vision often cemented by past successes.

And this is exactly the fresh breath of air that Japan needs. For example, its high-tech industry, once a crown jewel, has lost much of its competitiveness in recent decades as companies raced ahead to perfect technical specifications while leaving consumers' real-world needs on the starting grid. All those male executives with similar engineering backgrounds need a breath of fresh air, not the fumes from each other's tailpipes.

Moving away from nemawashi will require a drastic cultural shift in many Japanese companies, and top executives must start encouraging their staff members to respectfully and constructively challenge each other. It will take practice. But the rewards are more innovation and higher levels of engagement from all parties. Such an open debate culture will be an inclusive one for all minorities, including women.

One of the unexpected outcomes from Mori's misstep is a popular hashtag based on his use of the phrase *wakimaenai onna*, referring to women who do not understand their place. The original Japanese verb, *wakimaeru*, implies being an adult who understands the unwritten rules. But these rules are conveniently penned by the incumbent, powerful majority. In their world, women in the meetings are window dressing. The real decision-making happens before the meetings anyway. Now that these ill-conceived assumptions are exposed in broad daylight, we must consciously break them to move the needle for gender equality at work.

In the history of Japanese business and politics, there were pioneer women who charged ahead, untamed by patronizing men. Compared to our predecessors, we have the power of numbers. Although still a minority, Japanese women have a strong enough voice and sense of camaraderie; #wakimaenaionna has reached 1.3 million Twitter users in six days. If there is a silver lining to Mori's gaffe, it is that we now have a nifty name by which to call ourselves.

Kawaii Culture Hurts Japanese Women in Business

This column was originally published in Nikkei Asia *on July 17, 2020, and has been modified for the purpose of this book. The information contained in this article is correct at the time of publishing in* Nikkei Asia.

Last year on November 1, Hello Kitty turned 45. Being squarely middle-aged does not bother the snow-white cartoon kitten, whose contribution to Sanrio, the company that designs her, ranges from theme parks to international licensing business.

Hello Kitty embodies the Japanese concept of *kawaii,* or cuteness, but more than simply cute, kawaii suggests something cuddly and cherished for its innocence. Baby animals are the epitome of kawaii.

Kawaii has an economic and global dimension, too, supporting Japanese soft culture ranging from manga to emojis, but when mixed with Japanese society's expectations of women's demureness, it spells a curse lethal to the advancement of women in Japan.

Japan's lackluster performance in gender equality is not new. Public and private sectors are working to improve myriad factors, ranging from insufficient outside childcare capacity to rigid employment customs. Yet Japan was 121 out of 153 countries on the World Economic Forum's Global Gender Gap report 2020, down 11 from last year.[3]

But the curse of kawaii lurks at the bottom of this sticky issue. Because it is invisible, it is particularly tricky to tackle.

In the corporate world, reaching the age of 45 would suggest a person was about to take a step up into management. But in 2018, women comprised only 12% of managerial positions and 3% of board positions in Japan, the worst among the Group of Seven countries.[4]

Unsurprisingly, cuteness does not sit well with wanting to climb the career ladder. Can you credibly demonstrate leadership while being kawaii? Do your staff members look up to the cuddly you? The problem of being, or feigning, kawaii is that you are not taken seriously.

Therefore, around mid-career, professional women are faced with the choice of opting out of advanced workplace progression; becoming a mother, literally or as a nurturing figure within the company, or carving out a different leadership model as an adult woman.

To be fair, Japan is not alone with its obsession about female stereotypes dominated by youth. The US equally values the capital springing from youth. But there is a difference: when American culture typically associates women's youth with sexiness, Japan associates it with innocence. Unfortunately, Bambi is granted with even fewer shots at professional success than a vixen.

Why this persistence of kawaii? It is too easy to point out that the older generation of men expects women to be kawaii. Often, they think they have good intentions as they claim it is an act of chivalry. This patronizing attitude, however, leads to the unfair lack of opportunities resulting in the gender gap in promotion over time.

Then we must realize that society has made women complicit. By constantly processing the message that men expect us to be kawaii, our brains start telling us that kawaii is unequivocally good, and we have stretched the notion so far that now we can be kawaii for life.

How do we snap out of the mental inertia that women, even in professional contexts, need to be kawaii, adorable, and infantile?

The problem will fix itself only if we have a critical mass of senior-ranking women. They would not have gotten where they were by being cuddly. They are a kawaii repellent who can shoot down the woman-child coquettishness at work. But Japan lacks the critical mass to build the critical mass.

So, we need the all-hands-on-deck approach. Patronizing attitudes start at an early age. Parents need to avoid overprotecting their girls. In my childhood, my father used to tell me that cats hide their claws, that you should not flaunt your talent. Although there is gender-free merit to this wisdom, if consumed with the kawaii doctrine, a girl's claws may get dull by the time their male peers are miles ahead.

Next, employers need to evaluate the next generation based on merit. They need to avoid the double standard in which assertive males are favorably regarded while their female equivalents are not, because of their betrayal of the kawaii principle.

Last, there is self-help. Japanese women themselves need to unlearn the spell of kawaii. Is it not that, deep in our psyche, we find it easier to be kawaii because it relieves us of the burden of having to achieve? We should catch ourselves switching to higher, girl-like tones when talking to male peers. We must not be afraid to speak assertively in the meetings instead of just smiling and politely nodding.

Encouragingly, there are signs women are stepping out of the kawaii coma. Sato Kondo, a high-profile freelance newscaster, stopped using hair dye in her late 40s in 2018.[5] Given that anchorwomen in Japan achieve celebrity status for their intellect and youthful appearance, Kondo's gray hair in public was sensational. It was decidedly anti-kawaii—and positively received. Such statements in the media will continue to awaken Japan and its women from the spell of kawaii.

Business experts have long pointed out women's lack of self-promotion as a universal hindrance to their career, but in Japan, the fear of not appearing kawaii gives an extra reason for women to hold their tongue. It is obviously by design that Hello Kitty does not have a mouth. But women do. And it is time we spoke up and started breaking free of our kawaii obsession.

References

1. *Asahi Shimbun Company*. (2021). 「女性がたくさん入っている会議は
時間かかる」森喜朗氏 (Translation: "Meetings with many women
take longer." Yoshiro Mori). https://www.asahi.com/articles/
ASP235VY8P23UTQP011.html (accessed 20 June 2023).

2. *Nikkei*. (2021). スポーツ界、女性役員拡大　JOC やラグビーで理事 4 割
(Translation: Female executives increasing in the sports industry;
40% of directors in JOC and rugby, etc.). https://www.nikkei
.com/article/DGXZQODH255R90V20C21A6000000/ (accessed
20 June 2023).

3. World Economic Forum. (2019). Global gender gap 2020.
https://www.weforum.org/reports/gender-gap-2020-report-100-
years-pay-equality/ (accessed 19 June 2023).

4. *Nikkei*. (2019). 世界の女性管理職比率は 27%、ILO　日本は G7 最低
(Translation: ILO states percentage of women in management
globally is 27%; Japan is the lowest in G7). https://www.nikkei
.com/article/DGXMZO42179640X00C19A3EAF000/
(accessed 19 June 2023).

5. *Asahi Shimbun Company*. (2018). 白髪隠さない近藤サトさん「束縛から
楽になりすっきり」 (Translation: Sato Kondo, who doesn't hide her
gray hair, says, "It's refreshing to be removed from restrictions").
https://www.asahi.com/articles/ASL9B3628L9BUTFL001.html
(accessed 19 June 2023).

6 Leadership

Some are born to lead, and others stumble into leadership later in adult life, never fully escaping their self-doubt. Masami Katakura, chairwoman of EY ShinNihon, falls into the latter case. Thirty-two years of tenure in a male-dominated accounting industry has certainly taught her resilience, an ingredient for successful leadership. But it was not until Scott Halliday, then–area managing partner of Japan, discovered a hidden gem in her optimistic mindset that she woke up to her full potential as a leader of such a large organization as EY ShinNihon, which counts over 500 partners and over 5,500 staff members within its ranks.

That Halliday, who groomed Katakura to take over the role of EY ShinNihon chairwoman, is American is not a coincidence. Japanese culture remains patriarchal, evidenced by the recent flight of former princess Mako in 2021 from the imperial family to the United States. As I analyze in my column, "Former Princess Mako's Marriage Holds a Mirror to Japan," her marriage to a "commoner" meant losing her royal status whereas it would not have been the case were she a prince.

Moreover, even Japan's everyday language itself functions to accentuate the gender bias as I discuss in my other column, "Japan's Language Gender Divide Hurts Women at Work." It is no surprise that if such an omnipresent haze of gender bias exists, it may quietly cloud the eyes of conventional Japanese male leaders as they pick the candidates for the next generation of leaders.

Even if her ascent to the helm was not premeditated, Katakura did not simply wait to be discovered by an American boss, however. Her own assertiveness, despite headwinds, helped her. Even though being an audit partner in Japan never required English proficiency, her enthusiasm in taking early morning English lessons to communicate directly with Halliday reaffirmed his view that she was up for the bigger task. Now, as EY ShinNihon chairwoman, Katakura confidently represents the Japanese audit practice's interests in English-language meetings with other global leaders.

Learned leadership such as Katakura's is no less effective than natural leadership. Humility and resilience, the hallmarks of learned leadership, may enhance one's relatability and authenticity. Stepping up to grab an opportunity, which Katakura did less for her ego but rather to open paths for fellow women, proved to be the right thing to do, not only for her but for the organization as well.

Masami Katakura, Chairwoman and CEO of Ernst & Young (EY) ShinNihon

1968: Born in Tokyo, Japan

1991: Graduated from Meiji University with a degree in business administration

1991: Passed the CPA exam and started her career at Showa Ota & Co. (now EY ShinNihon)

2005–2007: Appointed as deputy director in the Information Policy Division, Commerce & Information Policy Bureau of the Ministry of Economy, Trade & Industry

2011: Promoted to senior partner at EY ShinNihon

2016: Appointed as executive board member of strategic planning and brand, marketing, and communication

2019: Appointed as chairwoman and CEO of EY ShinNihon, becoming the first female leader of a major accountancy firm in Japan

Masami Katakura Realizes Her Leadership Potential with Help from a Mentor

This article was originally published in the Japan Times *on February 24, 2022, and has been modified for the purpose of this book. The information contained in this article is correct at the time of publishing in the* Japan Times.

Masami Katakura, the first chairwoman of a Big Four accounting firm in Japan, is the face of Ernst & Young (EY) ShinNihon—literally. Mere steps after entering EY's Hibiya Midtown office in Tokyo, you are greeted by her radiant smile emanating from the covers of *Accountant's Magazine*, prominently stacked in rows on the office magazine rack.

"When the face of someone you know is pasted on the cover, it gets awkward tossing these copies in the recycling bin," joked 53-year-old Katakura when I mention this. "I'm forever stuck on display." Her unassuming laughter is infectious.

The chair of the partnership behind accounting firm EY ShinNihon is democratically elected by its 550 partners under a system of one-partner, one-vote. Katakura's glass ceiling–shattering victory in 2019 was a milestone for the Japanese accounting industry, known for its conservatism.

What motivated her to run for office in 2019? "I just wanted to pave the path for the women following behind me," explained Katakura humbly. "At first, I was reluctant because it would look like screaming 'me-me-me,' but in the end, I could not contradict what I was telling my female colleagues—to grab a chance and go for it." Breaking the glass ceiling is one way to pave a path—and her story contains real-life remedies against the social inertia that weighs women down in the professional services industry.

Growing up in a family where nearly all the women worked, Katakura found her vocation early. Throughout her childhood, spending time at the office of her aunt, a tax accountant's assistant, she was impressed with how small business owners were appreciative of professional service support. "They showered my aunt and her colleagues with thank-you gifts—the office was always filled with goodies every child would dream of, and I certainly liked that," she explained.

After graduating from Meiji University and passing the CPA examination in 1991, she joined Showa Ota & Co., now EY ShinNihon. It had been five years since the enactment of the Equal Employment Opportunity Act. "On our client's side [which tended to be middle to upper managers], it was 100% older men," she recalled. "They did not relegate to female accountants as much as they did to their own female subordinates to pouring tea at meetings," she continued, "but neither was it an equal professional footing for women and men."

First, some clients concocted remarkable reasons to fend off female professionals. Industries related to natural resources cited the superstition that having women on-site would invite celestial wrath and thus cause natural disasters. The construction sector, Katakura's desired sector, was out of her reach because her bosses deemed it required too much business travel and client entertainment for women to handle. And in manufacturing, factories did not welcome female accountants for inspections because it was "dangerous for ladies," when in fact, as Katakura dryly pointed out, "they had plenty of women working on the shop floor."

But what made women, including Katakura, more indignant than the clients' responses were the behaviors of their own male colleagues. She recalled her disbelief when overhearing a male boss bantering with his (male) client suggesting how truly annoying it was when a female accountant pointed out an issue. When it came to promotion, the cost of being a woman was undeniable—"it usually took three to four years to be a project leader for a man. A woman, without exception, needed four to five years." The unconscious bias is still there. She notes that employers expect more evidence for the promotion of women than for men.

While many of her female colleagues left frustrated—some of them going independent—Katakura stuck around. With her head low, she kept working and observing—the higher she climbed the corporate ladder, the more acutely she felt the old boys' network. At one point, she realized that "some women above me were totally out of the loop, only because they did not join the informal network and therefore missed out on the opportunity to build trust with those in power."

In the high-context culture of Japanese formal business, direct relationship-building often takes place offline over impromptu drinks after work. Katakura, married in her late 20s but childless, did not mind the last-minute invites. But many women, especially with children, are at a disadvantage as their informal exposure to colleagues and higher-ups is less frequent than their male peers.

Trotting the path of diligent client work and recognition by mostly male peers as "one of us"—Katakura was a rising star. Promoted to partner at the age of 35—she could have easily ended up as another seasoned female partner, well-compensated but outside the inner orbit of leadership. Her defining moment arrived in 2015 after the accounting fraud of a major client came to light, seriously tarnishing the brand of EY ShinNihon, its auditor. The firm found itself in a crisis, losing blue-chip clientele and replacing its senior leadership. In response, the global EY organization dispatched Scott Halliday, a seasoned American executive who formerly led its UK division, as a fixer to work alongside Koichi Tsuji, the newly appointed chairman of EY ShinNihon.

It was Halliday, assuming the role of Japan's area managing partner, who, according to Katakura, "brainwashed" her: "He kept telling me every day that I was destined to be a leader." On his side,

"I don't think she believed what was possible for her," Halliday, now retired in the US, reflected during our phone interview. Katakura impressed him with her intellectual curiosity and positive attitude—"you cannot be a pessimistic general," said Halliday. While EY ShinNihon scrambled to get back on its feet, Halliday saw in Katakura an engine for change. She was a hidden talent.

It took some convincing, however. "Women are not quick to pound their chest," noted Halliday, who said he "created a safe zone for her while feeding her intellectual curiosity." In an organization of EY's scale with 12,900 partners and more than 300,000 employees worldwide,[1] it is near impossible for a "line partner," a moniker for a partner without an internal leadership role, to be organically recognized by the global leadership. Fully aware of this handicap, Halliday organized one-on-one meetings for Katakura to connect with the global leaders.

At first, Katakura was even shy to communicate in English with Halliday. So, she kept taking early morning English lessons. Halliday recounted "a big moment" when Katakura came to talk to him one-on-one without a translator after about 10 meetings. The trust deepened.

Along with Koichi Tsuji, who would succeed Halliday as area managing partner of Japan and whose leadership position atop the assurance business Katakura later occupied, Halliday kept promoting Katakura into leadership positions such as the head of brand, marketing and communication, in 2016. The firm's marketing needed a serious facelift, and it needed to be globalized after ShinNihon was converted to EY ShinNihon, more visibly connected to the global EY network.

Perhaps for the first time in her career, being a woman had a tangible benefit for Katakura. "Because we were careful around the optics of gender balance, we kept positioning her alongside Tsuji in front of our partners," recounted Moriaki Kida, the current chairperson of EY Japan, who served as deputy to Tsuji at the time. By 2019, "there was no partner within the assurance business that didn't know her," observed Kida.

In 2019, after four years of turnaround leadership under Tsuji and Halliday, the firm was ready to put the fraud saga of EY ShinNihon's former client behind it. Katakura, once her mind was made up, made a calculation—"women leaders have a cleaner image in general. I wanted the world to acknowledge that EY ShinNihon had transformed and was about to make a new beginning with me, a woman, as our new chair."

Her intention was genuine, and she had enough exposure alongside the incumbent leadership. It also turned out that she was the only candidate running after the vetting of the nomination committee. Still, she needed to secure more than two-thirds of the vote of confidence, which made her nervous—"I was unable to read how many would be against me. It would have been humiliating to lose [the vote of confidence] as the only candidate. I seriously imagined that I would resign if that happened." The two-hour pre-vote session with her fellow 550 partners started lukewarmly, she recalled, but she felt that the tone turned positive midway as she answered all the questions with sincerity.

Katakura ran her campaign on two promises: bringing leaders and frontline staff closer together through communication and improving audit quality and work-life balance. Under her tenure, the service line started hosting two meetings a month for partners and a town hall meeting for all staff members. The attendance rate for partner meetings remains over 90%, high even discounting the effect of remote work under the pandemic. On ensuring audit quality and life quality for her organization, she pursues having the best of both worlds using technology. "When I started talking about using AI for audit [in 2019], people laughed that it was a pipe dream," she recounted. "Now it has become a reality." It convinced her that if you are right, the world will follow eventually.

Reflecting on her 30-year-long career, Katakura sounds ambivalent about progress on gender equity at work. "On the one hand, the position of Japanese women in the economy has certainly advanced, triggered by the Equal Opportunity Law," she observed, "but at the same time, after 30 years, it is embarrassing that we have only inched this far." According to the Gender Gap Index issued by the World Economic Forum, Japan ranked dismally at 120 in 2021, sinking to be the lowest among developed economies.[2] Even though the ground formally appears level set about gender, working women continue to fight an uphill battle against gender-based expectations. (See Table 6.1.)

Katakura has practical ideas to correct gender-biased societal expectations. Thirty years ago, in her cohort of newly certified accountants, women occupied 10%. Now the ratio has crept up

Table 6.1   Gender gap index ranking (index rank, 2023)

Country	Total	Economic Participation and Opportunity	Educational Attainment	Health and Survival	Political Empowerment
Iceland	1	14	79	128	1
Germany	6	88	82	64	5
UK	15	43	34	105	19
Canada	30	36	1	93	33
France	40	51	1	76	39
US	43	21	59	78	63
Thailand	74	24	61	42	120
Korea, Rep.	105	114	104	46	88
China	107	45	123	145	114
Japan	125	123	47	59	138

Note: Political and economic participation weighs down on Japan's gender gap index.

Source: Adapted from Gender gap index ranking (index rank, 2023)

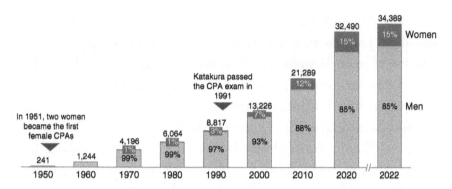

Figure 6.1   Number of certified public accountants (CPA) in Japan by gender

Notes: Becoming a CPA, typically considered a "male" certification, is an example of horizontal gender segregation.

The number of CPAs is treated as equal to the number of members of The Japanese Institute of Certified Public Accountants.

Adapted from The Japanese Institute of Certified Public Accountants (2023). 女性会計士活躍促進協議会の取組について (Translation: Initiatives of the Council for the Promotion of Women Accountants). https://jicpa.or.jp/cpainfo/introduction/cpa_women/about/ (accessed 24 June 2023).

to 25%. The proportion of women among the total population of certified public accountants in Japan has increased from 3% in 1990 to 15% in 2020 (see Figure 6.1). "Twenty-five percent [ratio of women among newly certified accountants] is still unacceptably low, and it stems from gender bias in college majors," asserted Katakura. Female students tend to favor "soft" majors such as literature over "hard" majors such as economics, accounting, management, and law. Katakura attributes the skew to the societal expectation for women: "We must start at a young age, such as teaching accounting to girls in middle school."

Then at work, the social norm, which Katakura describes as a "drinking-networking culture" must change. It requires a mindset change from the bottom up. Consciously building trust during an official, daytime work setting is one point; making men equally responsible for childcare is another. And she tries hard to avoid the unconscious bias in promotions where more conservatism is implicitly applied to female candidates. "I firmly request that the slate [for promotion] contain as many women as possible. We would be neutral in appraising them [against men], but I want these women at least to be on the slate when they meet the formal requirement."

Instilling a quota of 30% women in leadership positions in business as well as in politics is something that Katakura endorses. "We have done almost everything when it comes to rules. Japan's only gap [in contrast to other developed economies] is a quota."

Meanwhile, Katakura believes that women must improve their game as well. Observing senior professional women within and outside EY, she lamented that "many women have such untapped potential." Partly it may be due to lack of opportunities and mentors, such as Halliday was to Katakura, but she assesses that women are not pushing hard enough. "Perhaps men are afraid of the competition getting crowded if women also chase leadership positions," so men keep it to themselves, she mused. "We must encourage women to aim higher." Her remark resonates with a comment from Halliday: "women should always be prepared with elevator speeches [for bosses]."

Did Katakura experience any aha moments after assuming the current leadership role? "I think I was too preoccupied with the notion of typical male leadership," pondered Katakura, "that one has to be technically savvy and lead multiple big accounts and all that." Two years into the role, she is now more at ease with her own style. Halliday concurs that Katakura "balances femininity well," pointing to more empathy and caring for people. "Women can bring a breadth of leadership styles," observed Katakura, "because women have many faces—the office cannot be a single dominant existence," as it could be for men. The diversity of style encourages a virtuous cycle of creating a rich pipeline of aspiring women in the next generation.

In addition to her talent and her 30 years' worth of hard work, was there any luck in Katakura's story? She certainly was lucky to have been discovered by Halliday. But what is important is that her narrative presents a repeatable formula for any employer serious about tapping into the potential of women. Encourage a culture that is unbiased toward gender, and provide mentorship from the top for those hidden gems. These actions pay a hefty dividend when consistently and patiently applied on the ground.

Katakura's tale is one of a woman in professional services who survived the headwinds and, in the end, leveraged her minority status to her advantage—not to advance her personal agenda but to benefit the organization for which she dedicated her career.

"I hope that my journey encourages the next generation of women," Katakura said. I noticed that she deliberately chose her title to be *chairwoman* as opposed to *chairperson*. "We are all tired of being called the first woman of whatever, aren't we," she chuckled, "but it also benefits us for the attention it calls to us. So, why not chairwoman? I am unabashed."

Former Princess Mako's Marriage Holds a Mirror to Japan

This column was originally published in Nikkei Asia *on November 26, 2021, and has been modified for the purpose of this book. The information contained in this article is correct at the time of publishing in* Nikkei Asia.

Earlier this month former princess Mako, now Mrs. Mako Komuro and niece to Emperor Naruhito, left Narita for JFK Airport with her new husband and college sweetheart, Kei Komuro.

As far as royal marriages go, it was all very unusual: no wedding ceremony, rejection of the one-off allowance worth ¥152.5 million ($1.37 million), and the choice of New York City as the couple's new home.[3]

Ever since an unsettled financial dispute between Kei's mother and her former boyfriend boiled over in 2017, public criticism has mounted against the couple getting married.

Former princess Mako's drama can be interpreted in many ways. For romantics, she is a princess struck by true love. For those critical of social media, it is a cautionary tale of excessive celebrity bashing, with the former princess reportedly suffering from complex post-traumatic stress disorder.

For many, it is a commonplace story of a relationship-induced familial rift blown out of proportion due to the fact that one side has royal blood.

Although all these interpretations are valid, I see it as the story of a young woman's rebellion against the deep-seated patriarchy of Japan. The former princess' struggle mirrors our own, and her family status only brings our woes into painfully sharp focus due to its extremity.

When it comes to the imperial family, Japanese traditions must be reassessed according to changing times. And in modernizing the imperial family, we can also modernize ourselves. Three parallels can be drawn between the Mako saga and women's position in Japanese society.

First, the unwritten code of conduct is that women follow family expectations in major life events such as marriage. Men, although not exempt from that same pressure, generally have an easier time of it. In the former princess Mako's case, the family became synonymous with the public. When the masses of traditionalists deemed Kei and his family unfit as imperial in-laws, she was up against a wall.

Second, conservative societal and familial expectations are a familiar burden on women's shoulders. The desire to escape them is a key reason pushing young women into the big cities. Last year Tokyo added 21,000 women[4]—more than twice the number of men—resulting in more single women in Tokyo and more single men in the countryside.

Women who do decide to marry are then forced to renounce a part of their maiden identity. The *ie seido*, or family system, may have been officially abolished in 1947, but its patriarchal spirit is alive and well. It dictates that a house, the foundational unit of Japan, is governed by a male master. The marriage law, which binds a married couple with one surname—the husband's surname is chosen in 96% of marriages[5]—is a lingering manifestation of ie seido.

Because the imperial family encapsulates ie seido, it is little wonder imperial status comes with gender-biased baggage.

Under the Imperial House Law, only a male descendant of the emperor can ascend the throne. Imperial women automatically become commoners when they marry commoners, but not imperial men. Emperor Naruhito and his father both married commoners. Former princess Mako, however, kissed her royal title goodbye just by marrying for love.

Finally, patriarchy discourages female members of the imperial family from pursuing a career. According to Emperor Naruhito's sister, Mrs. Sayako Kuroda, whose 2005 book was published the same year that she married a commoner,[6] she "withheld from assuming long-term responsibilities for fear of stepping down midway" due to marriage.

Discouraging female labor has long-term consequences. An employer who expects less from women than from men may not offer them proper career advancement growth opportunities, which leads employers to expect even less down the road. How unsurprising that only 6.2% of Japanese board members are women.[7]

Japan faces serious structural challenges, such as revitalizing the regions, slowing population decline, and reinvigorating the workforce, to list just a few. Encouraging women to enjoy vibrant careers as well as having a family would go a long way toward addressing these challenges.

Reflection on former princess Mako's marriage suggests that the imperial family would be a great place to initiate change. Although many Japanese are ambivalent toward the imperial structure, we still respect the family as an icon; change at the top has the power to move the needle.

The imperial clock is ticking. Of the six under-40 imperial family members, excluding former princess Mako, five are women.[8] Insisting on patrilineal male succession poses an existential threat to the imperial family. Similarly, while trying to drag the country out of a long no-growth tunnel, failing to include half of the population is not an option.

Despite popular backing—87% of people approved of seeing a female emperor according to a Kyodo News poll conducted in March and April[9]—political elites are reluctant to change the law. Likewise, they drag their feet on allowing married women to retain their maiden names. But we must keep pushing for reform.

Former princess Mako's decision to relocate to the United States is a warning sign. It is time to make Japan a more welcoming place for her young women to stay and thrive in.

Japan's Language Gender Divide Hurts Women at Work

This column was originally published in Nikkei Asia *on May 22, 2020, and has been modified for the purpose of this book. The information contained in this article is correct at the time of publishing in* Nikkei Asia.

In Japanese, men and women eat differently. This is not a comment on table manners but on language: a man would *ku-u*, with connotations of devouring his food, and a woman may *taberu* or, even better, *itadaku*: to humbly consume.

Similarly, a man would call himself *boku* or *ore*, whereas a woman would say *watashi*. A woman might say *ii-wayo* for "that's OK," but from a man that would sound extremely feminine. Real men would mutter succinctly *ii-yo*.

This is not just a matter of linguistics: these gender-specific forms, with their different levels of assertiveness and politeness, and the societal expectations behind them, put women at a huge disadvantage against men, in life and particularly in the workplace.

Beyond specific words, gender language differences in Japanese are evident in how and what women say. Women are softer spoken and use more euphemisms. Unwritten rules for women's language reflect the acceptable features of women in Japan: never direct, always respectful.

Momoko Nakamura, professor at Kanto Gakuin University who studies the relationship of gender and language, points out that women's language in Japan is strongly tied to the myth that women deserve their own expressions because they are different from men.[10] The notion flies directly against the modern understanding that social expectations, not nature, shape gender stereotypes.

Classifying women as a different species implicitly justifies unequal treatment of men and women, from promotion in careers to role divisions at home. Moreover, for women, believing that we are naturally more delicate beings, as language tells us, becomes a self-imposed ball and chain for those who wish to explore the full potential of life and career.

This gender distinction presents a great handicap. Compared to Western languages, Japanese is inherently higher context, favoring innuendo instead of plain speaking. If women's Japanese is subtler than its male equivalent, it ends up being almost cryptic to untrained ears.

In a business context, even a senior-ranking woman would intentionally speak demurely to a male peer with a soft, soothing tone. Sadly, this is our survival tactic as well as our charm offensive. No wonder many educated Japanese women find English-speaking liberating. It allows us to be blunt even with men, a tall order when speaking the female Japanese language.

As effective as this demure speaking may seem in the short term, this strategy hurts Japanese women in the long run. First, it simply takes longer to coo "I'm afraid I am not good with numbers. Could they be really correct?" instead of saying, "These numbers are wrong."

Second, it forces us to trade off between being articulate and being demure. Although many women hone their skills over time, this is an exhausting exercise. Finally, acting in a "ladylike" manner can take you only so far in business. We should be able to shoot straight and not feel sorry about it.

It is therefore high time that we consciously parted with our irrational expectation of how women should speak. Its underlying assumption is that women need to be subtle to be attractive. But who says that they cannot be both direct and attractive?

Interestingly, Nakamura observes that the Japanese female language is most prominently represented in the Japanese translation of women's remarks in Western literature. For example, Hermione in the Harry Potter wizarding novels sounds much more ladylike in Japanese than a girl her age in Japan today would. In fact, Hermione speaks as briskly as her male peers in the original English.

But the translation sends a subliminal message that all women, even Western ones, should be speaking demurely. Intellectually we know that this is not true. Western professional women are much more outspoken, but they are not any less charming for that.

Some even argue that the delicate Japanese spoken by women represents the "true" Japanese because it embodies the sublime intricacy of the language. Indeed, one attribute of the female language is the abundant use of honorary speak, *keigo*, a reflection of the Japanese culture of respect and humility.

So is this a rare manifestation of diversity and inclusion? No, it is more of the same setting apart of the genders.

Japan's fight for gender equality is subtle and deeply cultural. In contrast to the Hollywood-style #MeToo movement, we have #KuToo, where women protest the mandatory wearing of high heels at work.[11] But even more deeply ingrained in society than dress codes is our language. As the air around us quietly affects our health, the language we use influences our psyche.

Speech should help us advance, not tie us down to stereotypes. It is time to face up to the discriminatory ways in which our words shape our worlds—and change them.

References

1. EY. (2021). EY value realized: Reporting progress on global impact 2021. https://www.ey.com/en_gl/news/2021/09/ey-publishes-annual-report-ey-value-realized-on-progress-toward-measuring-global-impact (accessed 15 June 2023).
2. World Economic Forum. (2021). Global gender gap report 2021. https://www.weforum.org/reports/global-gender-gap-report-2021 (accessed 16 June 2023).
3. *Bloomberg.* (2021). Japanese princess giving up $1.4 million to wed Fordham grad. https://www.bloomberg.com/news/articles/2021–10–01/japan-princess-said-to-give-up-1-4-million-to-wed-fordham-grad#xj4y7vzkg (accessed 19 June 2023).
4. Statistics Bureau of Japan. (2020). Report on internal migration in Japan. https://www.stat.go.jp/data/idou/ (accessed 19 June 2023).
5. Ministry of Health, Labour, and Welfare. (2016). Specified report of vital statistics. https://www.mhlw.go.jp/toukei/saikin/hw/jinkou/tokusyu/konin16/index.html (accessed 16 June 2023).
6. Kuroda, Sayako. (2005). ひと日を重ねて―紀宮さま 御歌とお言葉集 *(Translation: One day at a time—Princess Norinomiya's collection of songs and words).* Daito Publishing.
7. Gender Equality Bureau Cabinet Office. (2020). 上場企業の女性役員数の推移 (Translation: Number of female directors in listed companies). https://www.gender.go.jp/research/weekly_data/05.html (accessed 26 June 2023).
8. The Imperial Household Agency. (2023). Genealogy of the imperial family. https://www.kunaicho.go.jp/e-about/genealogy/koseizu.html (accessed 19 June 2023).

9. *Kyodo News*. (2021). 80% supportive of reigning empress amid shrinking pool of heirs: Poll. https://english.kyodonews.net/news/2021/05/8e4d8a69c832-80-supportive-of-reigning-empress-amid-shrinking-pool-of-heirs-poll.html (accessed 19 June 2023).

10. *Wezzy*. (2018). なぜ翻訳でステレオタイプな「女ことば」が多用される？　言語学者・中村桃子さんインタビュー (Translation: Interview with Momoko Nakamura, linguist: Why are stereotypical "female words" often used in translation?). https://wezz-y.com/archives/56597 (accessed 19 June 2023).

11. *Financial Times*. (2019). Japan's women say #KuToo and ditch high heels. https://www.ft.com/content/cb5a7210-0c50-11ea-bb52-34c8d9dc6d84 (accessed 19 June 2023).

7 Growth

In an era when professional self-reinvention every few years is encouraged, staying at the same company until retirement may seem like an old-fashioned concept. But it does not mean that you cannot have a meaningful career, rich with personal growth, within the walls of a single employer if new opportunities are in fresh supply. In fact, you benefit from the upside of lifetime employment, during which you can build an uninterrupted reputation within the company and a lifelong bond of trust.

Ryoko Nagata, a freshly retired lifer from Japan Tobacco, is one such story. Despite its name, Japan Tobacco is a conglomerate housing food and pharmaceutical businesses in addition to the core tobacco business. Her audacity to announce that she would prefer to stay out of the tobacco business during her recruiting interview set a theme throughout her 36-year career at Japan Tobacco.

Lifetime employment is like marriage—it takes constant effort on both sides to sustain. Japan Tobacco always looked out for new environments in which Nagata could flourish, who in turn repaid the favor by acting as a reputed "fixer" in nontobacco businesses. For Nagata, each stage—from managing a frozen food poisoning crisis, leading the beverage business, to launching a CSR program at corporate headquarters—presented a new set of challenges, from which she learned the requisite lessons to take her to the next chapter.

Just as Japan Tobacco experimented with nontobacco businesses—for example, establishing a joint venture with Burger King in 1996 but eventually exiting in 2001—Nagata's career path may also have been an experiment, and a successful one at that. The question is whether it is repeatable for others. As I argue in my column, "Japan Must Break the Glass Fence Keeping Mothers at Home," working mothers in Japan particularly find themselves in a bind between the societal expectation to stay at home with children and the risk of a prolonged professional career break.

Nagata argues that the social contract between an employer and an employee must be bespoke. She certainly was a successful example of such a social contract. My other column, "Japanese Companies Must Capitalize on the Gender Gap Disclosure Rule," argues that removing gender bias from these social contracts benefit both sides of signors: the employer and employee. And Nagata's career demonstrates that job hopping is not a requisite to a fruitful career; personal growth is possible if your employer invests in your long-term career.

Ryoko Nagata, Former Standing Audit and Supervisory Board Member of Japan Tobacco (JT)

1963: Born in Tokyo, Japan

1987: Graduated from Waseda University with a bachelor's degree in psychology

1987: Started her career at JT in the pharmaceutical business

1992–1994: Attended and graduated from University of Florida with a master of science in agricultural economics

1994: Returned to JT and worked on talent development in HR

1996: Seconded to Burger King Japan as training and marketing manager

1999: JT acquired the food business of Asahi Kasei Corporation to enter the frozen food business[1]

1999: Promoted to manager at the food business division in charge of product development of the frozen food business

2008: JT acquired majority stake in Katokichi, a frozen foods manufacturer[2]

2008: A food poisoning incident due to contaminated frozen dumplings sold by a JT subsidiary

2008: Promoted to executive officer and general manager of the beverage business

2013: Appointed as executive officer, corporate social responsibility (CSR)

2015: JT exited the beverage business[3]

2018: Appointed as standing audit and supervisory board member of JT

(continued)

2021: Appointed as outside director at Honda Motor Co., Ltd.

2023: Left JT

2023: Appointed as external corporate auditor at Medley, Inc.

2023: Appointed as outside director at UACJ Corporation

Ryoko Nagata Stays Clear of Cigarettes in a Tobacco Company

This article was originally published in the Japan Times *on December 21, 2021, and has been modified for the purpose of this book. The information contained in this article is correct at the time of publishing in the* Japan Times.

When I sat in front of the screen for a video interview with Ryoko Nagata from Japan Tobacco (JT), she was still mourning the recent passing of her 94-year-old mother. I have known Nagata for years and how close they were as mother and daughter—they had enjoyed sleepover domestic travels in luxury JR trains even as recently as this year.

At my condolences, she smiled tightly, "I am doing OK. And thank goodness for work! It sure takes your mind off things." And work has been kind to her. At 58, Nagata is the most senior-ranking full-time female executive at JT, a major global tobacco company whose market cap is over ¥4 trillion. She has sat on the board as its standing audit and supervisory board member since 2018. Sought after as one of the few high-ranking women in Japan Inc., she also now serves on the board of Honda Motors as a nonexecutive director.

A lifelong JT employee, she is not your typical high-flying Japanese middle-aged woman, bred on the vibrant cluster of foreign firms—finance and professional services representing two of the fertile sectors to produce this breed. Nor is she a hardened "male executive in a skirt" who gritted her teeth through daily chauvinism by playing golf and backroom politics. Nagata exudes the nonchalant confidence of someone comfortable being the honest and forthright person that she is and with the recognition that she deserves.

Her story, which Nagata herself describes as "quite unique," builds on a happy confluence of JT's long-term intention to nurture female talent and her ever-fresh resolve to take on new challenges— "every five years I seem to turn a corner."

When then-22-year-old Ryoko Nagata, before graduating from the prestigious Waseda University in 1987 with a degree in psychology, interviewed with her prospective employer, JT, she made a curious request. "I said, 'I am a nonsmoker and I want to work on something other than cigarettes,'" recalled Nagata.

This nonmainstream thinking and its verbalization is a hallmark of minority—in fact, I would find it hard to imagine a male student making the same request, as it would be interpreted as a failure to read the (proverbial smoke-filled) room. Luckily for Nagata, JT, who had begun to diversify its business portfolio to supplement the saturating cigarette business following the end of its domestic monopoly in 1985, welcomed her direction.

History of Japan Tobacco[4]

Privatization. Initially, the tobacco business in Japan was solely handled by the government, starting in 1898 when the Japanese Monopoly Bureau was established for the sale of leaf tobacco. This monopoly was extended to all tobacco businesses in 1949, and the bureau was named the Japan Tobacco and Salt Public Corporation (JTS). With the enactment of the Japan Tobacco Inc. Act in 1984, which abolished the tobacco monopoly, Japan Tobacco Inc. (JT) was founded as an entity the following year to succeed the operations of JTS.

Diversification and globalization. In response to the
saturating domestic tobacco business, JT focused on
diversifying its portfolio and globalization. The business
development division, which later became the food and
pharmaceutical business divisions, was established with
the founding of JT to expand into new nontobacco businesses. This was followed by a series of acquisitions to
strengthen the new business areas. Additionally, JT International, which handles JT's international tobacco business,
was founded in 1999 after the acquisition of the non-US
tobacco business of RJR Nabisco Inc., strengthening its
footprint globally. Recently in 2022, JT combined its
domestic and international tobacco business to form a single
global operating model.

The traditional career path within the cigarette business was well
paved with slow and steady progression. By contrast, the nontobacco
space served as a sandbox for JT, allowing experimentation with
business models and career paths. For Nagata, it meant cutting her
teeth with JT's fledging businesses from a Burger King joint venture
(dissolved in 2001) to the frozen food business that JT acquired from
Asahi Kasei in 1999.

It was when she was assigned to a managerial position in the
food business division, as a middle manager to run its frozen food
business, that she had her first serious challenge. With no prior experience in the processed food business, she found herself surrounded
by seasoned colleagues from Asahi Kasei.

It is not hard to imagine how her new colleagues, male and
middle-aged, rolled their eyes at their younger, female boss. Her
designated role as a change agent was a saving grace—she was not
supposed to be one of them but was tasked to instill change. In fact,

JT's intention after the acquisition was to pivot the food business from industrial use to consumer use to leverage JT's consumer branding capabilities.

For Nagata, it felt like pushing a rock uphill. To make matters worse, about the time of Nagata's arrival, performance was in decline, bringing the acquisition itself under scrutiny. The tension culminated when a male colleague from Asahi Kasei, peer to her level, declared in front of everyone, including herself, that Nagata was clearly unfit for the managerial role. "I was absolutely mortified on the spot," she recounted.

To her surprise, the one who sided with her was her boss, the head of the food business division and another lifer from JT; he defended her position as "a decision of his own making." Even though Nagata was wary of his micromanagement style, she recalled being saved by his support; JT had her back.

Was she upset about the personal attack? "I was definitely deflated, but I also knew he was right [that I lacked experience]. I was so nervous and eager to perform, I ended up spinning the wheels," admitted Nagata. Rather than being defensive, she took the criticism with a constructive attitude.

Her approach to compensate for lack of experience was to leverage her team. After the initial humiliation, she worked to gain the trust of those around her. "I took time for multiple one-on-one meetings with each of my seven direct reports" originally from Asahi Kasei, she recounted. "You really need the personal connection as foundation to mobilize someone."

By her third year in the frozen food business, performance was bouncing back. Increasingly, JT management viewed frozen food as a growth area for the group—so much so that in late 2007, JT was ready to acquire Katokichi, a branded frozen food manufacturer, planning to subsequently consolidate them with the frozen food business of Nissin Foods, a packaged food giant under the joint ownership of JT and Nissin Foods. The combined turnover of the hypothetical subsidiary would have been ¥260 billion, making it the largest domestic frozen food player,[5] and overseas expansion for the business was also in sight.

However, it was only a month after the successful takeover bid of Katokichi when a crisis struck, which eventually caused Nissin Foods to pull out of the scheme. Frozen dumplings of JT Foods, the food subsidiary of JT, imported from a Chinese supplier were blamed for food poisoning 10 Japanese consumers, 9 of whom were hospitalized. Pesticides were detected in the dumplings, resulting in a consumer uproar in Japan over food safety. Two years after the incident, a disgruntled Chinese employee at the local supplier was arrested as the culprit who contaminated the line.

For Nagata, the turmoil was a real-life exercise in crisis management. It was not without a revelation—"in the most unexpected moments, you meet people who wow you." She recounted that JT hired temporary hands to handle upset consumers' phone calls. Women who entertained at bars would come in to earn pocket money before starting their night job—"and they were just amazing with their listening skills." The experience taught her to be unbiased.

Emerging from the crisis, she was assigned to lead the beverage business from 2008 to 2013, where she successfully delivered a turnaround. By then, her reputation as a fixer in the nontobacco businesses was solid. What JT had in plan for her next was a corporate role—corporate social responsibility (CSR), a relatively new and growing field that required a strategic communication framework. Appointed to be an executive officer in charge of CSR, Nagata spent her energy on changing the executives' thought process. In contrast to the daily firefighting they were accustomed to, CSR required approaching societal challenges over a longer time horizon. Presenting a vision then back-casting to address today's problems, including facing their own deficiencies, was a mindset shift Nagata had to navigate her senior colleagues through.

Nagata described the challenge: "The management naturally dreaded disclosing anything incomplete—like sustainability KPIs—but the disclosure of work-in-progress is a must for CSR." Step by step, she nudged the management to break away from their comfort zone. "The cycle starts to run on its own when they get recognition [from disclosure], which pushes the boundary of their comfort zone a little further." The delicate balancing between pushing the cause and ensuring followership is something she learned from her previous career chapters.

Nagata affirmed that JT is a gender-equal employer and always has been. Out of the six women who joined the company out of school in her cohort as professionals, three remain including herself—a ratio relatively high for the generation. The other three retired on the occasion of marriage, a social norm at the time. Fast-forward to today, she marvels at the options available to women—"now mothers return to work 100% after maternity leave [at JT]. There is little physical or emotional constraint against [women] working." (See Figure 7.1. for Japan's national statistics.)

Encouragingly, the gender ratio in the incoming cohorts for JT is balanced. But I wondered whether with only Nagata and three other women, two being nonexecutive, serving on the board of 35 directors were too few models, possibly categorized as exceptional cases, to assure the young women today that the corporate ladder is not hostile. Nagata brushed off my concerns—"I think rather than focusing on gender, it is important to create your own individual story, the one and only," she emphasized. She argued that, although employers are responsible to flexibly support working in every life stage—from raising small children to tending to aging parents—the ultimate accountability lies with the individual to charter their career. The ideal engagement between the employer and the employee to

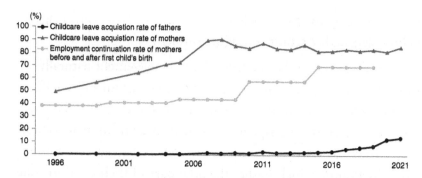

Figure 7.1 Childcare leave acquisition rate by gender and employment continuation rate after first child's birth in Japan (%)

Notes: Although taking childcare leave is a norm for mothers, it still takes major convincing for fathers.

The figures for employment continuation rate are averages over a time span of five years. It includes employees who took childcare leave and those who did not. Created by the author based on: Ministry of Health, Labour, and Welfare. (2021). Basic Survey of Gender Equality in Employment Management. https://www.mhlw .go.jp/toukei/list/dl/71-r03/03.pdf (accessed 9 May 2023); National Institute of Population and Social Security Research. (2021). The 16th Japanese National Fertility Survey. https://www.ipss.go.jp/ps-doukou/j/doukou16/JNFS16gaiyo.pdf (accessed 23 May 2023).

make it happen? "It comes down to a hybrid system," she mused, "a combination of platform as common denominator and on top a negotiation between the individual and the company."

When I spoke to Mutsuo Iwai, the deputy chairman of the board at JT and a long-term mentor figure to Nagata, he expressed a more reserved view than Nagata. He pointed at "the entrenched culture of the old boys club" of Japanese companies, including JT, as an inhibitor to successful mass replication of Nagata's story. The men would bond and exchange tips through late hours at the office and the drinking that ensues. If such an old boys' culture is alive in the mainstream businesses, the race there remains rigged for women. It is an uphill battle, even before factoring in the biological clock.

Iwai critically observed that "there is still such a narrow image of naturally accepted leadership styles in the organization—male and monolithic—which stifles diversity." Iwai frankly admitted to a gender diversity deficiency in the pipeline following Nagata.

The assignment of Nagata to the nontobacco business, therefore, was intentional, according to Iwai. JT reckoned that she "would enjoy more freedom in the new space than being with the tobacco business entrenched with the old boys' hierarchical culture."

For Japan Inc. to truly embrace the diversity of talent, this bedrock culture must change. In Nagata's case, her career path was carefully curated, so she experienced less of that culture. What she demonstrated beautifully over the three decades is that it is indeed possible for women to flourish in their corporate career if given the right opportunity to do so. Today, the challenge is for the companies, including JT, to ready the ground for many more women.

On the bright side, Iwai pointed out two factors that inadvertently work in women's favor. One is the work style change forced by COVID-19; face time at the office is irrelevant in the age of remote work. This, he suggested, undermines the culture of in-person camaraderie for better or worse.

The other factor he mentioned is more JT specific. Because of health awareness and the emergence of popular alternatives such as heated tobacco products, the stability of the conventional cigarette business evaporated over the recent years. "Command-and-control no longer works," admitted Iwai. "We now switch to trial-and-error, the bottom-up approach," which erodes the rigidness of patriarchy. This, he hopes, broadens the window of acceptance for leadership styles. "Only then can we expect a richer pipeline of female talent following Nagata."

Nagata had said, "I feel lucky . . . wherever I was assigned, a wind of change blew." Iwai later added a nuance to her sentiment—"we put her where we expected a wind. And indeed, she performed well every time." Iwai summarized Nagata's approach as her "survival"—"she understood what we expected of her and delivered—not in the old-fashioned way of bonding over late-night drinking, but in her own way of being in the trench and connecting with the line soldiers." It is a balancing act of accommodation and sticking to your guns.

JT's bet on Nagata was handsomely rewarded. The beverage and food businesses, once considered a hobby of a cash-rich tobacco company, continued to gain recognition in the overall JT portfolio. Later, putting Nagata in charge of CSR paid off, preparing JT for the increased attention on sustainability that is observed today. Iwai explained the rationale behind posting Nagata—"CSR at the time needed a major upgrade, requiring a trailblazer."

She counts it as her good fortune that she had many lives within a tenure with one company. Although her late mother, who worked full-time at the Bank of Japan as a young woman, exemplified an independent, professional working woman, the daughter's career is certainly more colorful.

The challenge for JT and Japanese society at large today is to replicate Nagata's success on a larger scale. It is a proof of concept that a talented woman can develop her own leadership style and thrive in a corporate environment. But a proof of concept is pointless if it remains a standalone case in a niche environment. We must work on democratizing her case until, as Nagata points out, focusing on gender becomes irrelevant.

Japan Must Break the Glass Fence Keeping Mothers at Home

This column was originally published in Nikkei Asia *on September 11, 2020, and has been modified for the purpose of this book. The information contained in this article is correct at the time of publishing in* Nikkei Asia.

It was the "potato salad tweet" that went viral across Japan.[6]

A Japanese woman who goes by the Twitter handle Mitsu_Bachi_Bee recounted a sardonic conversation she overheard at a local supermarket where an older man approached a young mother holding a ready-to-eat package of potato salad.

"You ought to be fixing at least potato salad if you are a mother," said the older man, with the mother looking down in shame as her accuser fled the scene. Mitsu_Bachi_Bee, herself with a daughter in tow, promptly picked up two packages of potato salad in front of the mother to show that it is okay to buy ready-made potato salad.

Predictably, the older man's offensive mansplaining triggered a wave of ire in cyberspace, with the tweet attracting 390,000 likes in a month. Clearly, the man had never made the deceptively simple potato salad himself. If he had, he would have known much time is required to prepare it.

What this supermarket pas-de-deux perfectly encapsulates is Japanese society's excessive and unfair demand on mothers.

Driven by economic pressure, there are twice as many double-income households as single-income households today.[7] Yet, Japanese women, on average, spend five times as much time doing the housework and taking care of family members as men.[8] This is the highest ratio among OECD countries, where women, on average spend twice as much time as men managing the household.

No wonder that Japan has a 23.5% gender pay gap, the second largest in the OECD.[9] Although women won equal employment opportunities 35 years ago with the enactment of the Japanese Equal Employment Opportunity Act in 1985, Japanese mothers are miles away from being on an equal footing at work. Japanese society expects mothers, working or not, to be the primary caregivers, locked up in the holy land of motherhood and walled off from the working world. So before Japanese women can aim at the glass ceiling, mothers must first shatter the glass fence surrounding motherhood.

When it comes to fencing mothers into the home, Japan stands as the prime example. First, because of low levels of immigration and high labor costs, securing a domestic helper or au pair is a luxury for most working families, even those earning above-average incomes.

Second, there is an emphasis on hands-on parenting. With so-called experts preaching that baby food must be homemade, those forced to rely on ready-made food or third-party help—mothers, by default—are made to feel guilty.

Finally, Japan's workplace culture automatically expects mothers to scale back. Although most women switch to shorter working time arrangements after the birth of a child, most employers would never even consider that new fathers should do the same.

The glass fence is equally bad news for men, who are relegated to passenger status when it comes to childcare. Not only do men lose out economically because their spouses are not advancing as quickly as men but also they miss out on shaping their children's formative years.

Meanwhile, with COVID-19 shaking so many core beliefs, the opportunity for change will be lost unless society can let go of its obsession with gender roles. With so many people now working from home, those chores which were mostly hidden from men are now on display for all to see. Encouragingly, we have started to see more fathers picking their kids up from daycare and enjoying it, too!

What Japan's government must do is reassess the arcane system of single-earner families, which is built on the spousal income tax deduction. Once and for all, we need to erase policy doublespeak, on the one hand calling for more women to reenter the workforce, and on the other hand penalizing them for earning when they do.

Employers must also start treating working parents equally. Unfortunately, it's those bosses managing young parents—mostly men in their 50s and 60s—who will be the hardest to convince, as they most likely delegated their own childcare responsibilities to their wives. In 2018, only 6% of men in the private sector took parental leave, compared to 82% of women.[10]

Last, society needs to understand that motherhood is not sacrosanct. Myths suggesting that children up to the age of three do best under the full-time care of mothers need to be punctured. We now know that small children benefit from having social interactions outside the family, and we need our leaders to start saying so.

Under the slogan of womenomics, Japan's Prime Minister Shinzo Abe has been busy rolling out policies to advance women's status in the working world. But setting goals and targets will be useless unless we first change the way most households are organized.

That old man who berated the young mother for not making her own potato salad not only revealed his ignorance when it comes to home cooking but also showed how oblivious he was regarding the unreasonable expectations borne by mothers, their families, and society.

Hopefully, the increased awareness afforded by the COVID-19 crisis provides an opportunity to break down the glass fence keeping mothers at home and preventing them from advancing at work.

Japanese Companies Must Capitalize on the Gender Gap Disclosure Rule

This column was originally published in Nikkei Asia *on October 26, 2022, and has been modified for the purpose of this book. The information contained in this article is correct at the time of publishing in* Nikkei Asia.

Otsubone-sama, now used to refer to controlling middle-aged women in the workplace, was originally the title for the female senior butler who supervised the shogun's mansion in imperial Japan's Edo period between the 17th and 19th centuries.

Akin to the American meme of Karen, otsubone-sama derogatorily describes a self-righteous woman with an overbearing, know-it-all attitude.

Most of the otsubone-sama I have met at client companies during my career as a management consultant in Japan have, in fact, been helpful women, well-armed with internal networks developed over many years.

These otsubone-sama knew how to navigate intricate administrative processes, alerting me to subtle power dynamics at play. Their male colleagues largely respected them. Otsubone-sama made the world go around, so it was unwise to make an enemy of them.

Over lunch with one such woman in her 40s, I was shocked to learn that she was paid much less than her male peers despite equivalent academic credentials and importance to her company.

The gender-based division of roles is clear in Japan. Men are common in customer-facing sales positions, while women are sequestered in back-office support jobs. Over time, compensation diverges, creating a pay gap between male and female staff members.

Starting next year, large Japanese companies will have to disclose gender-based pay differences.

German playwright Bertolt Brecht once wrote of "the difficulty of the plains" once the mountains are left behind as he reflected on the daunting task of creating a new society after the fight against fascism was won.[11]

His metaphor applies to the journey of elevating a disadvantaged group, in this case women. When such a group represents less than 10% of the whole, there is a strong imperative to stick together, but above that level, differences can appear, the imperative can be lost, and empowered interests, in this case men, may strike back.

As women now hold about 13% of managerial positions in Japan, the initial momentum for transformation has ebbed.[12]

But Japan cannot sit idle, because elevating women's social status can help address numerous structural challenges facing the country. Some 68% of the irregular workforce is female, while only 35% of those in regular employment are women.[13]

Bridging this difference is key, given Japan's dwindling labor supply. Regular employment can alleviate female poverty by allowing workers to build long-term savings to support their retirement. Improving women's status could also put the brakes on the country's free-falling birthrate, which has been hitting new annual lows.

Mari Kogiso, co-chief executive of impact investment fund SDG Impact Japan, expects the country's requirement to disclose gender pay gaps and the accompanying media attention to force blue-chip companies to "walk the talk."

"It prompts reflection on the employers' part regarding existing initiatives" to promote women, Kogiso told me. "Year-over-year disclosure forces a company to improve."

Advances by blue-chip companies could then set the tone for others, as seen in the UK since a transparency mandate for reporting pay differences by gender was introduced there in 2017.[14]

Valerie Frey, an economist with the Organisation for Economic Co-operation and Development who specializes in gender equity, stresses the importance of combining effective policies with supportive infrastructure to change societal norms and catalyze action. Incentivizing paternity leave to level the playing field for working mothers can be a good start, but is sustainable only if affordable childcare is in place, too.

Gender pay gap disclosure requirements can jump-start improvements. Corporate leaders who view such requirements as a differentiating opportunity, rather than another compliance box-checking exercise, will draw strategic road maps to narrow pay gaps and will require specific improvements across all levels of their organization, mandate unbiased performance reviews, and hold managers accountable.

More broadly, attention to the gender pay gap must be framed to trigger a mindset shift. The media has a prominent role to play.

As Frey points out, the disparity in compensation is reflected in the distribution of unpaid work at home. Gender-based fixed roles within families must be challenged and the skewed allocation of unpaid labor between husbands and wives adjusted. The momentum created by such conversations can fuel the political engine to generate new policies and shift norms.

Japan cannot afford to lag in its march to improve gender equity because it ranks just 116 among 146 countries in the size of its gender gap, according to an index published by the World Economic Forum, the lowest among East Asian and Pacific nations.[15]

Otsubone-sama—competent yet underpromoted women in the workplace—should not be labeled as mildly annoying Karens. They are the ones who keep grinding away, while many of their fellow women have given up and retired entirely. But kept firmly in support roles, they are victims of our societal failure to leverage their strength.

"All too often, we see competent women forever playing a supporting role," Kogiso observed. "Women tend to regard it as virtuous to work behind the scenes supporting the top dog."

Japan's gap stood at 24.5% in 2017, nearly double the OECD average of 13%.[16] Rather than a lack of leadership or a deficiency in women's education, this reflects societal norms that prevent women from reaching their full potential in Japan.

As Brecht pointed out, the difficulty of the plains ahead is undeniable. With the gender pay gap disclosure requirement, the Kishida administration has an opening to tackle the unfinished business of Shinzo Abe's womenomics.

References

1. Japan Tobacco. (2023). Our history. https://www.jt.com/about/history/index.html (accessed 15 June 2023).
2. Ibid.
3. Ibid.
4. Ibid.
5. Nissin Foods Holdings. (2007). 加ト吉、JT 及び日清食品における冷凍食品事業の統合について (Translation: Integration of the Frozen Food Business of Katokichi, Japan Tobacco and Nissin Foods). https://www.nissin.com/jp/news/2223 (accessed 15 June 2023).
6. Twitter. (2020). @mitsu_bachi_bee tweet on 8 July 2020. https://twitter.com/mitsu_bachi_bee/status/1280640234120568832 (accessed 19 June 2023).
7. Statistics Bureau of Japan. (2017). Employment Status Survey. https://www.stat.go.jp/data/shugyou/2017/ (accessed 19 June 2023).
8. OECD. (2016). Time use across the world. http://stats.oecd.org/Index.aspx?datasetcode=TIME_USE (accessed 19 June 2023).
9. OECD. (2018). Gender wage gap. https://www.oecd-ilibrary.org/employment/gender-wage-gap/indicator/english_7cee77aa-en (accessed 20 June 2023).
10. Ministry of Health, Labour, and Welfare. (2019). Basic Survey of Gender Equality in Employment Management. https://www.mhlw.go.jp/toukei/list/71-23.html (accessed 19 June 2023).
11. Open Access in Media Studies. (2019). The difficulty of the plains—6 theses on open access. https://oamediastudies.com/the-difficulty-of-the-plains-6-theses-on-open-access/ (accessed 20 June 2023).
12. OECD.stat. (2022). Employment: Share of female managers. https://stats.oecd.org/index.aspx?queryid=96330 (accessed 19 June 2023).

13. Statistics Bureau of Japan. (2022). Labour Force Survey. https://www.stat.go.jp/data/roudou/longtime/03roudou.html (accessed 19 June 2023).

14. The National Archives on Behalf of HM Government. (2017). The Equality Act 2010 (Gender Pay Gap Information) Regulations 2017. https://www.legislation.gov.uk/ukdsi/2017/9780111152010 (accessed 19 June 2023).

15. World Economic Forum. (2022). Global gender gap report 2022. https://jp.weforum.org/reports/global-gender-gap-report-2022 (accessed 19 June 2023).

16. OECD. (2017). Gender wage gap. https://data.oecd.org/earnwage/gender-wage-gap.htm (accessed 19 June 2023).

8 Curiosity

Some of us are born under a lucky star. It is tempting to believe that Noriko Osumi, vice president at Tohoku University, is indeed such a person—both of her parents are accomplished scientists, and she herself had a series of successes in her 38-year-long research career in science, most notably the discovery of the relationship between the *PAX6* gene and autism. At age 57, she was appointed as vice president of Tohoku University, one of the prestigious national universities in Japan.

Luck alone does not tell the entire story, however. Underlying Osumi's career is her zeal to uncover new and hidden themes, themes perhaps overlooked by others but that quietly speak to her of their worth. Discovering and framing an appropriate problem statement based on such a diamond in the rough can be the first step of successful academic research.

It is this intellectual curiosity that led to another lifelong project of hers: correcting the gender imbalance in science, technology, engineering, and mathematics (STEM) education. Osumi firmly believes that a lack of women in STEM is a national loss. And mature economies like Japan desperately need more STEM researchers, male and female, as explored in my column, "Japan Needs More STEM Research, Not Tours, to Revive Innovation."

It is a solvable dilemma, and everyone would be the better for it—scholarship in academia would benefit from increased diversity.

For example, the increased presence of busy women researchers with better time management skills challenges the culture of self-sacrifice with little regard to productivity, disappointingly prevalent in academia. Moreover, as I analyze in my column, "Women Can Help Revive Innovation for Japan Inc.," a diversity of perspectives improves innovation.

Osumi approaches the problem as she would a scientific hypothesis: by addressing the root causes. The systemic structure, which excludes women from STEM fields, is a persistent one as it exists in a self-reinforcing cycle; the lack of female role models leads to fewer women aspiring for STEM careers, which prevents the rise of more role models.

To break this self-fulfilling prophecy of a dearth of women in STEM, Osumi takes tangible action—for example, the Science Ambassadors program, which educates young female students about a STEM career, provides an immediate flow of role models for young girls, producing more than 900 Science Ambassadors cumulatively in its 18 years in existence.

Osumi's life story is one profoundly driven by curiosity. Whether it is about science or gender equity in the STEM fields, her work to address root causes advances the society at large.

Noriko Osumi, Vice President of Tohoku University

1960: Born in Kanagawa, Japan, to parents Seiji Ohsumi and Masako Osumi, who were both researchers

1985: Graduated from the Tokyo Medical and Dental University with a degree in dentistry

1989: Obtained a PhD at the Tokyo Medical and Dental University in craniofacial developmental biology; became a research associate

1996: Appointed as associate professor at the National Center of Neurology and Psychiatry

1997: Revealed in her research the role of the PAX6 gene in autism

1998: Appointed as professor at Tohoku University's School of Medicine, in the field of developmental neuroscience

2001: The Gender Equality Committee established at Tohoku University[1]

2006: Appointed as special advisor for gender equality

2006: The Gender Equality Committee launched the Tohoku Women's Hurdling Project supported by the government

2006: Launched the Science Angels (now Science Ambassadors) program to educate young female students on a STEM career

2008: Appointed as distinguished professor

2014: The Tohoku University Center for Gender Equality Promotion was established[2]

2018: Appointed as vice president of the university and director of Tohoku University Center for Gender Equality Promotion

2022: Appointed as vice president for public relations and diversity promotion

Noriko Osumi Normalizes Women in Science

This article was originally published in the Japan Times *on August 16, 2022, and has been modified for the purpose of this book. The information contained in this article is correct at the time of publishing in the* Japan Times.

Professor Noriko Osumi, 61, is one of the most eminent female scientists in Japan. Since 2018, she has served as vice president at Sendai-based Tohoku University—one of seven prestigious Japanese national universities—founded in 1907. Her academic achievements include seminal work on the PAX6 gene, important for eye, brain, and behavior development. Ultimately, her PAX6 work pivoted her research topic to explaining autism.

Within the male-dominated realm of science, Osumi has had an expansive career—guided by curiosity and sound judgment. It is not hard to imagine that she had to "strive much harder" than her male or Western female counterparts, according to Veronica van Heyningen—Osumi's mentor, an honorary professor at the University of Edinburgh and University College London (UCL), as well as a fellow of the Royal Society in the United Kingdom.

When I spoke to Osumi via video interview, far from seeming bitter or unsympathetic, she was soft-spoken, warm, and cordial while maintaining a precise use of language befitting a scientist. Without children of her own, she said, "I see my students as my kids now."

"I find her very evenhanded," commented van Heyningen, describing how Osumi treated both male and female PhD students alike with respect. Osumi is "such an all-rounder"—van Heyningen was impressed by Osumi's appetite for travel and her versatile cooking. "She cooks international food as well as Japanese."

It is hardly surprising news that gender diversity in Japan, far from blazing forward, is instead on a slow burn inching toward the center stage of business, politics, and academia. The challenge is particularly evident in the gender construct of talent with degrees in science, technology, engineering, and mathematics (STEM).

While Japanese women's participation in higher education has increased—44.5% of the new college students were women in 2021 compared to 36.2% in 2000—the ratio of those going into STEM fields has remained suppressed—only 17.8% of science and engineering university students in 2021 were women, slightly more than from 12.4% in 2000.[3] (See Figure 8.1.) Unsurprisingly, in 2019, Japan ranked at the bottom of the Organisation for Economic Co-operation and Development (OECD) countries for the ratio of female entrants to tertiary engineering education: 16% in Japan versus the OECD average of 26%.[4]

Osumi asserted that the extreme lack of gender diversity in STEM fields is "a tremendous loss to Japanese society." For one, it

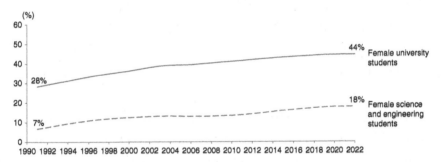

Figure 8.1   Proportion of female university students and female science and engineering students in Japan (%)

Notes: Science and engineering faculties struggle to attract women, who make up close to half of student body.

The data on female university students include all types of students enrolled in the universities. The data on female science and engineering students refer only to undergraduate students.

Created by the author based on: Ministry of Education, Culture, Sports, Science, and Technology. (2023). Basic School Survey. https://www.mext.go.jp/b_menu/toukei/chousa01/kihon/1267995.htm (accessed 2 June 2023); Ministry of Education, Culture, Sports, Science, and Technology (2023). Statistical abstract. https://www.mext.go.jp/b_menu/toukei/002/002b/koumoku.html (accessed 2 June 2023).

is a talent misallocation on a national scale. Competent women are systematically excluded from the growing fields of STEM, while, according to Osumi, less competent men—particularly deficient in time management of themselves and others—maintain their dominance.

Moreover, diversity of thinking, which can only benefit interdisciplinary studies, suffers from the male dominance of academia. "Individual differences exist within a gender," she affirmed, "and adding women's perspectives can only broaden the spectrum."

Her own career is a colorful one that kept pushing boundaries. Reflecting on her 37-year career, Osumi herself admitted to having the knack for "hunting" underexplored topics both within and outside her research. Uncovering those areas which are "interesting but to which few paid attention" is how she described the fortuitous development of her research topics.

Her undergraduate major in dentistry at Tokyo Medical and Dental University led her to start her researcher career in oral and maxillofacial pathology, which ignited her interest in the generation of the brain and nerves.

Along the way, in 1997, her work on the PAX6 gene, which is involved in brain and eye development, later pivoted her attention to the mechanism of autism. Using animal models, Osumi's work has revealed that PAX6 plays an important role in this disease when it is impaired. "Her career reflects how biology works," attested van Heyningen. "Biology is imbued with chance occurrences."

When Osumi earned her professorship at Tohoku University's School of Medicine in 1998, she was shocked to find herself the only woman at her first faculty meeting. Thus began her 25-year-long journey at Tohoku University to enhance gender diversity in STEM. Osumi reflected that it was her way of giving back now that she had achieved tenure. Moreover, similar to her research topics, the curious absence of female scientists in Japan struck her as an under-investigated yet worthy cause to tackle.

It is a mission she inherited from pioneering female researchers before her—Osumi considers herself to be the second generation of Tohoku University's female faculty members leading gender diversity enhancement at the institution. Historical presidents supported the effort, in the spirit of being the first national university to accept three female undergraduate students in 1913—the university's sixth year from inception.[5]

The first generation, represented by Miyoko Tsujimura, professor of constitutional law, established the Gender Equality Committee in 2001, which in turn founded the Research Encouragement Award on Gender Diversity.[6] Osumi and other professors in STEM fields at Tohoku University launched two successful initiatives—the Science Angel and Hurdling Support programs. Both programs address systemic barriers that prevent Japanese women from entering STEM career paths and thriving in these fields. Succeeding Tsujimura's leadership in 2006 with the support of the president at the time, Susumu Satomi, Tohoku University launched the Center for Gender Equality Promotion, which Osumi has led since 2018. Today, the committee and the center function as dual wheels, according to Osumi.

Science Ambassadors as Role Models

The lack of role models for women who major in science is a self-perpetuating challenge. Over a remote interview, Professor Mami Tanaka, faculty of engineering at Tohoku University, described the persisting invisibility of women in STEM career fields. "When schoolkids visit a plant, it is very likely that they meet women working as the plant's tour guides and rarely as the head of the plant," Tanaka observed.

However, when it came to herself, Osumi had no shortage of immediate role models in her family. In addition to her father, Seiji Ohsumi—an acclaimed researcher of whales who had been chairman of the Governing Council of Cetacean Population Studies—her mother, Masako Osumi, was a biologist specialized in yeast at Japan Women's University. In 1983, Masako, now 87, was crowned with the third Saruhashi Award, the highest honor given to female scientists in Japan.

The Saruhashi Award

The Saruhashi Award was established in 1980 to honor women scientists below age 50 in Japan for outstanding research achievements in the area of natural science.[7] (See Table 8.1.) It was established by Katsuko Saruhashi (1920–2007), a renowned Japanese geochemist, who was a pioneer in measuring carbon dioxide levels in seawater.[8] She is also recognized for her research in nuclear pollution in the ocean from nuclear testing, which triggered restrictions on experimentation activities.

Awards such as the Saruhashi Award that celebrate women scientists are vital in boosting their visibility in a male-dominated space. Globally, the L'Oréal-UNESCO for Women in Science International Awards, which started in 1998, awards five women researchers every year, one for each of the specified five regions, for their contribution to scientific progress.[9] Another such award is the Francis P. Garvan–John M. Olin Medal established in 1936, which recognizes women chemists in the US for their contributions to chemistry.[10]

Table 8.1 Historical recipients of the Saruhashi Award

Number	Year	Name	Institution	Research Area
1	1981	Tomoko Ohta	National Institute of Genetics	Theoretical study of population genetics at the molecular level
2	1982	Haruka Yamada	Kwansei Gakuin University	Laser Raman spectroscopy to study surface phenomena
3	1983	Masako Osumi	Japan Women's University	Research on microstructure and the function of yeast cells
...				
40	2020	Atsuko Ichikawa	Kyoto University	Elucidating the properties of neutrinos by accelerator-based long baseline neutrino experiment
41	2021	Mikiko Tanaka	Tokyo Institute of Technology	Research on the development and evolution of vertebrate limbs
42	2022	Kimiko Sekiguchi	Tokyo Institute of Technology	Experimental study of three-body force in nuclear physics

Adapted from Association for the Bright Future of Women Scientists (2022). 「猿橋賞」受賞者一覧 (Translation: Saruhashi Award Awardees List). https://saruhashisho.wordpress.com/list/ (accessed 24 June 2023).

Few women are born as privileged as Osumi was. She points out that the lack of role models affects average girls as early as primary or middle school: "60% of public primary school teachers in Japan are female—the majority of them majored in liberal arts," she said. (See Figure 8.2.) "This context is not conducive to encouraging girls to take interest in science." By the time they choose their high school, few girls opt for science and mathematics.

To ensure the girls' exposure to STEM role models, Osumi started organizing the Science Angels program. Renamed Science Ambassadors in 2022, the program is a volunteer network of female graduate students in STEM subjects at Tohoku University. They are dispatched to local science events or their alma mater high schools to meet younger students.

"Science Angels [now Science Ambassadors] can answer firsthand questions from young girls about what graduate school is and what a PhD in science means for women," Osumi explained, "thereby filling the information gap left by the teachers." At roughly 50 enrollments a year, the 18-year-old program has produced 900

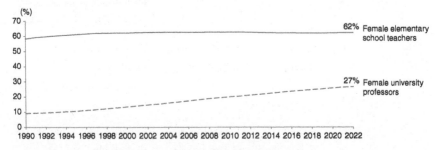

Figure 8.2   Proportion of female elementary school teachers and female university professors in Japan (%)

Note: Women teachers are overrepresented in elementary schools and underrepresented in university faculty.

Adapted from Ministry of Education, Culture, Sports, Science and Technology (2022). Basic School Survey. https://www.mext.go.jp/b_menu/toukei/chousa01/kihon/1267995.htm (accessed 9 May 2023).

Science Angels and Ambassadors cumulatively. "Some of the first-generation Science Angels have already become tenured faculty," Osumi noted proudly.

Hurdling Project to Assist Parents

Compounding the challenge of insufficient entrants into the field, the pipeline of women with a STEM career is leaky. The gender-based expectations to be the primary carer of the household discourage some women, especially mothers, from continuing on the time-consuming career paths. In fact, according to a research environment survey conducted by Tohoku University in 2020, 60% of women in research left their work due to parenting, while only 2% of men did so at the institute.

Under Osumi's leadership, Tohoku University started offering a series of tactical support efforts for parents, including funding part-time administrative resources for researchers who parent young children, subsidizing babysitters, and offering three on-campus nurseries. Those nurseries, the first established in 2005, now count a total capacity of 258 infants.[11] It was forward-thinking at the time—even today, childcare support such as nurseries on campus is considered progressive. Tanaka was a grateful beneficiary of the first nursery when she was an associate professor and a new mother.

The gender disparity remains unsolved, Osumi analyzed, unless men lean into childcare. To this end, Tohoku University implemented paid paternity leave of 15 days before the child reaches one year old, on top of the nationally mandated leave.

The skewed gender balance of STEM researchers in academia reflects a larger problem in the Japanese society. In 2018, an entrance examination manipulation was uncovered at a private medical school. The school had consistently tipped the scale for male candidates, resulting in a marked gender-based difference in acceptance rates.

The average woman is shown the door from the beginning, as the profession of a medical doctor is believed to require total dedication. To preserve the challenging work culture, the incumbent system chose to exclude inconveniences—specifically, women with anticipated career breaks due to changes in their stages of life were deemed unwelcome. But since the Ministry of Education, Culture, Sports, Science, and Technology intervened following the examination scandal, gender disparity in acceptance rates disappeared in 2021.[12]

Osumi shared her frustration about systemic sexism. "Not only do we underutilize the talent of competent women, it also allows a subset of incompetent men to continue occupying seats at the table. Without [systematically nurturing women in STEM], we have no way to get rid of these men," she said.

"The current system, which assumes the slave-like 24/7 devotion of up-and-coming researchers to their professor, conveniently masks the lack of management capabilities on the part of these senior men." Similarly, at university hospitals, the average overwork time for doctors sometimes exceeds 100 hours a month—a concern for medical errors and burn-out.[13] In Osumi's eyes, with better management skills and wider acceptance of a family-friendly workstyle, men and women should be equally able to function as researchers or medical doctors.

Then, there is the challenge of women's own agency. Osumi admitted that part-time and contract staff positions at Tohoku University are predominantly occupied by women. "Women would rather not take on a senior role for fear of jeopardizing family life," she reasoned. "Their male partners may not take it well."

It is an issue that Osumi takes personally. Despite her impeccable pedigree, the young Osumi also felt pressured to prioritize her family instead of her career during her marriage to her college boyfriend, which ended after seven years. During the marriage, "I once turned down a major promotion for fear of jumping ahead of my then-husband," she explained. "I prioritized marital peace" over career.

The marriage also cost her the chance to conduct research overseas. When the opportunity knocked, Osumi refused to leave her then-husband behind. The irony does not escape her that her mother, however, spent a year as research assistant at Southern Illinois University in 1962,[14] leaving a two-year-old Osumi and her husband behind in Japan.

Conservatism, with its ebbs and flows, manifests itself in different ways over generations. Van Heyningen, who also knew Osumi's mother as a fellow scientist, commented on how the senior Osumi seemed to divorce herself from Japanese culture, while the daughter embraced it. She recalled fondly how Osumi, donning a kimono, cooked Japanese food for her when she visited Japan with a group of researchers from overseas. Van Heyningen considered it a sign of maturity that the daughter could appreciate her native culture, decoupled from its chauvinistic undertone.

And the daughter Osumi chooses to see the glass half-full. "Because I never left Japan, I was able to gain visibility earlier within the domestic academic circle, which accelerated my independence," she explained, "and I consciously built my network by attending international conferences once a year at a minimum." She was her own boss at the age of 36 at the National Center of Neurology and Psychiatry—a position she held between 1996 and 1998 before arriving at Tohoku University.

In academia as well as in business, the family-unfriendly work norms and gender-based role expectations remain sticky. With the goal of gender equity in STEM careers coming closer but still far from being attained, Osumi has a succession plan in mind. "Professor Osumi was always clear with me that, with the 10-year age difference, I would receive the baton from her," recounted Tanaka, taking over the leadership for the center in 2022. Osumi mindfully groomed Tanaka as her successor over the years by assigning her various senior roles within the committee.

It is grim news that over three generations there was but one female faculty member per cohort to represent STEM. However, on a positive note, Osumi attested that the gender gap is, albeit its glacial speed, shrinking. Women in science are coming into sight more over the generations—"when I became a researcher, my supervising professor solemnly told me that a woman needs to work twice as hard as men," she recounted, noting that his comment would not be considered politically correct today. "But in Professor Tsujimura's era, 10 years before me, it was thrice as much. Twenty years before, I heard it was five times," she laughed. Tanaka seems no longer bound by such an expectation, even accounting for the need to be politically correct.

Meanwhile, the nature of diversity-related challenges is also evolving. Tanaka faces the modern complexity of gender fluidity and the LGBTQ+ community. It is for this reason that Science Angels was renamed as gender-neutral Science Ambassadors in April 2022.[15] "The kids today are becoming more unisex in their thinking," observed Osumi. She added, "while I am cognizant of the risk of overemphasizing the anatomical gender, I think it is still worth pushing for gender parity until the ratio of female students reaches 40% in STEM." The ratio for female doctoral students was 30.4% in total at Tohoku University in 2022.[16]

Osumi remains unwavering in her conviction. "Women are just as capable as scientists and medical doctors as men," Osumi declared, "but we must change the culture which penalizes women. The default still lacks equity."

Japan Needs More STEM Research, Not Tours, to Revive Innovation

This column was originally published in Nikkei Asia *on October 7, 2022, and has been modified for the purpose of this book. The information contained in this article is correct at the time of publishing in* Nikkei Asia.

When Koichi Hagiuda, then Japan's minister of economy, trade, and industry, announced a plan in July to dispatch 1,000 entrepreneurs to Silicon Valley over the next five years, debate quickly flared on social media.[17]

Japanese already immersed in the region's start-up ecosystem were particularly vocal in protest. Naotake Murayama, an experienced advisor to start-ups in San Francisco, worried that Japan-centric business pitches would be misaligned with the business interests of West Coast venture capital firms. Hagiuda's two-week visit program would effectively be a safari tour of business tourists gawking at exotic Big Tech and venture capitalists, he suggested.

The safari tour criticism obscures a bigger question: what key ingredient is now missing among Japanese entrepreneurs?

It is not capital. Japan has abundant capital that is chasing too few opportunities.

Neither is it will. Young businesspeople, especially 30-somethings with good educations and elite jobs aspiring to strike out on their own are increasingly common.

What today's Japan lacks is the nucleus of innovation: applied science and technology. Addressing this problem requires better treatment of PhDs in the STEM fields.

"The Japanese start-up scene revolves around buzzwords like SaaS, AI, and Web 3.0," observed MIT Sloan School of Management students Yuka Kojima, founder of eye-tracking technology venture

FOVE, and Akihiko Izu, cofounder of Multitude Insights, a start-up building intelligence tools for US police departments.

"By contrast, in the US, new ventures are framed with a goal to solve a societal problem by applying a technological solution," Izu said.

"Many PhDs at MIT try their hand at entrepreneurialism," added Kojima.

If the US provides Japan with a benchmark of sustainable entrepreneurship, this observation points to its formula for success: STEM innovation turned into solutions.

Deep technology is the application of scientific discoveries and innovative technologies, including artificial intelligence, robotics, and advanced material sciences, to solving key challenges, such as those facing the environment, health, food, and energy.

The good news for Japan is that the academic backgrounds of those who contribute to deep technology are usually in areas that are the country's traditional forte.

In fact, four of Japan's nine Nobel Prize laureates over the last decade specialized in STEM-related fields that contribute to deep technology.[18]

However, this glory belongs to the past. Today, doctoral candidates in Japan receive little support from the government and industry as compared with the prospective Silicon Valley tour group participants. This is not only bad for academia—the primary destination for Japanese PhDs—but also for industries running on a diminishing supply of vanguard scientists.

Japan's shrinking number of new PhDs is an anomaly among developed nations. The country produced about 15,000 doctorates in 2019.[19] Adjusted for population, Japan has one-third the number of doctoral graduates of Germany or the UK and two-fifths that of the US.[20]

The diminishing popularity of Japanese doctoral programs has been attributed primarily to poor financial viability. Only 10% of the 74,000 students in doctoral programs as of 2021 said they were receiving sufficient financial support.[21]

Their employment outlook is also bleak. Some 29% of 2018 PhD recipients remained in irregular and precarious postdoctoral positions as of 2020.[22]

How can we better support Japanese PhDs? First, ensuring financial security for candidates and graduates is essential. Although the government aims to provide financial support to 30% of eligible doctoral candidates,[23] that will be too late and too little to turn the tide.

Second, PhD graduates must be provided with better exit options. Nonacademic options can help bridge academic research with real-world applications and give graduates flexibility, making doctoral programs more attractive.

At the Fraunhofer Society's 76 laboratories and research centers in Germany, PhDs can adapt their research to commercial applications. Japan comes closest to this model with its Riken Research Institute, but although it emphasizes collaboration with industry, Riken's research scope leans toward more basic research than Fraunhofer.

More could be done at universities, too. Recognizing the complementary skills and mindsets of STEM PhDs and MBAs, top business schools are mixing MBAs with STEM doctoral candidates. Such collaborations can provide a safe test bed to commercialize innovation. For example, a popular course at MIT Sloan teams two MBA candidates with a PhD STEM student to work on a business plan.

In Japan, the Matsuo Lab run by professor Yutaka Matsuo of the University of Tokyo systematically guides students studying AI into becoming entrepreneurs.[24] The lab has produced more than a dozen start-ups, including PKSHA Technology, a software company focused on developing algorithms and licensing that went public in 2017 and has a market capitalization of ¥60 billion ($415.4 million). The Matsuo model could be replicated in other STEM disciplines.

The Kishida administration has christened 2022 as the beginning year of entrepreneurship in Japan, vowing to increase the number of start-ups tenfold within five years, with a particular emphasis on deep tech.[25] STEM awareness is palpable.

Momentum is building in the right direction, but deep-tech start-ups are rooted on the foundations of rigorous research. Japan will fail to meet its goals if it treats deep tech as yet another buzzword. The country must continuously invest in STEM higher education, produce a steady supply of STEM PhDs, and encourage them to apply their knowledge to solve societal problems. There can be no shortcut.

Women Can Help Revive Innovation for Japan Inc.

This column was originally published in Nikkei Asia *on August 26, 2022, and has been modified for the purpose of this book. The information contained in this article is correct at the time of publishing in* Nikkei Asia.

In 2020, chemists Emmanuelle Charpentier from the Max Planck Unit for the Science of Pathogens in Berlin and Jennifer Doudna of the University of California, Berkeley, jointly won the Nobel Prize in chemistry for their gene-editing technology, CRISPR-Cas9.[26]

The groundbreaking discovery by the duo of female scientists left a memorable impression because women are a minority in the STEM fields. In yet another manifestation of the gender-based expectations ingrained in many societies, especially in Japan, STEM careers, associated with brainpower, self-discipline, and a touch of geekiness, are typically reserved for men.

This imbalance has undermined our collective ability to innovate at a time when new solutions are desperately needed to tackle the world's existential problems, from climate change to the current food and energy crises.

Beyond academia, women in STEM are already playing an important role in everyday business. Consider, for example, the hand-touch sensor that is now a standard feature of the Gen 2 Premier, the bestselling elevator from the Japanese arm of global manufacturer Otis Worldwide. The sensor, which can prevent a child's finger or hand from accidentally slipping into the door pocket by automatically halting motion, was the brainchild of a diverse team including a woman engineer in her 20s.

According to Nippon Otis Elevator president Thibault Lefebure, the sensor demonstrates women's acumen in understanding user experience.

"Innovation today is a function of many things: hardware, software, user interface, internet connectivity and data visualization. It is no longer only about the hardware," he said. "I find that women, because intuitively they pay more attention to end users, are generally better at imagining creative solutions."

In addition to the obvious advantage of tapping into the other half of the population for new ideas, Lefebure stresses another reason why we must encourage the representation of women in STEM—the aptitude of women for modern innovation.

Despite this, a shortage of females in STEM persists. Veronica van Heyningen, a preeminent female geneticist in her mid-70s known for her work on eyes and a fellow of the UK's Royal Society, recalls that when she was considering her field of study she was told, "Girls don't go into physics because they don't like math."

Such banter would fail to raise an eyebrow in Japan even today. In 2019, Japan ranked at the bottom in terms of female tertiary graduates in engineering, manufacturing, and construction among Organisation for Economic Co-operation and Development members, at 16%.[27] Although the proportion among group members overall was 21%, both South Korea at 20% and Indonesia with 19% bested Japan.

In Japan, the whispering starts early. Professor Noriko Osumi, a geneticist and vice president of Tohoku University, blames structural bias in the education system. By the time students choose their high school, few girls opt for science or mathematics.

If the chronic dearth of women represents a missed opportunity for innovation both in academia and in industry, how can we accelerate the shift to equalize the gender balance in STEM?

In the short run, both the public and private sectors must highlight and encourage women's active participation in innovation. Now, some women can find it risky to offer ideas, according to a board member of the foundation that grants the German Sustainability Award, Europe's top award for ecological and social commitment.

In selecting female recipients for its prize celebrating game-changing technologies, he witnessed the challenge that younger nominees have faced.

"They have brilliant ideas, such as engineering-as-a-service, which overhauls chemical plant operations to make them more efficient and environment-friendly," he said. "But these ideas are often shot down by the old male guard, the would-be clients who think they knew everything from their decades of experience."

Both gender and generational discrimination can thus stand in the way of younger women trying to promote their ideas. Support from government, industry associations, and cross-industry awards such as the German prize could help further encourage female innovators.

In the long run, we must undo male dominance in STEM careers. Optics matters.

In Japan, conference panels on digital transformation, a popular topic of the day, are often monopolized by men to the extent that the moniker *manel* is heard even though plenty of women are riding the digital wave. Government can lead by example by setting a guideline for gender-balanced panels with its own programs.

To change the narrative for the younger generation, institutions of higher education and corporations can provide girls with real-life female STEM role models. Osumi's Science Angels program has sent 900 female graduate students to local science events or their alma mater high schools over the past 18 years.[28]

Japan, a country largely devoid of natural resources, particularly depends on innovation for its prosperity. Although the womenom-ics policies of former prime minister Shinzo Abe focused on tapping into women simply as an additional labor force to fill the gap left by a dwindling male working population, we must reframe our thinking about women to recognize them as a source of innovation.

By including women in the innovation equation and mixing the perceived work styles of men and women, the emulsion can do wonders. Innovation with gender diversity can present a path for Japan and other modern societies to bring out innovation vibrancy.

References

1. Tohoku University Center for Gender Equality Promotion. (2023). TUMUG history. http://tumug.tohoku.ac.jp/en/about/history/ (accessed 15 June 2023).

2. Ibid.

3. Ministry of Education, Culture, Sports, Science, and Technology. (2023). Basic School Survey. https://www.mext.go.jp/b_menu/toukei/chousa01/kihon/1267995.htm (accessed 2 June 2023).

4. OECD. (2021). Education at a glance 2021: OECD indicators. https://www.oecd-ilibrary.org/sites/1426642c-en/index .html?itemId=/content/component/1426642c-en (accessed 15 June 2023).

5. Tohoku University Center for Gender Equality Promotion. (2023). TUMUG history.

6. The Society of Polymer Science, Japan. (2010). Toward gender equality in the academic sphere. https://main.spsj.or.jp/danjo/message/tsujimura.pdf (accessed 15 June 2023).

7. Association for the Bright Future of Women Scientists. (2022). 猿橋賞 (Translation: Saruhashi award). https://saruhashisho .wordpress.com/ (accessed 19 June 2023).

8. Toho University. (2023). 女性科学者の先駆 猿橋勝子氏 (Translation: Katsuko Saruhashi, pioneer of female scientists). https://www .lab.toho-u.ac.jp/univ/diversity2/center/history/past.html (accessed 19 June 2023).

9. UNESCO. (2023). L'Oréal-UNESCO for Women in Science International Awards. https://www.unesco.org/en/prizes/women-science/awards (accessed 19 June 2023).

10. American Chemical Society. (2022). Francis P. Garvan–John M. Olin Medal. https://www.acs.org/funding/awards/francis-garvan-john-olin-medal.html (accessed 19 June 2023).

11. Tohoku University Center for Gender Equality Promotion. (2023). Message from the director of TUMUG. http://tumug .tohoku.ac.jp/about/message/ (accessed 15 June 2023).

12. *Nikkei.* (2022). 医学部入試「女性差別」、順天堂大に賠償命令　東京地裁 (Translation: Juntendo University ordered to pay compensation for "discrimination against women" in medical school entrance examinations by Tokyo District Court). https://www.nikkei .com/article/DGXZQOUE162L80W2A510C2000000/ (accessed 15 June 2023).

13. Ministry of Health, Labour, and Welfare. (2020). 医師の勤務実態 について (Translation: Working conditions of doctors). https:// www.mhlw.go.jp/content/10800000/000677264.pdf (accessed 15 June 2023).

14. Japan Science and Technology Agency. (2022). Masako Osumi research history. https://researchmap.jp/read0029386/research_ experience/22540644 (accessed 15 June 2023).

15. Tohoku University Center for Gender Equality Promotion. (2023). Tohoku University science ambassadors. http://tumug .tohoku.ac.jp/next_generation/sa/ (accessed 15 June 2023).

16. Tohoku University Center for Gender Equality Promotion. (2023). Percentage of female researchers. http://tumug.tohoku .ac.jp/public-relations/data/ (accessed 15 June 2023).

17. *Nikkei.* (2022). シリコンバレーで起業者育成、10 倍増へ　5 年で計 1000 人 (Translation: Nuturing enterpreneurs in Silicon Valley and aiming for a 10-times increase; 1000 people in 5 years). https:// www.nikkei.com/article/DGXZQOUA274WA0X20C2 2A7000000/ (accessed 26 June 2023).

18. *Forbes.* (2019). 歴代の日本人ノーベル賞受賞者は？ 1949 年から、数々の 快挙を振り返る (Translation: Who are the Japanese Nobel laureates? Looking back on many achievements since 1949). https:// forbesjapan.com/articles/detail/30481 (accessed 20 June 2023).

19. *Nikkei.* (2022). 大学院、博士人材の就職後押し　将来不安解消へ本腰 (Translation: Support employment of graduate school students;

serious efforts to eliminate uncertainty about the future). https://
www.nikkei.com/article/DGXZQOUE271S40X20C22A7000000/
(accessed 26 June 2023).

20. National Institute of Science and Technology Policy. (2013).
International comparison of degree holders. https://www
.nistep.go.jp/sti_indicator/2014_e/RM229E_34.html (accessed
26 June 2023).

21. *Nikkei Asia.* (2021). Japan to pay Ph.D. students in quest for
cutting-edge tech. https://asia.nikkei.com/Politics/Japan-to-
pay-Ph.D.-students-in-quest-for-cutting-edge-tech (accessed
19 June 2023).

22. *Nikkei.* (2022).「博士離れ」浮き彫り、学生 2 年連続減　就職状況厳しく
(Translation: Number of doctorate students decline for second
consecutive year, due to the difficulty of employment). https://
www.nikkei.com/article/DGXZQOUE236MY0T20C22A8000000/
(accessed 19 June 2023).

23. *Nikkei Asia.* (2021). Japan to pay Ph.D. students in quest for
cutting-edge tech.

24. Matsuo Lab University of Tokyo. (2023). Matsuo Lab startups.
https://weblab.t.u-tokyo.ac.jp/startups/ (accessed 26 June 2023).

25. Prime Minister's Office of Japan. (2023). 主要政策 (Translation:
Main policies). https://www.kantei.go.jp/jp/headline/seisaku_
kishida/seichousenryaku.html (accessed 26 June 2023).

26. The Nobel Prize. (2020). The Nobel Prize in Chemistry 2020.
https://www.nobelprize.org/prizes/chemistry/2020/summary/
(accessed 19 June 2023).

27. OECD. (2021). Education at a glance 2021. https://www.oecd-
ilibrary.org/education/education-at-a-glance-2021_b35a14e5-en
(accessed 19 June 2023).

28. Tohoku University Center for Gender Equality Promotion.
(2023). Tohoku University science ambassadors.

9 Ambition

Having a deeper calling at the outset of one's career is not a prerequisite for long-term success. Such realizations may retrospectively visit us in the middle of our career.

Yumi Narushima has built her career dedicated to the education industry—spending a combined 26 years at Benesse, an education conglomerate, sandwiching a five-year stint running a girls' junior and senior high school in Tokyo. Being an educator was not her original aspiration out of college—she stumbled into education not by choice but by chance.

Instead of a deeper calling, however, she had the ambition to quickly ascend within Benesse. Overturning Japanese cultural inducement toward modesty, especially for women, Narushima was never shy about announcing her ambitions.

Ambition, underpinned by Narushima's dedication to performance, which earned her a reputation in her early 30s as a fixer of struggling businesses within Benesse, paid off in two ways. First, it fueled her passion for the education industry, which she became convinced would be her life's work. Second, she honed her leadership skills and learned to leverage her staff members to enhance group-wide performance.

Even though Narushima achieved her professional success while simultaneously raising a family—she is married with a son—her life story is not about "having it all" in a perfectly balanced way. Her priority was clearly on professional success, on top of which she managed personal life events with help of others around her as well as her employer.

Her preference to engage in common-law marriage to maintain her maiden name is a personal protest to the current marriage laws. As I describe in my column, "Japan Must Reform Its Antiquated Marriage Laws," the current system forces a legally married couple to choose a common surname—usually the husband's—despite being unpopular with a large segment of Japanese population.

As my other column, "Japan's 'Miss Contests' Reflect Society's High Demands on Women" concludes, there are high expectations placed on modern women to be capable in both spheres of work and personal life. Being both tough and traditionally feminine at the same time is a tall order. Narushima's trajectory tells us that we can be strategically nonconformist, as evidenced by her decision to retain her surname by common-law marriage.

Japan is often described as a homogenous society where "a nail that sticks out gets hammered down." Narushima shows that it is possible to stick out and to keep on growing.

Yumi Narushima, Head of the Extracurricular Education Company of Benesse Corporation

1970: Born in Ibaraki Prefecture, Japan

1992: Graduated from Tokyo Woman's Christian University with a degree in Japanese history

1992: Started her career at Fukutake Shoten (now Benesse Corporation)

1994: Appointed as leader of the English division of Shinkenzemi for 9th grade

1996: Appointed as leader of the English division of Shinkenzemi for 11th grade

2000: Benesse listed on First Section of Tokyo Stock Exchange[1]

2002: Promoted to division manager of junior high school Shinkenzemi

2005: Promoted to be the youngest ever executive officer at Benesse

2012–2014: Led project MOON to digitalize Shinkenzemi

2014: Benesse launched Challenge Touch, the digital version of Shinkenzemi

2015–2017: Attended and graduated from Waseda Business School with an MBA

2017: Left Benesse and became principal of Otsuma Junior and Senior High School

2023: Returned to Benesse as head of the Extracurricular Education Company

Yumi Narushima Returns to Benesse After Running a Girls' School

This article was originally published in the Japan Times *on March 14, 2023, and has been modified for the purpose of this book. The information contained in this article is correct at the time of publishing in the* Japan Times.

Lifetime employment, the traditional hallmark of the Japanese labor system, has long lost its luster. The once sacred social contract between the employer and employee—lifelong loyalty to the organization compensated by unwavering job security—is frayed at best.

Not only did the economic stagnation from the late 1990s rationalize periodic downsizing for employers but also Japanese workers today often frame switching positively, searching for better opportunities and, hopefully, reaping better pay along the way.

However, there are occasional counterexamples, in which lifetime employment makes good sense, beyond its obvious benefit of stability. Consider a young recruit who grows up within a company, notching a growing list of accomplishments in their belt and solidifying a team of followers, while internalizing the purpose of the organization as they rise and mature as a professional.

Unlike the blind faith and inertia assumed in the conventional lifetime employment, the social contract in such a case is a dynamic one—while the employee strives to give their best at assignments, the company must recognize such talent early, provide them with opportunities, as well as senior air cover when necessary.

Yumi Narushima, 53, presents an example of an inhouse-grown corporate executive who managed to build a mutually rewarding and long-term relationship with her first and latest employer, albeit with a break in between. In 2022, she freshly returned to her mothership of Benesse Corporation, an education conglomerate with more than ¥400 billion turnover[2] and well-known for its correspondence course

for home study called Shinkenzemi (Zemi shortened for seminar)
covering elementary to high school education. Narushima returned to
lead their Extracurricular Education Company after a five-year stint
running a prestigious private girls junior and senior high school in
Tokyo as the school's principal.

Akin to successful marriages, the story of Narushima and Benesse
is one of mutual trust and constant endeavors. And like any long-
term marriage, it is with no shortage of turbulence along the way.

When Narushima joined Fukutake Shoten in 1992, to be
renamed Benesse Corporation in 1995, it was an outcome after "a
disastrous job search" according to the graduate from Tokyo Woman's
Christian University with a Japanese history major.

"I wanted to be a journalist or editor for women's fashion maga-
zines," Narushima told me in a recent interview, "doing something
creative. So, I applied to every opening in media—from print to
broadcast—and got dinged by them all." The bubble economy had
not burst just yet and media, with its glam and high compensation,
was a popular destination for both male and female graduates. She
was adamant that her being shown the door was never a gender-
biased decision. "I was just not good enough, including my English."

The irony is that Narushima, within a mere five years of joining
Benesse, ended up twice leading the English division of Shinkenzemi,
first for ninth graders in 1994 and then for junior high schoolers in
1996, earning the highest number of enrollments and continuation
rate ever in both cases.

"I told myself I'd commit myself on education [after joining
Benesse]. It was not the world of journalism as I wanted, but I feel
that the field of education fits me like fate," recalled Narushima
reflecting on her resolution 30 years ago. In the early 1990s, *Challenge*,
Shinkenzemi's main textbook, had about 800,000 readers for the
junior high school course targeting the age segment from 12 to 15,

a readership unmatched by any fashion magazine. "I thought of these students who await their monthly textbooks and magazine arrival, and I started to like what I am doing," told Narushima in an interview she gave in 2012 to a nonprofit women's network, J-Win.[3]

"From the beginning, I openly declared I'd be in top management within 10 years," says Narushima unabashedly. "More than anything, I wanted to put pressure on myself." Such naked ambition would be unpopular, particularly in the context of Japan's seniority-based corporate culture. But her bosses at Benesse responded by awarding her with what she describes as kingcraft—"I was given a series of tough assignments, one after another, and climbed up the ladder each time I was successful. They appreciated my ambition and treated me as a climber."

And never did she go at it alone. A self-described former "school queen" from Ibaraki, an agricultural prefecture outside Tokyo, Narushima always had a knack for leading the pack. Through her younger days, she refined a teamwork model, dubbed at Benesse as *Team Narushima*. Calling it "management by one dozen," Narushima described carefully selecting and empowering 12 or so direct reports in a *Nikkei Business* article published in 2011.[4] "The trust we built within Team Narushima remains strong to this day," Narushima told me.

Typically, the path to division manager takes on average 25 years, according to research conducted in 2010 by the Institute of Labour Administration with listed companies in Japan.[5] In her flying start, however, Narushima was made division manager—responsible for junior high school Shinkenzemi—in 2002, just 10 years after joining the company, fulfilling her self-declaration. She was promoted to executive officer in 2005 at 36, youngest ever at Benesse.

She also became a mother during this period. Having married a colleague, Narushima had her only child, a son, in 2003 at 33. The couple has a common-law marriage—she attributes the Japanese marriage law to force a single surname between a married couple to this decision. "We will legally marry as soon as having two surnames is possible." I asked whose last name the boy adopted. "Of course, mine," quickly replied Narushima. "I had him, didn't I?"

Benesse is advanced in caring for employees with a family, with a high ratio of employees returning to work after parental leave at 96% in 2020. Additionally, Benesse is serious about gender equality: 52% of total employees and 33% of those in management roles were female in 2022.[6] The national average ratio of those in management roles who were women in 2021 was 13.2%, according to statistics published by the Gender Equality Bureau Cabinet Office.[7] (See Figure 9.1.)

"In the education industry, we welcome the parental experience as it is directly beneficial for our work," contemplated Narushima in the 2012 J-Win interview,[8] "but you also have your own responsibility to organize a support infrastructure." Supporting Narushima's return to work two months post-labor, her husband, who still does a lion's share of the housework according to Narushima, took three months of paternity leave, unprecedented at the time at Benesse. Her son, now

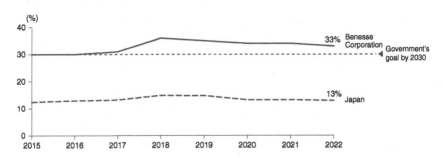

Figure 9.1   Proportion of women in management roles (%)

Notes: Benesse is advanced in female representation in leadership, already reaching the government's goal of 30% women representation in management roles by 2030. Benesse Corporation is the largest operating company under Benesse Holdings. Created by author based on: Benesse Holdings (2022). Benesse Report. https://www.benesse-hd.co.jp/ja/ir/library/ar/index.html (accessed 4 June 2023); Statistics Bureau of Japan (2023). Labour Force Survey. https://www.stat.go.jp/data/roudou/index.html (accessed 30 July 2023).

a freshman at Keio University, stayed under the care of Narushima's parents in Ibaraki before he started his elementary school.

After making executive officer, her most challenging assignment ever came in late 2012, when Narushima led the division to provide Shinkenzemi for elementary school children. A competitor developed a completely digital offering in an industry deeply steeped in paper-based culture—after all, Shinkenzemi had built its fame with its "red pen teachers," most of them stay-at-home mothers who check answers with advice, teaching them with neat penmanship as a side job.

The competitor's digital move "sent a chill down our spine," admitted Narushima in an interview for Benesse's employee brochure, "Baton." "We had a ¥70 billion business for elementary school in paper to protect," she reflected in our interview. "At the same time, management, in an emergency meeting, decided to invest more than ¥8 billion to digitalize Shinkenzemi. We vowed to avoid the fate of Kodak, who, despite its market leadership, died for lack of self-transformation."

The project was code-named *MOON* for its ambition to travel as high as the moon. Under such competitive pressure, management decided to launch their own digital product within a year starting from scratch.

The vision was to build a "school without a building," according to the article in Baton, where an enrolled student can navigate and self-teach. The problem: there was neither digital expertise nor hardware know-how within Benesse.

As a project manager, Narushima "was a force of nature," remembered Hitoshi Kobayashi, Benesse Holdings CEO from 2022 and then director of the company, in a recent interview. The gloves were off to meet the aggressive deadline—Project MOON involved procuring mid-career hires from gaming companies for coding, poaching an advisor from the competitor who was a step ahead, and negotiating with Panasonic to develop their own tablets.

"It was scary," admitted Narushima to me. "I am no digital expert. I asked the team to simplify so that even I could use it intuitively—I was as digital-savvy as a six-year-old using a tablet for the first time." Kobayashi counts this user orientation as Narushima's strength in addition to her savviness to woo new stakeholders into her projects.

"Our culture is rather docile and inward-looking," Kobayashi told me. "Her outgoingness by contrast is a great influence on our people. Of course, some managers end up unhappy to lose their own people to Team Narushima," confided Kobayashi to me, "but she shows outcome."

In April 2014, 16 months after the competitor's digital offering launch and 12 months after Project MOON's kick-off, Benesse launched Challenge Touch, the digital version of Shinkenzemi, online with multimedia. Although many competitors have jumped on the tablet bandwagon since then,[9] with tablet installs exceeding five million in 2022, Challenge Touch remains a de facto leader in digital education for elementary and junior high school in Japan.

"You need to take the bull by the horns," Narushima told me. "The competitor's new offering, although far from being perfect, was the cusp of a wave we could have been too late to catch."

Although Narushima built her reputation as a fixer—she arrested the long-term decline in Shinkenzemi enrollments—and a builder for new business such as Challenge Touch, the external environment continued to deteriorate for Benesse. The number of children in Japan under 15 started to decline in 1982,[10] and the correspondence education market was saturated. (See Figure 9.2.) "The adverse conditions were slowly and surely gnawing at Benesse," described to me Kazunari Uchida, a retired management consultant and professor from Waseda Business School who taught Narushima from 2015 to 2017. "Then they were dealt a sharper crisis on top everything else."

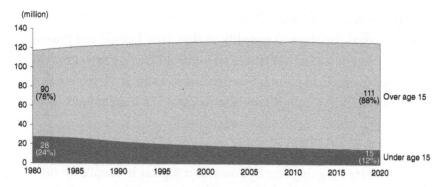

Figure 9.2   Population of youth in Japan (million)

Note: Decline in the number of youth poses existential threat to Japanese education sector.

Adapted from Statistics Bureau of Japan (2022). Population Estimates. https://www.stat.go.jp/data/jinsui/ (accessed 3 June 2023).

In June 2014, shortly after Challenge Touch's launch in April, Benesse received a phone call. On investigation, they found that more than 35 million individuals' personal data—names, addresses, dates of birth—were stolen and sold to outside vendors by a contracted system engineer. The data leak immediately made headlines in Japan.

"There is no question that our sensitivity to data protection was insufficient," admitted Narushima to me. "There was a hole in how we stored data." Being responsible for the Shinkenzemi business at the time, Narushima was hugely affected by the incident. "I apologized to so many places," she recalled, "and only then did it home in on me, the magnitude of societal impact we were making. The data leaked amounted to the size of a quarter of Japan's population. We were a social infrastructure."

It was dark times at Benesse. With financial loss mounting, an early retirement program as part of restructuring was announced at the end of 2014.[11] Almost all employees helped to respond to calls from anxious customers, but "some left because of depression," said Narushima. Management was equally shaken. The top management went through a major reshuffle, and new blood was brought in externally at the executive officer level—to a debatable success in the end.[12]

Although she remained at Benesse, Narushima's position also changed. The scandal derailed the unstoppable ascent of her star with its latest achievement of Challenge Touch. It was in this time of patience that she started and graduated in 2017 from Waseda Business School's evening program with encouragement from Benesse, and more importantly she received an unexpected invitation from the Otsuma Junior and Senior High School to be their principal.

Established in 1908 by Kotaka Otsuma, an educator of humble background from Hiroshima, Otsuma is a girls-only private junior and senior high school in the Chiyoda ward, the heart of Tokyo, with about 290 students per class year. With her aunt being a graduate, Narushima was on the board supporting the plan to differentiate the school from the competition when the chairman of the board at the time approached her. "He gave me a biography of Kotaka Otsuma, and I saw that I was born on the day she died—January 3, 1970," recalled Narushima to me. "It felt a bit like fate."

"She was heavily debating whether to leave Benesse for Otsuma and rightly so," Uchida told me, who consulted her personally at Waseda Business School at the time. "While still in the education industry, running a school is a 90-degree pivot from running a for-profit business," he explained. "The ultimate objective is growing young people versus increasing profit. Moreover, schoolteachers are far more diverse in their motivation than corporate staff, which makes building alignment challenging. Therefore, school transformation is hard and takes years."

When she finally decided to leave Benesse and join Otsuma, Benesse CEO Kobayashi supported her decision. "Shinkenzemi is a consumer business through textbooks," he explained. "Being on the frontline of school is a different experience. And [although she resigned from Benesse] we anticipated that she'd eventually be back with that experience" although nothing was promised.

In separate interviews, both Narushima and CEO Kobayashi musingly recounted the day when Kobayashi voluntarily offered to accompany Narushima to meet with the board chairman at Otsuma, "I felt like a father sending off a daughter to a marriage," said Kobayashi. Narushima reasoned that, because Kobayashi was also a come-back case to the mainstream from having spent 12 years in the nursing home business within the Benesse group, he saw the benefit of outside experience.

According to Narushima, Otsuma leaders "must have liked my restructuring experiences, reviving Shinkenzemi for junior high school." Indeed, she found Otsuma "complacent with long history, left in the dust while aggressive newcomer schools advanced by leaps and bounds in popularity." "At Otsuma, it was as if time stood still," recalled Narushima in our interview. She laid out her transforma-tion plan, organized into the three steps of a student life cycle: entry, student in-school, and post-graduation.

At the entry, Narushima added an entrance exam date of February 5 in addition to their traditional February 1 to 3, after most schools hold their exams during this period. The result of the exam is usually available on the same day. "We were not a top-notch school, often chosen as a second choice," explained Narushima. "We wanted to offer a chance to those girls who refuse to give up [after being unsuccessful with their top pick]." This decision of adding an extra exam date was highly successful and boosted Otsuma's competitive-ness significantly. The ratio of applicant numbers to open seats shot up from about 1:1 before the change to nearly 8:1 for the added February 5 date, reflecting an extraordinarily high popularity.

Despite its declining popularity against co-ed options, she believes in same-sex education for junior and senior high school. "If you install the right mindset at this critical phase [teenage years], an all-girls' school can be a springboard for young women," Narushima emphasized. "You talk your hearts out, woman-to-woman, and you learn to lead without relying on men. This is where you make your lifelong friends."

For in-school Otsuma girls between the age of 12 and 18, Narushima tried to open their eyes to the possibilities. "In the digital age, teachers' value-add no longer lies in filling knowledge asymmetry but in motivating students," she said. Through her network from Benesse, she invited high-caliber working adults, including AI and robotics specialists, to inspire Otsuma students with possibilities.[13]

At the same time, she wanted the girls to harbor no illusions about the real world, in which the cards are stacked against women. "I delivered this New Year speech in 2022 about the truth of women," said Narushima. "Based on current stats, only one to two of 10 Otsuma graduates will end up as lifetime housewife. I wanted them to self-help, to never give up work, and to be strategic about the choices they make in life—career or partner." From her own experience, she knows how important it is to have a partner who shares the same values and supports his wife. "It's hard, frankly," she told me, "being a mother, an employee, a wife, a daughter-in-law, all-in-one. You need support."

Last, she aimed to make sure that the Otsuma graduates left Otsuma with the right trajectory. Particularly, Narushima aimed to arm Otsuma students for STEM careers beyond graduation. STEM, traditionally affiliated with maleness, is long known to be a hard sell for girls in Japan. "Having worked in private sector, I know STEM credentials—say, data science or AI—boosts your marketability in the job market," Narushima explained in an interview with Asahi Shimbun in 2021.[14] "I want my students to have indispensable skills that help them to weather shifts in life."

Otsuma students now learn to code and can enlist in a prep course for medical school. "We increased the ratio of graduating students who major STEM to 50% from what was 30% under my predecessor," she said proudly.

Although she set out to complete two terms, a total of six years, at Otsuma, Benesse needed her back a little sooner, at the five-year mark. Since January 2023, Narushima has been the head of the Extracurricular Education Company of Benesse Corporation overseeing correspondence courses and Shinkenzemi for elementary, junior high, and high school, a core business for Benesse with a ¥150 billion turnover.

"We sent her off to Otsuma open-ended," explained CEO Kobayashi, "and stayed in touch. I knew she always cared about Benesse. With her coming to terms with the limit of what she can realistically do at Otsuma, in 2021, I asked her if she could come back" to Benesse.

Kobayashi said that Benesse now needs radical self-transformation as the backdrop of education broadly needing an overhaul. The conventional education system has proved to be hopelessly insufficient to fully educate 18- to 22-year-olds for a decades-long career within dynamic environments. The greater the requirement for teachers, the less appealing the profession appears. As a leading education company, Benesse must demolish its internal silos and redefine what it can do for the broadest definition of education beyond Shinkenzemi for students.

While at Otsuma, Narushima saw the vision of Benesse occupying the role of "a second place," a comfortable place besides school, which provides good education and information. "Benesse should be the professional of children and students," she told me, citing her surprise witnessing the insecurity of teenagers at Otsuma. "The nurse's office is full of students," Narushima told me. "Being healthy both mentally and physically is the priority, before you can focus on studies. And there is just not enough care for that part today, including the number of counselors. This is a void Benesse can and must fill."

"I trust that Narushima-san will lead the transformation for Benesse with increasing responsibilities," said Kobayashi. "After leading Otsuma, I find her a better listener, in addition to her outgoing leadership skills." Narushima currently leads negotiations with external stakeholders to start new virtual reality learning services.

Historically women at Benesse thrive and there is "no [gender-based] discrimination," Kobayashi affirmed. Uchida concurred that Benesse is "a great place to work for women. It is inclusive of any workstyle—whether you want to go slow or fast."

Meanwhile, Kobayashi also observed that women tended to stick to on-the-ground execution and shied away from top management roles such as board membership—"many women are satisfied at executive officer level [responsible for execution]." He finds this unfortunate. "Management is an extension of execution," he told me in our interview, "when you resonate with and internalize our vision [Benesse means *well-being*], the natural step is to become management from within." He finds a perfect role model in Narushima—"Women should absolutely drive decision-making in a company like ours."

Was Narushima's rocket ascent to top management and leaving and returning to the mothership after turmoil possible because she is special? "She would have done well in any company where you deal with people," observed Uchida in the interview. "She is a natural reader of people and never hesitates to lend a helping hand."

What I do find most uncommon in her journey, though, is the early declaration of ambition, which is hardly Japanese, let alone lady-like. But this strategy led her to climb up the ladder at Benesse, where a perfect pas-de-deux took place between the grateful employer and the eager employee—a successful case of lifetime employment, even with a significant break in between.

By contrast, too many talented young women end up slipping under the radar early in their career as they keep their heads low, work hard, and yet never get recognized by the employer while their male counterparts leap ahead. It is a hard habit to unlearn, because women in Japan are taught that modesty is a virtue. By the time they are mid-career, the distance from the leaders of the pack is wide.

Narushima's success story is a testimony that an ambitious woman can flourish just as well as a male equivalent. And it took Benesse, her counterpart in the pas-de-deux, to recognize and nurture her career all the way.

Had she started as an assistant editor to a women's fashion magazine, she could have been equally successful, just in a different way. But now she has found her calling in education, a decision that is a fortunate asset for Benesse.

Japan Must Reform Its Antiquated Marriage Laws

This column was originally published in Nikkei Asia *on April 30, 2021, and has been modified for the purpose of this book. The information contained in this article is correct at the time of publishing in* Nikkei Asia.

How does the reign of a particular system, be it societal or religious, withstand the test of time?

One way is to stick to its original set of values and try to weather the turbulence. Another is to be flexible enough to adapt to changing times. The conundrum for any incumbent system is that neither way is foolproof. Marriage rules in Japan are no exception.

For the past 120 years, Article 750 of Japan's civil code has stipulated that "a husband and wife shall adopt the surname of the husband or wife in accordance with that which is decided at the time of marriage."[15] Even though the rule is gender-neutral, 96% of couples adopt the husband's surname.[16]

Moves to challenge this requirement are gaining intensity inside the ruling Liberal Democratic Party ahead of a general election that will be held later this year. Liberals are pushing for the introduction of a dual-surname option that saves mostly women from the loss of identity that comes with taking their husband's name and eases the administrative burden. Conservatives are pushing back, saying that allowing dual surnames would weaken family ties.

At best, the family unity argument is a sincerely held belief, but lacks any empirical evidence to support it. At worst, this argument is camouflage to hide the true value set that conservatives wish to preserve—the patriarchal hierarchy soaking every cubic inch of Japanese air.

Contextualizing this debate as a metaphor for the fight against entrenched male and senior superiority is crucial. By allowing the optional dual surname in marriage, Japan must make the right step toward an inclusive society that empowers all individuals regardless of gender.

According to the Japan In-House Lawyers Association, Article 750, which binds a married couple by one surname, finds its root in the *ie seido*, or house system, established in 1898.[17] It explains that a house governed by its male master is a foundational unit of Japan. A woman who enters a man's house by marriage by giving up her maiden name is subordinate. From then on, she is expected to follow her husband, and later her male children, regarding any life decision.

Technically, the house system was abolished in 1947 for having encouraged wartime authoritarianism. But 75 years later, its patriarchal spirit lives on. A house governed by a father, symbolically united by his surname, is analogous to the nation governed by the male-only emperor.

The symmetry is also observed in the lifetime employment system, which, despite being weakened by enhanced mobility in the labor market, sees an employee devote their life to one company in return for lifetime protection. Obedience is a virtue. The house system pins people to a fixed status in society. There is no opting out. That resonates with staunch conservatives opposing moves to allow dual surnames.

The patriarchal spirit of the house system subordinates women and young people to their male seniors, the incumbent power elite.

Take Yoshiro Mori, the ex-prime minister and former Olympic organizing committee president, was forced to step down over his derogatory remarks about women.[18] He made a backhanded compliment about his female director colleagues *wakimaeru*, meaning knowing their places, in meetings. It was a blatant attempt to tap into the house system.

If patriarchy is the spiritual keystone of Japanese society, could adopting dual surnames ultimately bring about the collapse of the entire system? Sugarcoated by their cries about the loss of family unity, this is actually the worst fear of conservatives.

Unsurprisingly, the loss of patriarchal order is most damaging in the eyes of the incumbent—in this case, senior Japanese men who represent the most conservative pillar of society. But their vision is tinted by their nostalgia—a shining image of Japan's miraculous post-WWII ascent.

The totalitarian approach honed during the war may have maximized organizational efficiency during Japan's economic ascent through the 1970s and 1980s, when the spirit of the house system functioned best. But it no longer guarantees success when assumptions have completely shifted.

In fact, I would argue that today's Japan has much to gain by openly embracing more egalitarian values. For two decades or more, we have moved into the era of postindustrial capitalism, where creativity trumps militaristic rigor. It is common knowledge today that a confluence of ideas drawn from different backgrounds fosters innovation. Insularity, on the contrary, breeds myopia and arrogance.

With women only occupying 12% of managerial positions[19] and juniors expected to fall in line with the senior members in the organization, Japan Inc.'s vitality is clearly handicapped.

In a tradition-honoring culture like Japan, inertia favors old values. But when those values are deemed irreversibly outdated, we must take the courage to renew them. In this light, adopting the optional dual-surname system in marriage is a step toward a modern, egalitarian Japan. It symbolizes a conscious departure from the patriarchal mindset paralyzing the country and preventing it from unlocking its true potential.

Japan's Miss Contests Reflect Society's High Demands on Women

This column was originally published in Nikkei Asia *on January 30, 2023, and has been modified for the purpose of this book. The information contained in this article is correct at the time of publishing in* Nikkei Asia.

Why do women still take part in beauty contests?

This is an important question, as the Miss Contest pageants held at many Japanese universities are now drawing attention from international media.

Popularized in the late 1970s, Miss Contests have so far survived feminist bashing as well as bouts of #MeToo-esque scandals. They continue to draw a steady following and are organized by student groups at some of Japan's most prestigious universities.

The recent feature article "Beauty over Brains: Japan's Skin-Deep University Pageants" in the *New York Times* posited that the pageants, nicknamed *Miss Cons*, objectify young women. The article concluded that their unabashed lookism reflects a sexist cultural emphasis on "beauty over brains."[20]

Writing in the article "Japan's 'Miss Contests' Are Hardly Swimsuit Competitions" published in *Nikkei Asia* last month, Tokyo resident Stephen Givens framed Miss Cons as "complex personality contests" that "push young Japanese, often brought up to be shy and reticent, to present themselves in bold and unaccustomed ways."[21]

Both analyses, however, tread only lightly on the basic question of why a young woman would go through a weeks-long competition centered on appearance-focused public scrutiny.

Classic beauty pageants may have given aspiring women from underprivileged backgrounds a golden ticket to climb the social ladder. Not so with the Miss Cons held at top schools, including the

University of Tokyo and Sophia University. Although some universities have adapted the Miss Cons to respond to criticism of lookism,
such as by creating a new contest that aims to focus less on looks, the
ambitious young students who participate here are out to prove that
they have both brains and beauty.

Japan, along with South Korea and China, is infamous for its
competitive education system, which emphasizes finding the right
answer rather than asking creative questions.

Students at top universities are survivors of this system who have
conformed well to the expectations set by their elders. Some students
with better looks apply for Miss Cons as an extension of conformity,
in effect, responding to a dog whistle from society.

German philosopher Rebekka Reinhard conceptually divides the
world into a "hard sphere" of capitalism and business ruled by men
and a "soft sphere" of home, family, and personal lanes governed by
women in her recently published book that carries the translated title,
*The Headquarters of Responsibilities: 20 Survival Strategies for Women
Between Wanting, Should, and Must.*[22]

In modern Western societies, including Japan, gender-based
borders are blurred. Women now have to prove their worth in both
spheres with a combination of intelligence and the traditionally
praised feminine qualities of being pretty, sweet, caring, loving, and
seductive. "The oscillation between the two spheres," Reinhard writes,
"is difficult and stressful."

Men, however, have been conspicuously slow to claim the soft
sphere. Consider *iku-men*, a recent addition to the Japanese vocabu-
lary, which refers to an exotic species of father, "men who tend to
child care."

There is no equivalent term for women—they are simply
called mothers.

Unsurprisingly, to be a superwoman who can achieve the holy grail of dual-sphere happiness is a tall ask, in Reinhard's words, "an illusory promise."

If a woman opts out of this model due to excess stress, she can either aim to be successful in the hard sphere like her male counterparts and remain single, exempt from the wifely expectations of society, or she can forget the hard sphere entirely. But being a full-time Japanese housewife can mean forfeiting lifelong earnings of about ¥200 million ($1.5 million), according to calculations by the Japan Institute for Labour Policy and Training, a government research center.[23]

The first scenario contributes to the high rate of women who postpone or give up on marriage. As of 2020, according to government statistics, 23.6% of Japanese women between 35 and 39 had never been married, compared to just 10% in 1995.[24]

The average number of children a Japanese woman has over her lifetime continues to plummet, sliding from 1.42 to 1.33 over the same period.[25]

Choosing to stay home, however, is increasingly risky when the financial prospects of husbands are more and more precarious.

Either path is suboptimal for society.

So what can we do to chip away at the unreasonably high expectations to which society holds women accountable? Reinhard advocates "strategic nonconformism"; just because we can win Miss Cons, be a CEO, and be a perfect mother does not mean that we must.

I would add two more recommendations.

First, we must raise awareness about gender-based asymmetry. For example, let us catch ourselves before asking only working mothers if they want to leave early to pick up the kids. Hypothesizing gender reversal is a good exercise to question our bias.

Second, optics matter. Demonstrating the wide range of women who are markedly successful in either sphere of activity will help to break the notion that a woman must be perfect across the two spheres.

Take the hard sphere. As Givens rightly points out, Japan has its share of vibrant women active in diverse professional fields. Yet there is a gross underrepresentation in public of women who fall outside the narrow category of "young and pretty," the unofficial credo of Miss Cons. Men, however, are spared from such underrepresentation.

In promotional materials for business panels, my eyes automatically search for women. Higher consciousness of gender balance leaves few panels as "manels" these days. But too often, women appear only as moderators, and nearly all of these are freelance anchorwomen. Although there is nothing wrong with the profession, they represent but a fraction of qualified women.

Rather than reflect the strong sexist culture of Japan, which begins at a young age, I would argue that the conforming students who join Miss Cons diligently self-optimize for what society expects: superwomen with both brains and beauty. But this expectation is universal.

References

1. Benesse Holdings. (2023). Group history. https://www.benesse-hd.co.jp/en/about/history.html (accessed 15 June 2023).
2. Benesse Holdings. (2023). Financial performance. https://www.benesse-hd.co.jp/ja/ir/finance/chart.html (accessed 16 June 2023).
3. Japan Women's Innovative Network. (2012). 投げられた試練、受け続け36歳役員に 成島由美さん (Translation: Yumi Narushima kept taking the trials thrown at her, becoming an executive officer at 36). https://ameblo.jp/japhic-c/entry-11133431050.html (accessed 15 June 2023).
4. *Nikkei Business*. (2011). ブレないリーダー、ブレない生き方 (Translation: Unshakeable leader, unshakeable way of life). In 実践!ビジョナリー経営 (Translation: *Practice! Visionary management*), 80–83. Nikkei Business.
5. The Institute of Labour Administration. (2010). 役職別昇進年齢の実態と昇進スピード変化の動向 (Translation: The promotion age by position and trends in promotion speed changes). https://www.rosei.or.jp/attach/labo/research/pdf/000008216.pdf (accessed 15 June 2023).
6. Benesse Holdings. (2022). Benesse report 2022. https://pdf.irpocket.com/C9783/ba4w/Nsv6/SLoT.pdf (accessed 25 June 2023).
7. Gender Equality Bureau Cabinet Office. (2022). White paper on gender equality 2022. https://www.gender.go.jp/about_danjo/whitepaper/r04/zentai/html/honpen/b1_s01_04.html (accessed 15 June 2023).
8. Japan Women's Innovative Network. (2012).
9. *Nikkei*. (2014). 新規参入も続々、タブレット通信教育で子供争奪戦 (Translation: New entrants continue to compete for children in the tablet online learning market). https://www.nikkei.com/article/DGXNASFK1300Z_T10C14A5000000/ (accessed 15 June 2023).

10. Statistics Bureau of Japan. (2022). Population estimates. https://www.stat.go.jp/data/jinsui/topics/topi1311.html#aI-1 (accessed 15 June 2023).
11. *Nikkei*. (2014). ベネッセが希望退職 300 人　月内募集、通信教育リストラ (Translation: Benesse seeks 300 voluntary retirees within this month; online education restructuring). https://www.nikkei.com/article/DGXLASDZ02H2N_S4A201C1MM0000/ (accessed 15 June 2023).
12. *Nikkei*. (2014). ベネッセ、内部管理に甘さ　情報漏洩許した「過信」 (Translation: Benesse; laxity in internal management—"overconfidence" allowed information leaks). https://www.nikkei.com/article/DGXLASDZ13007_T10C14A9TJC000/ (accessed 15 June 2023).
13. *Asahi Shimbun Company*. (2021). 大妻中高校長・成島由美さん「女子に『21 世紀のお針箱』を授けたい」 (Translation: Yumi Narushima, principal of Otsuma Junior and Senior High School, "I want to give girls a 'sewing box for the 21st century'"). https://www.asahi.com/edua/article/14458453 (accessed 15 June 2023).
14. Ibid.
15. *Nikkei Asia*. (2020). Debate over surnames hinders reform agenda of Japanese PM. https://asia.nikkei.com/Politics/Inside-Japanese-politics/Debate-over-surnames-hinders-reform-agenda-of-Japanese-PM (accessed 19 June 2023).
16. Ministry of Health, Labour, and Welfare. (2016). Marriage Statistics, Specified Report of Vital Statistics. https://www.mhlw.go.jp/toukei/saikin/hw/jinkou/tokusyu/konin16/index.html (accessed 16 June 2023).
17. Japan In-House Lawyers Association. (2021). 夫婦別姓制度の導入に関する理事長声明 (Translation: President's statement on the introduction of a dual-surname marital system). https://jila.jp/wp/wp-content/uploads/2021/03/seimei20210310.pdf (accessed 19 June 2023).

18. *Asahi Shimbun Company.* (2021). 「女性がたくさん入っている会議は時間かかる」森喜朗氏 (Translation: "Meetings with many women take longer." Yoshiro Mori). https://www.asahi.com/articles/ASP235VY8P23UTQP011.html (accessed 20 June 2023).

19. Ministry of Health, Labour, and Welfare. (2019). Basic Survey of Gender Equality in Employment Management. https://www.mhlw.go.jp/toukei/list/dl/71-30r/06.pdf (accessed 19 June 2023).

20. *New York Times.* (2022). Beauty over brains: Japan's skin-deep university pageants. https://www.nytimes.com/2022/11/27/world/asia/japan-university-pageants.html (accessed 19 June 2023).

21. *Nikkei Asia.* (2022). Japan's "Miss Contests" are hardly swimsuit competitions. https://asia.nikkei.com/Opinion/Japan-s-Miss-Contests-are-hardly-swimsuit-competitions (accessed 19 June 2023).

22. *Frankfurter Allgemeine Zeitung.* (2023). Die Emanzipation, die wir uns wünschen, ist in Perversion umgeschlagen (Translation: The emancipation we desire has turned into perversion). https://www.faz.net/aktuell/stil/leib-seele/rebekka-reinhardt-emanzipation-ist-in-perversion-umgeschlagen-18576449.html (accessed 20 June 2023).

23. The Japan Institute for Labour Policy and Training. (2022). ユースフル労働統計 2022 (Translation: Useful labour statistics 2022). https://www.jil.go.jp/kokunai/statistics/kako/2022/documents/useful2022.pdf (accessed 19 June 2023).

24. Statistics Bureau of Japan. (2020). National census. https://www.stat.go.jp/data/kokusei/2020/index.html (accessed 19 June 2023).

25. Ministry of Health, Labour, and Welfare. (2020). Vital statistics. https://www.mhlw.go.jp/toukei/saikin/hw/jinkou/kakutei20/index.html (accessed 19 June 2023).

10 Competence

Competence, the critical core skills you build your professional value proposition on, is often an elusive concept. Particularly with Japanese companies, which prefer to groom generalists than functional specialists—a philosophy aligned with the traditional lifetime employment system—few employees can succinctly define their competence. In Japan, you hardly need to define it—the train of your career will keep moving along with you sitting inside as a quiet passenger.

However, Masae Yamanaka, vice president at Panasonic Connect, enjoyed no such luxury. She started her career in sales at IBM Japan, a multinational technology company operating in Japan, but she found herself loathing the classic sales tactics of drinking heavily and entertaining exhaustively. Instead, she invented and refined her own scheme for logical selling, which became her hallmark and competence.

Competence comes to life most vividly when it is put to the test of repeatability—would it work equally well in other situations? Now onto her fourth employer, Yamanaka has proven her method to be brilliantly repeatable; her method works with any company, IT or manufacturing, multinational or Japanese, when applied in a business-to-business (B2B) sales context. Indeed, over the course of her career, Japanese companies also transformed themselves to embrace outside talent, as I analyze in my column, "C-Suite: the Last Frontier for Foreigners Eyeing Japan Inc." And tapping into the underused Japanese talent, from highly educated women to retirees, is a sensible path to augmenting the declining workforce, as my other column, "Can Japan Have Prosperity Without Growth?" argues.

Today, Yamanaka is not coy about her marketability—there are few women senior executives in Japan who understand both IT and digital as well as having been in the trenches in B2B sales. She counts high-profile senior executives as her close allies. Naturally she is coveted for independent nonexecutive board positions, two of which she occupies today.

If competence in sales is an acquired hard skill for her, Yamanaka instead inherited her inner drive from her mother, who instilled in her young daughters the ideas that women must gain financial independence and that execution matters. Her career, therefore, is about more than successful execution and the digital transformation of Japan Inc., where she finds her platform in her late career. It is also about an emotional story of a daughter living up to her late mother's standards.

Masae Yamanaka, Vice President of Panasonic Connect

1963: Born in Aichi Prefecture, Japan

1987: Graduated from Keio University with a degree in literature

1987: Started her career at IBM Japan in the sales department

2003: Awarded the top sales award in IBM Japan

2004: Appointed as executive assistant to the president for IBM Asia Pacific

2005: Appointed as sales manager for general business manufacturing

2009: Joined Microsoft Japan and appointed as general manager for the distribution and services industry division

2014: Joined LIXIL as executive officer for sales development

2015: Appointed as executive officer in charge of sales for special demands for major housebuilders at LIXIL

2017: Joined Panasonic Connected Solutions (now Panasonic Connect) and appointed as managing officer of sales promotion division

2021: Appointed as external director at Sanrio

2021: Panasonic acquired the US supply chain application provider, Blue Yonder

2022: Panasonic reorganized its structure to a holdings structure, and Panasonic Connected Solutions was reconstructed as Panasonic Connect

2022: Appointed as vice president of Panasonic Connect in charge of the collaboration with Blue Yonder Japan, and executive vice president of Gemba Solutions Company (a division within Panasonic Connect)

2022: Appointed as external director at JTB

Masae Yamanaka Builds Career in Sales Traversing Four Companies

This article was originally published in the Japan Times *on August 3, 2023, and has been modified for the purpose of this book. The information contained in this article is correct at the time of publishing in the* Japan Times.

"I am after all a product of my late mother's curses," 59-year-old Masae Yamanaka cheerfully told me. I was sitting in the smartly furnished conference room of the newly renovated Shiodome office with Yamanaka, vice president at Panasonic Connect, a group company under Panasonic Holdings specializing in system development for corporate clients with a turnover of ¥1.1 trillion.[1]

For one, Yamanaka's mother preached to her daughters, Yamanaka and her younger sister, "to be financially independent." The financial situation of her family prevented Yamanaka's mother from advancing to college. After marriage to her father, who operated his own business, Yamanaka suspected that the lack of financial independence remained a chip on her mother's shoulder, even though it was the norm for married women to stay at home at the time.

Second, Yamanaka's mother taught her daughters to be realists. Yamanaka recalled being a child watching with her mother, a documentary about children suffering from famine in Africa. The atrocity made her eyes well up. "My mother snapped that my tears would not change a thing in the world, that without actions, emotion meant nothing," she recalled. This remark left a lasting impact on the young girl—"I became obsessed with execution." The conviction later brew into the backbone of her approach to sales in professional life; she faithfully translated her plans to actions while never making commitments she could not keep.

Convinced that she must always be self-reliant, Yamanaka made work a sacred and central theme to her life. She also has a 10-year-old son, who was born when she was 49. Her devotion has paid off handsomely—after two decades of a formative sales career at IBM Japan where she established herself as a star performer, Yamanaka steadily climbed the career ladder through Microsoft Japan, LIXIL, a Japanese home equipment manufacturer with ¥1.5 trillion turnover,[2] and now Panasonic Connect, where she serves as a managing executive officer. Two themes emerge through her career of 36 years.

First is about her core expertise. Yamanaka's success demonstrates the importance of shaping and sticking to what you do best. Her core remains the systemic B2B sales approach that she crafted and refined through practice at IBM Japan, where she spent the first 22 years of her career.

On the technical side, Yamanaka sells technology as customized solutions rather than generic off-the-shelf products. She learned early on that this is only possible through deep understanding of the client situation and constant refreshing of her knowledge about IT tools.

On the emotional side, she is aware that trust with clients takes a long time to build—committed to execution, Yamanaka vows never to promise anything she cannot deliver. After the deployment of an IT solution, the technical team recedes while the sales team stays with the client to address any issues. She follows up intensely. Combining both these technical and emotional factors, her holistic sales approach has proved versatile throughout her four employers, two multinationals and two Japanese companies.

The second theme, perhaps less intentional than the first, is about her perennial quest for the best environment to flourish in, signaling a new career model, especially for Japanese white-collar workers. Deep down, two factors drive her: one is the confidence she built in her core skills—"I can perform anywhere as long as there are B2B sales"—and the other her fear of stagnation in professional growth, which speaks to her more loudly than any sense of comfort or familiarity.

Overlaying on top of these personal drivers is the Zeitgeist. Her pivot from non-Japanese companies operating in Japan (IBM and Microsoft Japan) to working for Japan headquarters of globalized Japanese companies (LIXIL and Panasonic Connect) reflects the changing nature of business in Japan for global players over the past three decades. As Japan's relative economic stature waned, so did the importance of over-indexing on the Japanese market, which had previously justified heavy localization to access the then-second largest IT market in the world, until Japan was taken over by China in 2013.[3]

In parallel, the business model of IT also shifted to being cloud-based, where the global headquarters makes the lion's share of decisions to drive a global standard. Combined, these forces result in far fewer degrees of freedom for local management at non-Japanese IT companies compared to the 1990s, the early years of Yamanaka's career at IBM Japan.

During the same period, Japanese companies have been pushing to leverage digital technology to modernize their front- and back-end business operations. This is where Yamanaka found her perfect playground.

As labor mobility increases in Japan, traditionally known for life-time employment, her career story signifies a triumph for both herself and her employers. For Yamanaka, a long, exciting career with multiple employers, and for her employers, the handsome reward arising from introducing diversity into key leadership positions. Her mother's curses turned out to be a blessing, after all.

Reinventing Corporate Sales at IBM Japan

When Yamanaka entered IBM Japan in 1987 with a degree in literature from the prestigious Keio University, it was not due to foresight into the future growth of IT industry—"I had no interest in computers"—but rather thanks to her desire for long tenure.

"To choose an employer where I could be happy working for years, I looked for a gender-equal culture with no gender pay gap. Foreign companies sounded like a good idea and IBM Japan was the top pick for women college recruits at the time," explained Yamanaka.

IBM Japan, a wholly-owned subsidiary of IBM, was established in 1937 and was already a giant in the local IT industry by the late 1980s.[4] Yamanaka's cohort counted approximately 1,600 fresh graduates, among which 350 were women. The Equal Employment Opportunity Act had just taken effect a year before in 1986—young women with higher education entered the workforce with high hopes for a career on equal footing with men.

Except that it was still very much a dark era for professional women, even at IBM Japan. "After three to four years, the 11 women in my cohort assigned to the sales department dwindled to just one, myself," recounted Yamanaka. "Sexual and power harassment was rampant—young saleswomen would be forced to dance cheek-to-cheek with older male clients while male colleagues looked the other way." Back then, few employers expected young women to work much longer beyond the age of 30, certainly not after marriage, and therefore never seriously invested in them. Their well-being was never a priority for the management. Such extreme ageism for women at work has since diminished, and more women are staying in the workplace. (See Figure 10.1.)

The sales tactics were macho and old-fashioned. "You drank to win work," Yamanaka put bluntly. Committed to stick it out—her mother's teaching ringing in her head—she refused to give up. When she "hated it but somehow survived the first couple of years," a penny dropped for her. "I decided to use my brain for my sales approach." She tried alternatives to drinking.

It was not a slam dunk from the beginning. "I tried silly tactics, including insisting on starting a group journal with my client counterpart, which I put in the machine room," she chuckled.

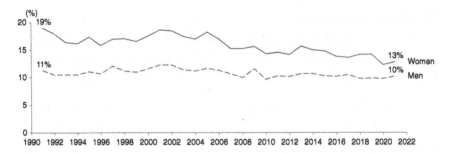

Figure 10.1   Turnover rate by gender for full-time employees in Japan (%)

Note: More women are staying in the workplace compared to a few decades ago because they continue to work after life events such as marriage and childbirth. Adapted from Ministry of Health, Labour and Welfare (2022). Survey on Employment Trends. https://www.mhlw.go.jp/toukei/itiran/roudou/koyou/doukou/22-2/index.html (accessed 24 June 2023).

"No entry from the other side for months naturally, until finally, I was elated to find a message, which read—Ms. Yamanaka, we need three more cables."

Eventually, she set her eyes on the account plan, the annual projection of account activities, and the resulting account P&L put forward by the account team. She found that barely half of the activities promised were executed. "It is such a big hoopla when you make the account plans, then after the presentation to the management they gather dust in the desk drawer." Instead, for her account plan, Yamanaka vowed to execute. "I broke the annual account plan down to quarterly-, monthly-, weekly-, and daily-level to-dos, so execution is enforced."

At the same time, Yamanaka insisted on being strategic and not only tactical; "30% of daily activities I tried to spend on things that would differentiate us from our competitors," she said. "I'd pore through investor disclosure reports, benchmark my accounts against their peers, and whispered the talking points into my superiors' ears so they could talk to their senior counterpart at clients."

In front of clients, she ensured accountability by presenting the monthly plan directly to the client's person in charge, for example, the vice president of information systems. "I'd ask them if we are meeting their expectations. Once our monthly meetings became a routine, they would open up more, and I would get more intel than my competitors. The quality of work obviously improved."

Her performance did not go unnoticed by the IBM Japan management. "I was in my 20s when they gave me a chance to present my new method to the board," she recalled. The culmination of her efforts was a three-year contract worth ¥10 billion from a major new client in retail for which she oversaw sales—this was the "most challenging project" of her IBM career. Based on her various accomplishments, she was awarded the top sales award in IBM Japan at 39 years old in 2003. To this day, Yamanaka remains the only woman sales professional to have received this honor.

It was in her last five years out of her two decades spent with IBM Japan that she led sales for general business manufacturing, a particularly male-dominated sector. The division was known for poor performance and persistently missing budget. She diagnosed the root cause to be short-termism and number-chasing. It was distracting the salesforce from targeting the right set of accounts with long-term upside, creating a vicious cycle of underperformance. "To this day, I never chase numbers," she declared. But the sales cycle was long—10 to 12 months—and further bleeding was inevitable with a pivot in target accounts.

"I knew I wouldn't get fired for further temporary sinking," Yamanaka revealed her calculation with me. "I was a woman and a high-potential candidate for management." When she bit the bullet and went through the investment period, the team was able to meet the quarterly budget in the fourth quarter, followed by the annual budget the next year. The motivation on the ground ameliorated as did performance.

A Younger Multinational: Microsoft Japan

When an executive search firm reached out to Yamanaka in 2009 for an introduction to Yasuyuki Higuchi, then 51-year-old serving as CEO of Microsoft Japan since 2008 after an illustrious career in IT at Hewlett-Packard Japan and others, the then 45-year-old was at the top of her game at IBM Japan. She was certainly not looking. "I only went [to meet with Higuchi] because the search firm assured me it was OK just to have a coffee" with him, she explained, "and I was curious to meet the celebrity CEO."

Higuchi also recalled that Yamanaka "had no intention of leaving" when they first met. "She clearly loved IBM, which is known for lifers." But she was a perfect fit for the transformation of Microsoft Japan he had in mind, from a business-to-consumer (B2C) company to a B2B company. To grow the B2B business, "I was looking for someone with an affinity for Japanese companies," Higuchi explained. In his eyes, IBM Japan had the right mixture of non-Japanese and Japanese culture, committed to results yet respectful.

Unexpectedly for Yamanaka, the meeting with Higuchi led to two revelations; that there were other possibilities for her outside IBM Japan and that, perhaps more important, she was getting too comfortable with her then-employer. "I knew by experience that only through tough assignments did people grow as professionals," she explained, "but things were getting too cozy for me back then [at IBM Japan]. I knew I had to change something."

Compared to IBM Japan, Microsoft Japan was "even less Japanese," described Yamanaka. It was "younger" to begin with. Lay-offs due to position closures were normal at Microsoft Japan, while IBM Japan tried to honor the social contract of employment and retain staff members. Her assignment as general manager for the distribution and services industry division meant she would lead a team who knew nothing about her glorious past at IBM Japan.

"People were skeptical [of me] at first," admitted Yamanaka. She proved herself by winning clients. "I was comfortable speaking with CIOs." The division, the second smallest amongst the six divisions in 2009 when Yamanaka joined, grew their sales by double digits annually to be the second largest in five years.

"She was able to align the value proposition of Microsoft Japan with the vision of the client," recalled Higuchi in our recent interview, "which was a departure from a product-oriented sales approach." What made her resonate with the C-suite of the client companies, Higuchi analyzed, was her "positive power" on top of her fluency in applications and solutions. "Things must get tough, being in direct sales as a woman," Higuchi commented, "but Yamanaka has the mental strength to laugh them off."

Japanese Company in Global Transformation: LIXIL

By 2014, "I was starting to feel as if ready to move on from the world of multinationals [such as Microsoft Japan]," reflected Yamanaka. "Japan is but a sales office. At the end of the day, transactional revenue counts more than addressing clients' issues holistically. This meant I couldn't fully capitalize on all my knowledge in solutions such as customer relationship management (CRM) or business process reengineering (BPR)." An opportunity with LIXIL, a Japanese company in process of globalizing, offered a breakthrough.

In 2014, an executive search firm introduced her to Yoshiaki Fujimori, then CEO of LIXIL. Fujimori was already a renowned senior executive in Japan, belonging to the new breed of "professional management" like Higuchi. After starting his career at Nissho Iwai, now Sojitz, a major Japanese trading conglomerate, he honed his career at GE culminating it with the position of CEO of GE Japan in 2008.

When introduced to Yamanaka, Fujimori was already a few years into his role as LIXIL CEO from 2011. Prior to his onboarding,

LIXIL was a mostly domestic, family-owned business with a strong network of domestic distributors. Fujimori's vision was to globalize the company for discontinuous growth in overseas markets using acquisitions as a tool. Large-scale transactions such as American Standard (2013) and GROHE (2014) took place during Fujimori's tenure.[5]

"Yamanaka was a perfect match with the three leadership traits I wanted at LIXIL at the time," Fujimori told me. First, he was looking for a change agent who could paint a big picture, communicate, and execute. Then, he wanted a leader with a stretch goal mindset and a sense of accountability. Finally, he or she had to have a "global mindset," which Fujimori explained as embracing diversity and meritocracy. "I was transforming a company which used to be 99% domestic," he recalled, "to earning a third of revenue from outside Japan."

"Global mindset" in Fujimori's mind is a personal frame of mind that is not automatically earned through long years of living abroad. Yamanaka could articulate herself without being held back by her minority gender status, while being aware of the gender inequality.

Diversity, Fujimori defines, is about respecting different cultures. And seldom is it more starkly expressed than in the case of traversing between Japanese and multinational companies. Having experienced both himself, Fujimori describes the Japanese work culture as diligent, dedicated, and hard-working with its talent generally capable. "They are equipped with the fundamentals to fight overseas."

Where multinationals do better, according to Yamanaka in reflection, is in instilling the sense of individual professionalism. Commitment to numbers where "performance is ultimately prioritized over what your boss may want," constantly honing one's area of expertise based on the job description, which often in Japanese cases remains unclear, and the conscious assessment of one's market value are the three points Yamanaka took away from working for two multinational tech giants.

That she was a woman in sales was significant. "Her appointment would have symbolic power to change the company," Fujimori explained. Although it is relatively easy to find women executives to lead corporate functions such as communications, human resources (HR), or investor relations (IR), "it is hard to find [senior] women in sales. Her success is extra-special," according to Fujimori; "it was a big-deal assignment."

At LIXIL, she enjoyed the sense of freedom to make her own decisions, which had been inaccessible at her prior companies. After IBM and Microsoft Japan, she was confident that her sales model was versatile. As the executive officer in charge of sales for special demands for major housebuilders, typically facing general contractors in rural Japan, which is "the utmost symbol of a male-dominated society," according to Fujimori, Yamanaka introduced systemic changes including salesforce automation (SFA), which led to a jump in bookings.

Ultimately, her tenure at LIXIL lasted less than three years, as she found that the management style had changed after Fujimori and his close allies in the management stepped down in 2016. Yamanaka soon started looking for a new environment where she could flourish.

Second Japanese Company After Deliberation: Panasonic Connect

Never down for long, Yamanaka was ready to sign an offer letter with a large, multinational medical equipment company when Higuchi contacted her via text on a messenger. In 2017, he had returned to Panasonic to lead Panasonic Connected Solutions Company, one of the four companies within the Panasonic group at the time, as CEO. It meant a homecoming after 25 years for Higuchi, who worked for a succession of multinationals after a 12-year post-college career starting in 1980 with Panasonic. "The next day was to be my last day at LIXIL when he messaged me," Yamanaka recalled.

"I suggested that we talk if she was leaving [LIXIL]," Higuchi said, "and I didn't invite her [to Panasonic] out of my ego. I genuinely thought it would be a better choice for her." He understood that she wanted a long and stable tenure. Traditionally a hardware company, Panasonic was shifting its B2B business direction to solution-based with its tip of the spear, Panasonic Connected Solutions Company, to be reconstructed as Panasonic Connect. The specialized operating company would be established in 2022 under Panasonic Holdings, consolidating other B2B businesses within Panasonic group. Higuchi knew it would be a multiyear journey in the trenches and he needed a trustworthy partner-in-crime such as Yamanaka.

"Gone is the era when Japanese companies [such as Panasonic] could overwhelm competitors by quality and affordability of stand-alone hardware," explained Higuchi. "We must pivot to the solution business orchestrating applications and hardware to address clients' needs." The transformation, which Panasonic Connect spearheads within the group, requires a whole new sales approach based on understanding the client's business agenda. In Higuchi's eyes, Yamanaka personified that vision.

Blue Yonder, a US-headquartered supply chain application provider that Panasonic acquired for ¥860 billion in 2021,[6] is a symbolic piece in the hardware-to-solution transformation of the Panasonic Group and a centerpiece for Panasonic Connect. "Blue Yonder Japan (BYJ, where Higuchi serves as representative director and chairman after the Blue Yonder acquisition) is still a fledgling organization," admitted Higuchi. "We are building capabilities from scratch."

Leading collaboration between Panasonic Connect, BYJ, and Panasonic, Yamanaka thinks strategically in unlocking Blue Yonder Japan's potential by introducing a delivery model that leverages outside partners such as system integrators and consulting firms—"BYJ was too bent on in-house delivery." Higuchi described her approach: "She presents a vision, the staff builds brick-by-brick."

However, transfusing outside mid- to senior-level talent into a homogenous organization is a gamble not without its risks. "Strong medicine must be taken in moderation," Higuchi cautioned—you want to rock the boat, but not break it. He understands it is hard for external hires such as Yamanaka to fully function without his endorsement. "It is a balancing act," he admitted, "between letting the hired guns be as aggressive as they are and controlling the reception on the ground." He is aware of his role to "get in the middle" in the case of escalations.

Because such top-down care is badly needed in Japanese companies for successful senior-level hires, such as in Yamanaka's case, Fujimori argued, his recommendation at the time was that she would be better off at a multinational, whose acceptance of diversity was more systematic and leader independent. Her post-LIXIL decision to join Panasonic, to the contrary of his advice, which she took seriously, signaled her level of confidence in hindsight, Fujimori told me.

Although Yamanaka chose a Japanese company, Panasonic, over Fujimori's advice, the incident never soured their mentor-mentee relationship. "I was impressed that she kept contacting me [after joining Panasonic]," Fujimori mentioned. Her zeal for self-development impresses him—"despite her busy schedule, she would often host a dinner inviting me and someone senior from her network. I meet interesting people through her, and I can see that she tries to learn from our conversations." Yamanaka, however, earnestly calls Fujimori her mentor.

Freeze Your Eggs

The biological clock presents a challenge for working women serious on building a professional career. The prime time for starting a family—late 20s to 30s—overlaps with career acceleration. Yamanaka, who ultimately had her baby boy at 49 while at Microsoft Japan after years of infertility treatment, has some practical advice. "I'd say, if the possibility [of giving birth] is not zero, women should freeze their eggs early," she told me straightforwardly. "You may change your mind. You could be over 40 when you finally decide that you want kids." Egg-freezing will be an insurance.

Yamanaka approached her childbirth with such efficiency that it surprised her Microsoft colleagues including Higuchi. "I worked till the eleventh hour on my hospital bed, had a caesarean section and was back at the computer in three and a half hours," chuckled Yamanaka. During the two-month maternity leave post-birth, she arranged a full-time sitter. "She was back to work in no time," recounted Higuchi with a hint of amazement. "it was radical."

Yamanaka uses every support available for childcare, from sitters to nursery schools to soliciting help from her fellow mom friends. Raising a child while working is more than another exercise of project management—eventually, it affected her state of mind, Yamanaka admits—"I think I slowed down a bit after having a child. I have become more considerate for others now that I see that what goes around comes around—I help some, you help some."

Working mothers in senior positions such as Yamanaka are key poster children for Japan, which encourages more women to stay in the workforce to stabilize, if not reverse, the falling total fertility rate, which currently stands at a precarious 1.26 in 2022.[7] (See Figure 10.2.) Curiously, Yamanaka downplays this part. "We never advertised the working mother bit," Fujimori told me even though her first and only child was still in infancy while she worked under him for LIXIL. "I think she took [working motherhood] as something quite normal."

Still, Higuchi described Yamanaka as a role model for female staff members. "Sometimes they argue that she is in a different league [and therefore unrelatable]," he told me, "But I try to tell them that she has been through a lot to become who she is today. It is not as if

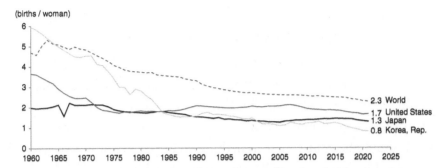

Figure 10.2   Total fertility rate by country (births per woman)

Note: The total fertility rate decline is common among developed economies, particularly pronounced for Japan and Korea without a large immigration influx. Adapted from The World Bank (2023). Fertility rate, total (births per woman). https://data.worldbank.org/indicator/SP.DYN.TFRT.IN?end=2021&name_desc=false&start=1960&view=chart (accessed 24 June 2023).

she had some superhuman abilities." Her motherhood, according to Higuchi, is an antithesis to the oft-heard murmur against successful women, that their ascent was only possible because they are childless and single.

Close to concluding her sixth year at Panasonic, Yamanaka finds her impact reaching beyond the immediate employer. With encouragement from Higuchi, she sits on two boards, those of Sanrio, a Japanese entertainment company that sells and licenses products of characters including Hello Kitty, since 2021, and JTB, the largest travel agency in Japan, since 2022. "The management at these companies are appreciative that she articulates the essence without reservations," Higuchi commented. "With limited information, she is able to see the big picture."

Vice versa, Yamanaka appreciates the learning experiences she receives by sitting on the boards of B2C companies such as Sanrio and JTB. She remains clear-eyed about her desirability as a nonexecutive board member. "I am a woman, have been always on the frontline in B2B sales, and I understand IT and digital," crisply analyzed

Yamanaka. "This combination is flaggable" for any prospective employer or companies looking to add new board members.

And consciously designing such scarcity is what she recommends for anyone building a career. "We should all find the inner axis that would serve the world," she said. "There are more possibilities than ever [for such axes] in the current environment with great uncertainty. What should be your core is something you need to find for yourself, however, because no one will conveniently hand it over to you."

Yamanaka's mother led her daughters to continue working and commit to actions. Yamanaka's loyalty to the mantra led to a rising career built over three and a half decades in sales in tech. But even without the mother's "curses," as Yamanaka calls them, her drive for personal growth is innate and genuine, which flourished in the form of a successful career constantly fueled by the mandate for self-reliance.

"When I won the sales award at IBM Japan in 2003, my mother was as happy as if I had achieved her life dream in her stead," recounted Yamanaka. Were the mother alive today, what Yamanaka has since further achieved would make one very proud mother indeed.

C-Suite: The Last Frontier for Foreigners Eyeing Japan Inc.

This column was originally published in Nikkei Asia *on December 8, 2020, and has been modified for the purpose of this book. The information contained in this article is correct at the time of publishing in* Nikkei Asia.

When Japan's top chemical company Mitsubishi Chemical Holdings appointed Belgian-born Jean-Marc Gilson as its next CEO in October,[8] it marked the first time a foreign national had been chosen to lead a blue-chip Mitsubishi group company.

It should come as no surprise that Mitsubishi Chemical, which earned 42% of its consolidated revenue from overseas in the fiscal year ended in March, recruited a CEO with Gilson's pedigree of leading the French food and pharmaceutical ingredients maker Roquette.[9]

But it is big news in Japan, where 99% of CEOs of companies on the Nikkei Stock Average are Japanese men. According to global executive recruiters Spencer Stuart, foreign nationals occupied only 5.1% of board seats for Topix100 companies in 2019.[10]

Although Gilson's appointment stands as something of an anomaly today, I would argue that the trend of recruiting foreign nationals to lead Japanese companies will gradually start to gain momentum. The main reason is that such appointments reflect the irreversible trend in corporate Japan: coming to terms with the idea that seniority-based, insular leadership does not always work best, even when it comes to Japan Inc.'s crown jewels.

Over the last 30 years, Japan has fallen steadily behind in global relevance, while China has ascended to become the Asian superpower. When I first joined the workforce in the late 1990s, in the aftermath of the bursting of the asset price bubble, I witnessed firsthand the collective psyche of Japan Inc. as it cycled through the five stages of grief—starting with denial, followed by anger, bargaining, and depression. Having lost its status as the post–World War II economic wunderkind, only now do Japan's corporate leaders seem to be reaching the final stage of grief: acceptance.

This does not mean, however, that Japanese businesses should be considered has-beens. Seeking growth outside a shrinking domestic market, many of Japan's larger companies now have a global footprint. Their stakeholders, including customers, suppliers, and shareholders, are truly international. The only part of the corporate structure that has been stubborn to admit outsiders is the C-suite.

Compared to insiders, who can harness all their inside knowledge to guide a company into the future, outside executives can bring fresh air. Especially if non-Japanese, outside executives' global vision can often complement a detail-obsessed Japanese mentality. When combined with forceful top-down decisions, this approach can dramatically enhance a company's competitiveness, at least in theory. With top management seats reserved for homegrown talent well into this century, those prized positions represented the crowning glory of a successful career within the seniority-based system.

But the signs of a thaw are growing. Japanese executives today who are just entering upper management ranks are in their early 50s, meaning that they have spent their entire career in the so-called lost three decades. It is easier for them than the generations before them to question the virtue of Japan's insular management system. This humility is not a weakness. Companies should look at the world of professional sports where Japan's rugby team, currently ranked ninth in the world, began its ascent only after inviting A-level coaches from abroad.

At a few prestigious Japanese companies, such as Shiseido and LIXIL Group, there are CEOs who are still Japanese but at least were recruited from outside the company. And it is not uncommon to appoint locals to lead overseas subsidiaries.

A good example is Takeda Pharmaceutical, which promoted former GlaxoSmithKline executive Christopher Weber from chief operating officer to CEO in 2015. Now, 14 out of 18 Takeda executives are non-Japanese.[11] With its 2019 takeover of Shire, Takeda solidified its position as a global pharmaceutical player.

Make no mistake, there are special challenges with bringing in outside—especially foreign—talent into the top ranks of a Japanese corporation. First, Japanese CEOs on average are underpaid compared to their Western counterparts. According to 2020 research by Willis Towers Watson, Japanese large company CEOs earn less than half in total compared to their European, let alone American peers.[12]

Second, Japanese management's tribal nature is difficult for an outsider to break into. Japan prioritizes cultural understanding as a prerequisite for its leaders. The ability to speak Japanese, literally and culturally, is important, and not having the language is a major handicap for external executives.

Still, these issues are not insurmountable. Takeda, for example, moved with extraordinary speed when it decided to promote an outsider. Once people here fully accept that we are far removed from the era when a seniority-based path to the top was considered the global best practice, it is only a small step to conclude that casting the net as wide as possible for CEO candidates, Japanese or non-Japanese, in-house or external, makes the most sense. As we know from our personal experiences, acceptance, the final stage of loss and grief, can be a hopeful one.

Can Japan Have Prosperity Without Growth?

This column was originally published in Nikkei Asia *on June 26, 2021, and has been modified for the purpose of this book. The information contained in this article is correct at the time of publishing in* Nikkei Asia.

Around the world, the countdown to humanity's numerical demise is audible. Under the influence of the pandemic, both China[13] and the US[14] recently posted their slowest rates of population growth respectively since the early 1960s and 1900s.

If any country is ahead of the curve in terms of shrinking demographics, it is Japan, where the population started its descent in 2008. The birthrate in 2019 at 1.36 is far from the 2.07 level necessary to maintain its current population of 126 million.[15] As a result of Japan's lower birthrate and longer life span, 28.7% of Japanese are aged over 65, making Japan the oldest population in the world.[16]

Does this mean that Japan is doomed to a downward economic spiral as its working age population shrinks? If a growing population is synonymous with prosperity—as conventional wisdom suggests—then Japan appears destined to a bleak future, consigned to serve as a cautionary tale of how a series of policy oversights brought the population, and therefore the country, down.

Yet, there is an alternative path for Japan. Rather than fight to reverse a falling birthrate, Japan has the power to reframe the narrative by instead focusing on how its people can maintain the same quality of life they enjoy now.

Of course, the first step is to make it easier for couples who want to have kids. But so far, developed countries have had little or no success using parent-friendly policies to reverse declining birthrates. Those who have succeeded have done so, though perhaps unintentionally, via an infusion of migrants, like Germany.

The old days where most parents had three to four children—in 1957, the average number of children in Japan peaked at 3.6[17]—are gone, especially with today's highly educated women having so many career choices. But it is not all doom and gloom. Fewer children means more attention from parents.

If a declining population is a given in a maturing society, it is unwise to fight against the grain. In fact, capping population growth was once officially endorsed by Japan's government, with the first Japan Population Conference in 1974 recommending limiting households to two children each.[18]

The conference highlighted the limitation of a model for growth tied to a rising population. It recommended focusing on mental, not material, well-being once an acceptable standard of living had been reached.

Half a century later, we are still trapped in the growth-oriented model but with no alternative. The question is: can we find one?

The greatest fear is that a falling population means that fewer young people will not be able to support the bigger, older cohorts once they stop working. So first, we must change the way we work.

Those people often relegated to the sidelines—highly educated women, retirees, persons with disabilities—must step into center stage. Thanks to increased digitization and automation, workplaces can now accommodate them.

Companies such as NGK Insulators, a ceramics manufacturer with ¥450 billion ($4.2 billion) in turnover since 2017, extend a full-time, fully compensated offer to their over-60 employees.[19] Such initiatives contribute to sustaining the workforce and give a sense of purpose for older people who might relish the opportunity to continue to make a positive contribution.

If the demographic shift can accelerate work reform, so can it nudge family reform. One of the major problems with our aging population is that they are too often isolated. With one in two Japanese households with a person over 65,[20] the higher their level of engagement, the better is their physical and mental well-being.

To this end, localism helps, too. A broadly connected community with cross-generational networks encourages the social engagement of the elderly. Over the long run, this trend may challenge the modern notion of family, from an isolated nuclear family to a community-based one.

Unsurprisingly, such a community forms more easily in regional cities than megacities such as Tokyo. The pandemic could emerge as an unexpected enabler, driving people away from crowded urban environments. Last year Japan saw the largest outflow of Tokyoites since 2014, a 5% increase from 2019.[21]

Underlying these changes is a shift in mindset. Although financial gain remains an important motivator, it should not be the only one influencing life choices. Mental well-being is important, and so is the gratification that comes with helping others.

If Japan manages to become a more charitable and supportive society despite its falling population, it can be a light unto the rest of the world and no longer a demographic cautionary tale.

Still, the existential question remains. If Japan is the short-term torchbearer of finding the right balance between shrinking demographics and improving collective well-being, what will happen to its population over the long run?

A flexible work style is friendly to parents. Localism leads to having neighbors as extended family who care for the children. These trends resonate positively with parenthood.

Will these trends be powerful enough to stabilize the birthrate decline? This is anyone's guess for now. But I am convinced that, instead of magically trying to save the birthrate, focusing on improving the happiness of those of us who are here already is a much better way to go.

References

1. Panasonic Connect. (2023). Company overview. https://connect
   .panasonic.com/en/about/profile (accessed 25 June 2023).
2. LIXIL Corporation. (2023). Consolidated financial results for
   the fiscal year ended March 31, 2023. https://ssl4.eir-parts.net/
   doc/5938/tdnet/2268023/00.pdf (accessed 25 June 2023).
3. *Computerworld.* (2013). China passes Japan to become world's
   2nd largest IT market. https://www.computerworld.com/
   article/2486456/china-passes-japan-to-become-world-s-2nd-
   largest-it-market.html (accessed 25 June 2023).
4. IBM. (2023). About IBM Japan. https://www.ibm.com/jp-ja/
   about?lnk=flathl (accessed 25 June 2023).
5. LIXIL Corporation. (2023). Our history. https://www.lixil.com/
   en/about/history.html (accessed 25 June 2023).
6. *Nikkei.* (2021). パナソニック、米社買収を完了　供給網支援を強化
   (Translation: Panasonic completes acquisition of US company
   to strengthen supply network services). https://www.nikkei.com/
   article/DGXZQOUF177VE0X10C21A9000000/ (accessed
   25 June 2023).
7. Ministry of Health, Labour, and Welfare. (2022). Vital statistics.
   https://www.mhlw.go.jp/toukei/saikin/hw/jinkou/geppo/
   nengai22/ (accessed 25 June 2023).
8. *Nikkei Asia.* (2020). Mitsubishi Chemical names Belgian as first
   foreign CEO. https://asia.nikkei.com/Business/Companies/
   Mitsubishi-Chemical-names-Belgian-as-first-foreign-CEO
   (accessed 19 June 2023).
9. Mitsubishi Chemical. (2020). Medium-term business management meeting. https://www.mcgc.com/ir/pdf/00889/00997.pdf
   (accessed 19 June 2023).
10. Spencer Stuart. (2019). Spencer Stuart Board Index. https://
    www.spencerstuart.com/-/media/2020/february/ssbi_jpn2019_
    web.pdf (accessed 19 June 2023).

11. Takeda Pharmaceutical Company. (2023). Leadership. https://www.takeda.com/about/leadership/ (accessed 29 June 2023).

12. Willis Towers Watson. (2020). 『日米欧 CEO 報酬比較』2020 年調査結果を発表 (Translation: Japan-U.S.-Europe CEO Compensation Comparison 2020 survey). https://www.wtwco.com/ja-jp/news/2020/07/report-fy2019-japan-us-europe-ceo-compensation-comparison (accessed 19 June 2023).

13. The World Bank. (2022). Population growth (annual %)—China. https://data.worldbank.org/indicator/SP.POP.GROW?locations=CN (accessed 29 June 2023).

14. *The Brookings Institution.* (2021). What the 2020 census will reveal about America: Stagnating growth, an aging population, and youthful diversity. https://www.brookings.edu/articles/what-the-2020-census-will-reveal-about-america-stagnating-growth-an-aging-population-and-youthful-diversity/ (accessed 29 June 2023).

15. Ministry of Health, Labour, and Welfare. (2021). Vital statistics. https://www.mhlw.go.jp/toukei/saikin/hw/jinkou/kakutei21/dl/tfr.pdf (accessed 29 June 2023).

16. Statistics Bureau of Japan. (2021). Population estimates. https://www.stat.go.jp/data/jinsui/pdf/202101.pdf (accessed 29 June 2023).

17. National Institute of Population and Social Security Research. (2015). The 15th Japanese National Fertility Survey. https://www.ipss.go.jp/ps-doukou/j/doukou15/gaiyou15html/NFS15G_html07.html#h3%202-2-1 (accessed 29 June 2023).

18. National Institute of Population and Social Security Research. (1974). 第 1 回日本人口会議の概要 (Translation: Summary of the first Japan Population Conference). https://www.ipss.go.jp/syoushika/bunken/data/pdf/14213805.pdf (accessed 29 June 2023).

19. NGK Insulators. (2017). 全従業員に 65 歳定年制を導入 (Translation: Retirement age of 65 introduced for all employees). https://www.ngk.co.jp/news/20170317_7764.html (accessed 29 June 2023).

20. Cabinet Office. (2020). Annual report on the ageing society. https://www8.cao.go.jp/kourei/whitepaper/w-2020/html/zenbun/s1_1_3.html (accessed 29 June 2023).
21. Statistics Bureau of Japan. (2021). Report on internal migration in Japan. https://www.stat.go.jp/data/idou/4.html (accessed 29 June 2023).

11 Homecoming

When we are young, ambitious, and filled with youthful hope, we haven an innate desire to explore the world. Particularly strong was the exploratory desire of Chikako Matsumoto, a first-generation college graduate hailing from Osaka where her father had founded and operated a small business. Her desire motivated her to follow the path of Sadako Ogata, former United Nations High Commissioner for Refugees. Hard work, reinforced by determination, led her to Harvard Kennedy School and eventually to a permanent position at the World Bank in Washington, DC.

Counter to one's exploratory desire is a gravitational force pulling people back to their roots. A wish for proximity to family and a sense of duty to contribute at home never fully disappears, however hundreds of miles away from home one may be. Matsumoto never forgets that she stands on the foundation of previous generations, both personally and as a nation; as a child she lived through the economic ascent of post-WWII industrialized Japan, the backdrop on which her father's manufacturing export business prospered.

Eighteen years later, after she left Japan for Harvard Kennedy School, Matsumoto made a homecoming, girded with nine years of working experience at the World Bank under her belt. What was originally a temporary return ended up becoming permanent. Ultimately, the juxtaposition of these two opposing forces—one out to the wider world and one back to Japan—resulted in a happy ending. Matsumoto, who has built her life's passion on sustainability finance, found a viable platform at Sumitomo Mitsui Trust Bank, a blue-chip trust bank in Japan. The employer hides none of their joy in recruiting a high-profile global talent who is singlehandedly accelerating their sustainability strategy.

Matsumoto's successful homecoming gives me reason for optimism. The increase in mobility is irreversible, as I discuss in my column, "Japanese Companies Can No Longer Expect Lifetime Loyalty from Workers." The younger generation has a low tolerance for initial years of grunt work and now want to enjoy a rich selection of outside opportunities in their 20s to 30s. In response, their employers start to offer lifelong connections with their alumni—the once rigid walls of lifetime employment are now more porous.

The course of a meaningful career requires a minimum of two actors to synchronize: the protagonist and the environment. In Matsumoto's case, both changed significantly over the two decades of her career, which was spent abroad. She matured professionally through years of working for financial institutions on America's East Coast. Japanese companies also have modernized their thinking in how to welcome diverse talent, as I analyze in my column, "Gender Equity Is Coming to Japan's Workplaces." Reflecting that the Japanese companies—looking at Matsumoto as a female master's degree holder at the "late" age of 25—failed to offer her a starting position let alone access to a global career in finance, both Matsumoto and Japan Inc. have come a long way.

Chikako Matsumoto, Executive Officer and Head of the ESG Strategy and Solutions Office at Sumitomo Mitsui Trust Bank (SMTB)

1963: Born in Osaka, Japan, where her father ran a family business of industrial fasteners

1985: Graduated from Sophia University with a degree in French literature

1985–1986: Studied at Institut des Hautes Etudes Européennes in France aided by a Rotary Foundation scholarship

1988: Graduated from Hitotsubashi University with a master's in international relations

1988: Started her career at the Japan office of Indosuez Asset Management

1989: Returned to Osaka to work at the family company

1992–1994: Attended and graduated from Harvard Kennedy School, obtaining a master's in public policy

1994: Joined the Inter-American Development Bank (IDB) in the US

2001: Joined the World Bank as a senior financial officer

2018: Joined EY Japan as an associate partner

2020: Joined Sumitomo Mitsui Trust Bank (SMTB) as the head of the ESG Strategy and Solutions Office

2022: Promoted to executive officer at SMTB

2023: Promoted to executive officer at Sumitomo Mitsui Trust Holdings

Chikako Matsumoto, World Bank Alum, Thrives at Japanese Trust Bank

This article was originally published in the Japan Times *on June 13, 2023, and has been modified for the purpose of this book. The information contained in this article is correct at the time of publishing in the* Japan Times.

Chikako Matsumoto, executive officer at Sumitomo Mitsui Trust Bank (SMTB), spent her Osaka childhood during the go-go era of economic boom times in Japan. When she graduated from a Tokyo college in 1985, the economy was on the cusp of entering a four-plus-year-long bubble, which gave the nation a false impression that the only way forward was up.

After Japan slipped into decades-long deflation when the bubble burst in 1991, Matsumoto spent much of her working years in Washington, DC, observing her homeland from afar, until she finally returned to a much-changed country first in 2010 through a leave of absence from the World Bank, and then permanently in 2014.

Her story invites multiple interpretations. One interpretation is that of social mobility: her parents, who worked their way up from nothing by managing a small workshop, Matsumoto Nut Manufacturing, gladly financed their eldest daughter's higher education, which enabled her to achieve a career in international finance.

Another is about a quiet determination: Matsumoto decided early on to make an impact through international finance and doggedly followed her calling. Or it could also be about a value-driven career; after supporting developing nations through international development finance at the World Bank, she is now turning her attention to making an impact on sustainability through finance at SMTB.

The most interesting narrative to me, however, is in the decades-long dynamic of push-and-pull between Matsumoto and Japan, during which both transformed. She exited Japan in the early 1990s, when women with a master's degree were largely unwelcome at Japanese workplaces due to their age. However, throughout her career in Washington, DC, now and then, a gravitational pull toward her roots would tug her sleeve in the form of an ailing family member.

Eventually, she would be homebound, with an American husband in tow. The Japan of the 2020s, much more embracing of competent women, gave her space to further build on her success. The long-distance relationship between Matsumoto and her home country concludes with a happy ending.

"I Am Grateful for the Past Generation"

"My late father hailed from the poorest family in his village and could graduate only from a middle school in Osaka," Matsumoto matter-of-factly recounted of her parents' background. "My mother was also from a humble working-class family."

Borrowing the seed money from relatives, her father started a small machine shop for industrial fasteners in 1953.[1] The family business grew in tandem with the Japanese economic ascent of the 1960s and 1970s, increasingly exporting its products. "Growing up, I lived in an economic environment that radically changed just over the course of a single generation, my own," described Matsumoto. "This got me interested in economic development of countries." Contrary to her parents, who had to make do with only a basic public school education, Matsumoto attended a private girl's school and held no doubts about advancing to college.

The seed of independence was planted early. "My mother, who cared about women's societal stature in general, encouraged me to be economically self-reliant," Matsumoto said. Seeing her father's struggles with the export business to the US—anti-dumping lawsuits against cost-competitive made-in-Japan products were prevalent against Japanese exporters—the young girl was impressed with the importance of law and language. "From elementary school days, I vowed to go abroad," she recalled.

Finding Her North Star, Sadako Ogata

Matsumoto chose to enroll in 1981 in Sophia University, a prestigious private college in Tokyo. The school had a high reputation for language education, and she chose French literature. There, she met her lifelong role model, the late Sadako Ogata (1927–2019), a high-profile as well as glass-ceiling-breaking diplomat in Japan. Ogata held the office of United Nations High Commissioner for Refugees from 1991 to 2000 and later served as president for the Japan International Cooperation Agency from 2003 to 2012.

In 1981, Ogata had just returned from her mission at the UN as Envoy Extraordinary and Minister Plenipotentiary. "Her lectures were thoroughly rooted in real-world experiences, not textbooks," Matsumoto reminisced. Inspired by Ogata, Matsumoto started considering the UN and the World Bank for her own career.

"Professor Ogata was of course in a totally different league [from mine]," she was quick to add, referring to Ogata's elite family background. Ogata's father was a career diplomat; her mother was granddaughter of Prime Minister Tsuyoshi Inukai, assassinated in 1932 due to his opposition to the rising militarism of Japan. "Nevertheless, Professor Ogata was my inspiration who shaped and personified my dream," Matsumoto remembered.

While at Hitotsubashi University, a top-league national university known for its liberal arts, where she would earn an MA in international relations, Matsumoto also studied at Institut des Hautes Etudes Européennes, Universite de Strasbourg III, (now Institut d'Études Politiques de Strasbourg) aided by a Rotary Foundation scholarship in 1985–1986. "It was tough," she recounted these years candidly. Not only was all the study material in French, her second foreign language, the French institution emphasized historical studies tracing back to the political philosophies of the 17th century. "It taught me that now is never absolute," said Matsumoto, "which is humbling." The time in Strasbourg also instilled in her the quality of life enjoyed by the French, which would counterbalance the American preoccupation with efficiency to which she would be exposed in later years.

Convinced she would like to contribute directly to society, as did Ogata, Matsumoto had decided to pivot from academia. The then-25-year-old found employment at the Japan office of Indosuez Asset Management, thinking it would be a step toward an international organization—"in those days, Japanese companies shunned women over the age of 25 with master's degrees." (See Figure 11.1.)

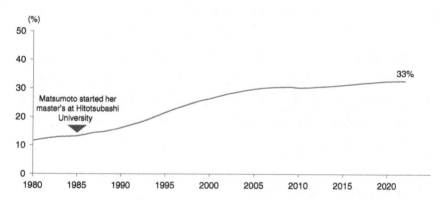

Figure 11.1   Proportion of female students in graduate universities in Japan (%)

Notes: Women with graduate degrees in the 1980s were rare, making up only 13% of total graduate students when Matsumoto started her master's.
The data includes master's students, doctorate students, and professional graduate school students.
Adapted from Ministry of Education, Culture, Sports, Science and Technology (2023). Basic School Survey. https://www.mext.go.jp/b_menu/toukei/chousa01/kihon/1267995.htm (accessed 4 June 2023).

However, her first employment did not last long, as her family in Osaka beckoned her. Her father had a recurrence of cancer and needed her to come back. On return to Osaka, Matsumoto worked to support the company in cleaning up its financials, cost accounting, and negotiating loan terms for export finance—she recalled with a chuckle in my recent interview how she toiled in the accounting department. "I was up to my neck with the nuts and bolts of cost accounting." Given her aspirations, "staying here for a long time would not be a great situation," she told herself. She knew she had to earn an education in an English-speaking country to enter the World Bank, which became her focus as a career destination.

In 1992, after spending three years working for the family business, Matsumoto eventually found her way to the World Bank via Harvard Kennedy School in Cambridge, Massachusetts, where she majored in public policy. She recounted the environment at Kennedy School as "very competitive—even among students, it was more about getting ahead than anything else."

That said, she also learned over time that the comments made by her fellow students in the class—Harvard Kennedy School employs the case method—are not "always right answers. They were masters of concocting logics and stories on the spot." She took to heart the art of communication.

Career in International Finance

The master's degree from Harvard Kennedy School gave Matsumoto an entry ticket to the professional world of development finance in the US. The starting point was the Inter-American Development Bank (IDB), where she worked from 1994 to 2001, eventually as a senior finance officer in Washington, DC, responsible for financial analyses and planning and risk management for the IDB. She started as a short-term consultant to be promoted to full-time after about a year.

The IDB, which some people call the Amigo Bank due to its affinity with Latin America, is much smaller in size—2,000 staff members of which the majority are of Latin American and Caribbean origin—compared to the World Bank's over 15,000 staff members. Working in a smaller international organization had an unexpected upside; it exposed her directly to the heat of political dramas.

"At the IDB, I witnessed the real face of international politics," commented Matsumoto. In 1998, she was an IDB lead financial analyst to support the negotiations for new funding of concessional finance operations. Beneath the surface reported by the media, the individual negotiation between the US, the largest shareholding country, and Brazil unfolded for months, in the middle of which she found herself receiving calls almost 24/7 including direct calls from the US Treasury Department. "I saw the underbelly of glitzy international politics," recalled Matsumoto.

As her profile rose at IDB—"the top management started recognizing me"—Matsumoto "realized that your internal network does impact your outcome. And making sure that people recognize your achievements is important," a lesson she took to her next stage, the World Bank.

In 2001, after seven years at IDB, Matsumoto acted on a friend's tip to interview for a senior financial officer role at the World Bank to finally realize her long-term career aspiration inspired by Ogata. Getting into the World Bank is notoriously competitive—"for every open position, we receive 400–500 CVs," explained Tenzing Sharchok, who is currently the lead financial officer of derivatives and structured finance at the World Bank and was Matsumoto's colleague during her tenure from 2001 to 2014—"Chika was technically smart and came with the [IDB] experience."

More than technical competence, it was the humane side of Matsumoto that made a lasting impression on Sharchok. He described her prominent characteristic as "having wisdom," which was "different from knowledge or experience." Matsumoto's wisdom, Sharchok surmised, came from somewhere deeper, her spiritual world view, which enabled her to have compassion and patience for people—"I was always surprised at the level of patience Chika had."

Although Sharchok tentatively associated Matsumoto's wisdom with Buddhism, I suspect that her upbringing, which coincided with the steep economic ascent of Japan, may have affected her outlook on life; the sense that she owes her present to the huge endeavors of her parents and their generation at large, and that the present moment, however prosperous it may be, is perpetually fleeting.

Matsumoto's wisdom, according to Sharchok, manifested itself in her lifestyle. "She was very aware of how she lived, reflecting her values." Her eventual pivot to focus on climate change and sustainability, Sharchok and I discussed, may be an outcome of deep care for the environment and future generations.

Meanwhile, the World Bank impressed Matsumoto with its diversity—"you work with people from all countries in the world"— and its high degree of professionalism. (See Figure 11.2 for a view of the regions where the World Bank staff are from.) "The accumulation of intellectual prowess as an organization is a source of great advantage for the World Bank," described Matsumoto. "The World Bank has been well positioned in understanding various risks associated with doing business in developing countries, which gives them an edge to manage projects and its loan portfolio better." Matsumoto was proud to "create something new," such as financial products tied to natural disasters or green bonds during her tenure.

Within the small Washington, DC, community of professional Japanese people, Matsumoto stood out. It was about 2000 that Toshihide Endo, former commissioner of the Financial Service Agency (FSA) from 2018 to 2020, who now serves post-FSA as senior advisor to a few Japanese blue-chip corporations such as Sony, met with Matsumoto at a CSIS seminar. From 1998 to 2002, Endo was

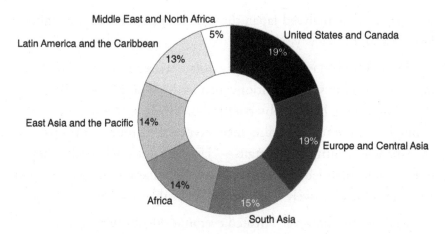

Figure 11.2   Breakdown of the World Bank staff by region, 2015 (%)

Notes: The World Bank is a highly diverse organization, with staff from all over the world.

The data includes all staff members globally.

Adapted from The World Bank (2015). Where Is Our Staff From? https://www.worldbank.org/en/news/infographic/2015/10/27/where-is-staff-from (accessed 4 June 2023).

seconded from the Ministry of Finance, which FSA would spin off from in 2000, to the International Monetary Fund (IMF) as deputy director of the Asia and Pacific department.

In the seminar Matsumoto raised a question from the audience— "at first I never imagined she was Japanese," recounted Endo to me in an interview, "as she presented herself so well in English." Harvard Kennedy School days and subsequent years of working at international organizations had clearly honed her communication style.

Later, on learning that she was Japanese, Endo invited Matsumoto to a group email exchange with 10–20 fellow Ministry of Finance secondees, codenamed *Group J*, to discuss a variety of topics from developmental aid to pension problems in Japan. Matsumoto played a key role in the group, impressing Endo with her insights that analyzed Japan through US perspectives. The online group lasted for a few years.

Endo found Matsumoto clearly differentiated from the typical Japanese local hires at institutions such as the World Bank. "They are an interesting breed," observed Endo. "Their individualism is so strong to the point of breeding incoherence as a group unified by the Japanese identity." Such traits—"Japanese don't help each other out"—Endo analyzed, allowed Indian and Chinese colleagues to band together more effectively to act on behalf of their nations.

Matsumoto, however, "treated everyone equally with respect, whether they be a civil servant secondee like me or another local hire," according to Endo. "She was both humble in spite of her track record and was yet totally comfortable with herself."

"Years spent at a progressive workplace such as the World Bank helped my mental development," recalled Matsumoto. There was little ethnic discrimination and much less consideration for gender. "What shocked me in the early days in the US was that women could be strong [and that it was considered a good thing]," she said. "When a female friend told me that I was strong as a compliment, it stuck in my mind."

Working abroad immersed in a different culture affects one's perspectives regardless of the duration. "Even if it was a short four years that I spent in DC, the American lifestyle changed my perspective," recalled Endo. "On return to Tokyo, I refused the life solely dedicated to the Ministry and moved my family to Karuizawa, a resort town 150 km from Tokyo, to raise our two kids born in DC." That working hard is not incongruous to fully enjoying your private life is what he took away from observing his fellow American professionals at the IMF.

Homecoming

In DC, Matsumoto had met her husband, Rob, a US Navy officer, whom she married at the end of 2008. "Finding the right partner is so important, especially for career women," stressed Matsumoto. "Like many other women, I have also had my dating history, through which I learned the hard way that a man one is attracted to and a man with whom one wants to build a life together may not be the same."

However, there was a sliver of overlap in her romance Venn diagram in which she ultimately found a husband. Through marriage, "I learned to balance work and life, both of us making compromises at times," she reflected.

It was the marriage that triggered her return to Japan—Rob was reassigned to Japan in 2010. Although she took a leave of absence from the World Bank, Matsumoto continued to work as an independent consultant, hoping eventually to return to DC and pick up where she left off.

Life threw a curve ball then, which tied her future more permanently to Japan. Her mother's health deteriorated. "It was now harder to return to DC," according to Matsumoto. About the same time, Rob had decided to retire from the military and found his next career opportunity in Japan.

Professionally, her interests in developmental finance had never been about pure finance, but rather about solving social issues through finance. "Climate change had become a hot topic. Living in the US for a long time, I had been concerned with the extremeness of capitalism—the [wealth] inequality was so dire that the underprivileged population seemed to no longer be treated as decent human beings," Matsumoto said. She was interested in working with the private sector to benefit multiple stakeholders beyond investors—employees, society, and the environment.

In the late 2010s, ESG was much debated by the management class in Japan as well as by investors. "I wanted to understand how large Japanese corporations operated," explained Matsumoto about her rationale for applying to work at EY Japan, one of the Big Four professional service firms in Japan, in 2018. I was her colleague in this brief period, although in a different service line.

Making an Impact from Japan

Matsumoto had not worked for more than two years at EY Japan, where she "learned that logic alone does not cut it at Japanese clients," when SMTB, a blue-chip trust bank at the heart of the world's oldest business consortium, *zaibatsu*, tapped her on the shoulder via an executive search firm to head their ESG strategy and solutions office.

When Matsumoto shared with me the news of moving to SMTB, I was skeptical of how well she would fit into a traditional Japanese organization typically known for rigid hierarchy and conservatism. I could not have been more wrong. "SMTB was full of pleasant surprises," Matsumoto told me. "The management gives me a big canvas with autonomy and is fast in decision-making."

Shigeki Tanaka, executive officer of Sumitomo Mitsui Trust Holdings, the parent company of the trust bank and deputy president of SMTB and Matsumoto's direct supervisor, is proud that SMTB has been pioneering ESG since 1999 among Japanese financial institutions.[2] What started small as managing a corporate social responsibility (CSR) fund expanded in scope to include sustainability finance and consulting on the Task Force on Climate-related Financial Disclosures (TCFD). In Matsumoto they found someone who knew green finance—from the World Bank—and consulting—from EY Japan.

"Her ability to breakthrough and execute" was Tanaka's answer when I asked him what he appreciated most about Matsumoto. "Years of survival in the tough professional environment of the US must have formed her," he speculated. "Backed by finance knowledge and her global network, she can persuade the organization, though compliance-heavy and risk-averse, effectively with a sense of balance."

One such example is the investment in Breakthrough Energy Catalyst,[3] a fund launched by Bill Gates to invest in innovative green-tech projects that use key emerging climate technologies such as green hydrogen and sustainable aviation fuel. What excited Matsumoto was the unique mechanism of the fund to play its namesake Catalyst role in leveraging private funding and working with governments—by providing the capital "we wanted to learn its mechanism," she explained. Through the trust bank's internal contact, she accessed Breakthrough Energy, which never searched for investors openly. It took her six months to make a business case within SMTB, starting with her own team.

"We were late to the game," confessed Tanaka, "and we were first routed to the second close." Matsumoto did not let up, however. "It was her game from there," recalled Tanaka of the negotiation. Her pitch on behalf of the bank to the Breakthrough Energy management was convincing enough so that SMTB was able to secure a position in the first close as an exception.

It made SMTB the first Japanese financial organization to participate in Catalyst, and the second Japanese organization in addition to Mitsubishi Corporation. Prior to the transaction announced in late November 2022, Matsumoto was invited as a panelist at the Breakthrough Energy Summit as well as one of the two Japanese guests invited to a private dinner hosted by Bill Gates.

Matsumoto also works as a talent magnet for SMTB. What started as a four-person ESG strategy and solutions team when she joined grew to 16 staff members during her tenure of three years. "Beyond expectations" is how Tanaka described her achievement in fortifying her team. It also helped that SMTB always had a reputation for respecting meritocracy and welcoming mid-career hires since 1985.

The sustainability talent pool in Japan is small. Matsumoto recruits through her own network both financial and nonfinancial talent—Kaori Miyake, formerly sustainability officer at Aeon, the largest retail chain in Japan with ¥9 trillion operating revenue,[4] is one such example who joined SMTB at the personal encouragement of Matsumoto.

"At SMTB, we put sustainability at the heart of our strategy," Tanaka told me. "Beyond lending [to green business], we offer investors a full spectrum of opportunities in sustainability finance." To this end, they need experienced hires with expertise—Matsumoto is the center of gravity, whipping up a virtuous cycle of recruitment and reputation.

Of the team of 16, 5 are women including Matsumoto and Miyake, both of whom were promoted to executive officers at the bank after about a year or so of their joining. "It is only natural that competent women take leadership now that it is about working smart rather than hard," observed Tanaka, "Men tend to be hierarchical and read the room too much. Women, by contrast, lead better even without authority and senior men are happy to let them."

If women's audacity is a survival skill linked to their minority status, we agreed that their advantage may be temporary as the gender ratio is gradually balanced. But for the time being, why not bank on it? It is clearly working out for both Matsumoto and SMTB who hired her.

Is there jealousy within SMTB for her steep ascent? "Maybe there is, but I am too busy to bother," laughed Matsumoto. "There is so much to do." For her, continuing to work is important in the context of raising women's status in Japan. And doing so for the next generation is very much on her mind.

"A third of the reason why I work is for the next generation," she recounted, pointing out how important it is for her to build an environment for her team to keep growing on. "Another third is for myself. And the final third is for the previous generation before me."

Although Matsumoto shaped her career at IDB and the World Bank, her working-class family roots with the fasteners factory in Osaka never left her consciousness. In an alternate universe, where she never achieved escape velocity from the orbit of her family business, she could be presiding over the family business out of Osaka today, no doubt with considerable success. In real life, she proved herself in a world-class professional environment in DC, always with compassion for the underprivileged, until Japan became her domicile of choice again after two decades spent on the East Coast.

During her absence, Japan had also changed considerably for the better for working women. "I wouldn't be surprised if we were talking about the need for affirmative actions to promote more men into management in the future," Tanaka, Matsumoto's boss, said with a smile. "When it is no longer about working around the clock [which advantaged men], we find our women to be so competent."

The combination of local Zeitgeist—much more accepting of competent women in senior positions than the 1990s when she left Japan—and the progressive employer she found in SMTB allows her to spread her wings. "I used to have a nagging sense that I ran away from Japan without putting up a good enough fight," Matsumoto told me. "But now I made peace with the fact that I went overseas."

Japanese Companies Can No Longer Expect Lifetime Loyalty from Workers

This column was originally published in Nikkei Asia *on April 3, 2020, and has been modified for the purpose of this book. The information contained in this article is correct at the time of publishing in* Nikkei Asia.

In Japanese companies, lifetime employment for a fresh cohort of graduate recruits was an implicit part of the social contract; each company believed loyal company men were the essential ingredient of the enterprise's success. But now that part of the social contract is fraying.

Take the large trading companies. They still rank high as popular destinations for graduates from top schools. Yet their middle managers lament, with an air of disbelief, that 20-somethings are freely forgoing the prestige to join start-ups instead.

A CEO of a major trading conglomerate said in 2018 that 30% of new joiners from college left a top-league peer within five years. This is consistent with the government statistic that the three-year attrition rate for college hires has risen to 25% for the class of 2016, up five points from the class of 2009.[5]

Why do millennials leave enviable blue-chip employers? First, compared to their predecessors, they have much less patience for the first years of apprenticeship baked into the career of a traditional Japanese company. Grunt work, once a rite of passage to becoming a full-fledged manager, no longer interests the generation used to the instant gratification from a Google search.

Then there are ample external opportunities. Technology giants, start-ups and foreign professional service companies all compete for the young, well-educated workforce. They promise a much steeper learning curve.

From young employees' perspectives, more options are better. No longer are you bound forever by the choice you make at the age of 22, which used to be true for those on the job-for-life track at Japanese companies.

For their employers, this is an inconvenient truth. Some tweak career progression to offer a better compensation track as a sweetener; others threaten leavers that there will be no place to come back to, should their next venture fail. This is, however, a systemic issue that requires a systemic solution.

First, companies need to reassess the need for grunt work. Twenty years ago, the task of efficiently making photocopies with the staple at a 45-degree angle in the upper-left corner may have been good mental, if not meaningful, training for white-collar work. But so much manual operation can be replaced by technology today.

What inhibits real change is the mentality of the senior management of Japanese companies. For example, one prestigious business insists on running a parallel process of digital authorization and a paper twin version, just in case any senior executive is uncomfortable with a digital signoff, to the exasperation of the staff members. Modernizing operations not only enhances productivity but also would be welcomed by workers.

Second, employers should snap out of the "don't leave me" threats-and-pleading mentality of clingy lovers. If increased talent mobility is a given, it is more productive to think of how to use its power.

Sumitomo Corp., one of the six largest trading conglomerates or *keiretsu*, started the SC Alumni Network, or SCAN, last year to maintain and strengthen ties with those who left.[6] Granted, the idea of building a web of affiliates is nothing new to the trading companies. Their executives have always been dispatched from the parent to keiretsu companies to foster the network effect.

What is new is that Sumitomo has expanded the concept to the 20- and 30-somethings who leave for opportunities outside the keiretsu. This benefits not only the parent company but also the alumni who support each other in the next chapter of their career.

Finally, the employer should recognize the benefit of talent mobility by making the most of mid-career hires. While mid-career hiring has become the norm, Japanese companies are not good at integration.

This is because the traditional upbringing of a manager in a Japanese company assumed the mechanism of *doki*, or a single cohort of graduates entering the workforce in any one year. They are a source of information about internal politics for each other and keep members appraised of the bigger picture. Similar to a cohort in the Swiss army, they stick together through thick and thin.

The mid-career hires without the benefit of a doki, therefore, can be disadvantaged. Structured mentoring and integration programs need to overcome this handicap. If mid-career hires succeed based on a culture of meritocracy, it is positive news to aspiring junior staff members. After all, if the outside comes to you, why bother to go outside?

I can sympathize with incumbent management griping over the loss of their grip on their up-and-coming employees. The generation now in power, who are in their late 50s to 60s, equated their individual identity with that of the employer. But that was only natural because in their junior years the employer was growing, along with the Japanese economy. With that assumption no longer true, we must accept the new reality.

But we gain while we lose. The longevity of employees also meant that grievances stewed in Japanese organizations. Not only harmful to the day-to-day morale, they can blow up in an unpleasant way and hurt the company, just as toxic gas in a steel can might suddenly explode the whole thing.

In the new world of increased mobility, we may have less of a cozy community, but we can instead enjoy meritocracy and openness.

Gender Equity Is Coming to Japan's Workplaces

This column was originally published in Nikkei Asia *on May 28, 2023, and has been modified for the purpose of this book. The information contained in this article is correct at the time of publishing in* Nikkei Asia.

The statistics for gender equity in Japan are sobering.

Japanese women occupy a mere 13% of managerial positions in the private and public sectors,[7] according to government figures, the lowest among the Group of Seven nations. The World Economic Forum's global gender gap index consistently snubs Japan, placing the country at a lowly 116 out of 146 countries last year.[8]

Patriarchal culture, with embedded gender stereotypes, has been long identified as a culprit with no apparent antidote.

The outlook, however, is not so gloomy. We may be standing at the threshold of a new era in Japan, in which it will simply be the norm for women to build a career on equal footing with men, thanks to three tailwinds: workstyle reform, increased paternal involvement in childcare, and rising gender neutrality.

Women, though, must be their own change agents to capitalize on this momentum. The progressive employers who let women do so will benefit from their leadership.

Japanese workers, especially women, are already being liberated from the constraints of presenteeism. Measures the government launched in 2019 as part of a policy of work reform[9] have taken effect at unexpected speed with the normalization of remote work. The trend has led to a hybrid workstyle for many since the lifting of COVID-19 control measures.

A senior Japanese bank executive in his late 50s recently reminisced how in his younger days, he worked day and night, often through the weekend. Back then, macho toughness was a prerequisite for career success. Now that it is much less relevant, he said, women are thriving on producing value-added output through a more flexible workstyle.

At the same time, there is increased pressure on working fathers to be active participants in child-rearing. With Prime Minister Fumio Kishida describing Japan's declining fertility rate as an existential threat, the sense of urgency to involve fathers has been heightened.

It has been long known that skewed child-rearing responsibilities sitting on mothers' shoulders force young women to confront a binary choice of a full-time career or motherhood, ultimately putting downward pressure on the fertility rate.

With the recognition that fathers' participation in child-rearing is key to breaking this binary paradigm, societal norms are changing. Paternity leave is becoming increasingly common. A survey by the Ministry of Health, Labour, and Welfare found that in 2021, 14% of new fathers took paternity leave, compared to just 6% in 2018.[10]

Finally, there is an undeniable cultural undercurrent of gender neutrality that is dismantling the foundations of gender-based segregation.

Japan, with its traditionally patriarchal culture, is a tightly wound coil, primed to pop. Although gender-neutral fashions, including makeup for men, are at the forefront of this trend, some gender-based customs are already unwinding.

Valentine's Day in Japan no longer evokes confessions from women to men. It is now a celebration of gender-agnostic friendship. Japanese schools are increasingly introducing trousers as a uniform option for girls, even if skirts for boys are yet to become an alternative.

The shift toward a more balanced environment is great for the upcoming generation of women. But more senior women, the next-in-the-pipeline leaders, are also positioned to experience the benefits. While Japan is in a transition period, they possess the advantage of being leaders from a rising minority. Because they have always been outsiders to the world of men, Japanese women can lead the room without excessively reading the room.

"Men are inherently attuned to the hierarchy," said the banker. "Minding the presence of their seniors, they become tongue-tied." Women, however, are less hierarchical, relying on their often-superior communication skills to get their messages across, in his view.

Now that we have more women in the professional world, however, the zone of acceptance is wider. We can be both respectful and impactful. Smart use of this minority advantage can create a virtuous cycle, with more competent women rising to senior positions and the corporate world encouraging the trend. This has already been set in motion by corporate governance reform.

As a thought experiment, we may wonder what would happen if women were no longer a minority in the workplace beyond the middle ranks or if gender neutrality became dominant. Our outsider instincts might diminish, and our collective identity could be diluted; Japanese women's minority advantage that allows them to lead the room would evaporate.

But by such a time, I hope that Japanese men will be liberated from the rigid pyramidal structure that stifles active debate across cohorts. In other words, the feminization of men should result in better-quality discussion—a win for both genders. The wheels are in motion. The lifetime employment system is fast crumbling, challenging seniority-based pyramids.

"Soon, we will be talking about introducing a male quota for gender ratios in management to ensure diversity," the banker half-joked. This may seem preposterous given Japan's track record, but gender equity is already emerging at the starting line; 46% of Japanese college students in 2022 were women, according to government figures.[11]

Building on women's current minority advantage, a force to be multiplied by strong societal tail winds, we may well be standing at an inflection point leading to gender equity in Japanese workplaces.

References

1. Matsumoto Nut Industries. (2023). Company profile. http://www.matsumoto-nut.co.jp/company/index.shtml#01 (accessed 16 June 2023).

2. Sumitomo Mitsui Trust Holdings. (2023). ESG investment. https://www.smth.jp/english/sustainability/Initiatives_achievements/esgi (accessed 16 June 2023).

3. Breakthrough Energy. (2023). Breakthrough Energy Catalyst. https://breakthroughenergy.org/our-work/catalyst/ (accessed 16 June 2023).

4. AEON. (2023). Financial highlights. https://www.aeon.info/en/ir/finance/highlight/ (accessed 16 June 2023).

5. Ministry of Health, Labour, and Welfare. (2021). 新規大卒就職者の事業所規模別就職後 3 年以内の離職率の推移 (Translation: Job turnover rate within 3 years of employment of new graduates by size of company). https://www.mhlw.go.jp/content/11800000/001006119.pdf (accessed 29 June 2023).

6. Sumitomo Corporation. (2019). 「SC Alumni Network」の設立および第一回総会の実施について (Translation: The establishment of the SC Alumni Network and the organization of its first meeting). https://www.sumitomocorp.com/ja/jp/news/release/2019/group/12450 (accessed 29 June 2023).

7. Gender Equality Bureau Cabinet Office. (2022). White paper on gender equality 2022. https://www.gender.go.jp/about_danjo/whitepaper/r04/zentai/html/zuhyo/zuhyo01-18.html (accessed 19 June 2023).

8. World Economic Forum. (2022). Global gender gap report 2022. https://www.weforum.org/reports/global-gender-gap-report-2022 (accessed 19 June 2023).

9. Ministry of Health, Labour, and Welfare. (2022). 「働き方改革」の実現に向けて (Translation: Towards the realization of "work style reform"). https://www.mhlw.go.jp/stf/seisakunitsuite/bunya/0000148322.html (accessed 19 June 2023).

10. Ministry of Health, Labour, and Welfare. (2021). Basic Survey of Gender Equality in Employment Management. https://www .mhlw.go.jp/toukei/list/71-23c.html (accessed 19 June 2023).

11. Ministry of Education, Culture, Sports, Science, and Technology. (2022). Basic School Survey. https://www.mext .go.jp/b_menu/toukei/chousa01/kihon/1267995.htm (accessed 19 June 2023).

12 Resilience

Yasuko Gotoh, who started her career in 1980 as the first female career bureaucrat recruited by what was then the Ministry of Transport, is a front-row witness to how Japanese society's attitude toward working women has evolved over the last four-plus decades. It has been a 180-degree transition from women being second-class citizens at the workplace to being heralded as symbols of diversity and, therefore, progressiveness.

Still, the journey toward gender equity at the workplace is far from complete. As I argue in my column, "Japanese Businesswomen Need More Than a Place at the Table," increasing women's presence in senior positions can be interpreted by corporations as an exercise in compliance to satisfy the mere optics of diversity.

That said, the Japan Inc. of 2023, in both its public and private sectors, is a much friendlier place than it was when the Equal Employment Opportunity Act was first enacted in 1985. In these days, Gotoh and her female colleagues at the Ministry had to double as office waitresses, preparing tea in the morning and pouring alcohol at night.

But the turnaround of the external environment alone does not explain Gotoh's eventual success in honing her career in the tourism industry. Against considerable headwinds, she demonstrated resilience over the years—never quitting work and always being open to the next opportunity.

The sources of her resilience can be summarized in two parts. One is her innate openness to trust those around her—her faith in people translates into her caring leadership style and her willingness to help others.

The other is her accumulation of broad experiences. As a career bureaucrat Gotoh was thrown into a series of assignments, even including such diverse situations as handling an international maritime crisis at the Japan Coast Guard involving a North Korean vessel. Self-doubt can be an impediment to career progression for a variety of reasons—for young Gotoh, the main culprit for self-doubt was the misogyny, which she naively mistook as a product of her own shortcoming. The antidote to self-doubt is rough and tumble in tough assignments, as I analyze in my piece, "Employers Should Encourage Risk-Taking to Beat Imposter Syndrome."

Gotoh's career began with an initial dark period but steadily acquires a lighter hue thanks to her resilience and the rising changes of the world around her. It resonates the aphorism, "what doesn't kill you makes you stronger."

Yasuko Gotoh, Former Career Bureaucrat at the Ministry of Land, Infrastructure, Transport and Tourism (MLIT)

1958: Born in Aichi Prefecture, Japan

1980: Graduated from the University of Tokyo with a degree in law

1980: Started her career at the Ministry of Transport (now MLIT) as the first female career bureaucrat recruit at the ministry

1997: Moved to Kyushu as general manager of the planning department at Kyushu District Transport Bureau for a year

2001: Appointed as international crisis management officer at the Japan Coast Guard (JCG)

2004: Moved to New York as the head of the Japan National Tourism Organization's New York office

2005: Returned to Japan, as a deputy governor of Yamagata Prefecture

2008: Appointed as the director of Regional Transport Bureau of Hokuriku and Shinetsu regions

2010: Returned to Tokyo and appointed as assistant vice-minister at MLIT

2013: Appointed as director of the Policy Research Institute for MLIT

2014: Retired from the ministry and moved to Kyushu as an advisor of Kyushu Railway Company (JR Kyushu)

2015: Appointed as board member in charge of the Travel Services business

2017: Promoted to chief financial officer at JR Kyushu after its initial public offering

2019: Appointed as external audit and supervisory board member of Shiseido Company, Limited

(*continued*)

2019: Appointed as external audit and supervisory board member of DENSO CORPORATION

2023: Appointed as visiting professor of Kokugakuin

University, Faculty of Tourism and Community Development

2023: Appointed as external audit and supervisory board member of Mitsui Chemicals, Inc.

Yasuko Gotoh Breaks Ground for Women Career Bureaucrats

This article was originally published in the Japan Times *on May 9, 2023, and has been modified for the purpose of this book. The information contained in this article is correct at the time of publishing in the* Japan Times.

Career bureaucrats, particularly those who support the national, as opposed to the regional, administration, embody the core elite of Japan. Although the career's popularity is declining, having been eclipsed by increasingly lucrative offers from the private sector, passing the national exam to work "for the nation" at one of the Government Ministries in Kasumigaseki, the nerve center of Japanese policymaking, remains a respectable aspiration for many graduates from top universities. According to the National Personnel Authority, in 2022 spring, 1,873 candidates passed the Comprehensive Service recruitment examination, representing a pass rate of 12.2%. Of those successful candidates, 30.6% were women.[1]

Yasuko Gotoh is among the first generation of women to enter Kasumigaseki. She joined the then Ministry of Transport, the predecessor to the current Ministry of Land, Infrastructure, Transport and Tourism (MLIT), with a law degree from the University of Tokyo in 1980. Joining five years before the enactment of the Equal Employment Opportunity Act, Gotoh was the first female career bureaucrat to be recruited by the Ministry. "Some male colleagues went as far to denounce in my face that the government had no need for women," recalled Gotoh in a recent interview.

Fast-forward to 2023, Gotoh has followed an illustrious 40-plus-year career in both the public and private sectors with stints in Tokyo, New York, and the regions of Kyushu and Yamagata. Gotoh, now 65, sits on the boards as a nonexecutive director for two Japanese blue-chip companies, Shiseido, a beauty giant with revenue of over ¥1 trillion,[2] and DENSO, a ¥5.5 trillion[3] automotive part conglomerate.

Gotoh is a survivor. Her career is a story of patience rewarded by an unexpected turning point in her mid-40s, after which she slowly learned to spread her wings. It is also a story of redefining femininity in professional contexts from a liability to an asset. Although Gotoh was relegated to second-class citizenship at the workplace in her 20–30s, she found that her collaborative and people-oriented leadership style was highly effective in her 40s and beyond.

The rapid-fire succession of government posts, each associated with obligatory long-distance moves for high-class bureaucrats—Gotoh counts a total of 25 moves in her 65-year life—these helped Gotoh develop a rich stratum of personal connections all over Japan. She continues to cultivate this network and give back to it recreationally with delight to this day.

Traumatic Start: The Ministry of Transport

"I have a blackhole of memory in my 20s and 30s," a straight-faced Gotoh told me. Just as trauma victims instinctively wipe out painful recollections to protect themselves, the headwind against young women career bureaucrats was such in the 1980s that Gotoh instinctively recoils at recalling details from work in her early days.

The number of female undergraduate students from national universities increased slowly during this period, reaching 22% of the undergraduate students in 1980, compared to 19% in 1970, according to government statistics.[4] (See Figure 12.1.) Ministries, then the

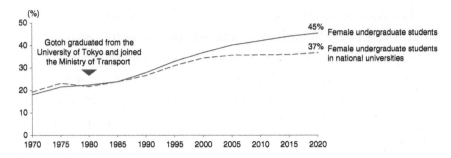

Figure 12.1   Proportion of female undergraduate students in national universities (%)

Notes: Female representation in national universities, which includes prestigious institutions such as the University of Tokyo, is still below 40%.
Data shown for every five years.
Adapted from Ministry of Education, Culture, Sports, Science and Technology (2023). Basic School Survey. https://www.mext.go.jp/b_menu/toukei/chousa01/kihon/1267995.htm (accessed 4 June 2023).

destination for the best and brightest, were gingerly starting to recruit successful female candidates, albeit with a varying degree of eagerness. The Ministry of Labor, whose women leaders were already senior by the time they helped pen the Equal Employment Opportunity Act in 1985, was the most progressive. The Ministry of Transport, however, was a laggard.

Gotoh credibly suspects today that the decision to recruit her in 1980 as the first woman college graduate at the Ministry of Transport, was the outcome of a kitchen table conversation between a political power couple at the time. Mayumi Moriyama (1927–2021), then already a senior bureaucrat at the Ministry of Labor, who later turned into a legendary stateswoman and whose significant cabinet posts included those of Minister of Education (1992–1993) and Minister of Justice (2001–2003), nudged her college sweetheart husband, Kinji Moriyama (1917–1987), then Minister of Transport (1978–1979), to start recruiting women into his Ministry.

"Originally I was thinking of joining the women-friendly Ministry of Labor," Gotoh told me, "but because of behind-the-scenes maneuvering by the Moriyamas, I ended up in the Ministry of Transport. I was full of hope and eager to start my career there."

Every day, large and small aggressions against Gotoh as the sole woman were the norm. "People blatantly told me how the Ministry never meant to hire me [because I am a woman]," Gotoh told me, "and the well-intended advice I received back then was to work twice as hard as the men."

After Gotoh's entry, it took the Ministry of Transport another three years to hire the second woman, followed by another three out of a total of 50 or so entrants per cohort. The interval was subsequently shortened to two years. It was only after 1993 that they started recruiting multiple women every year.

Yuri Furusawa, who joined the Ministry six years after Gotoh as the third generation of women entrants and retired in 2019, also commented on the prevalent gender-based practices of those days. When Gotoh entered the Ministry, female staff members would be required to come an hour before the official work start times to clean the office space and prepare tea for their male colleagues.

After working hours, people would often drink at the office. Women had to pour alcohol for the bosses—"only after they were done drinking and went home did we go back to our desks to do more work. It would be unimaginable today," said Furusawa, referring to both drinking at the workplace and subjugating women colleagues to waitressing duties.

Being the pioneer, Gotoh was an elder sister figure to her fellow women colleagues. Before the Ministry was consolidated with others to become MLIT in 2001, "the 10 or so women who joined the Ministry of Transport really stuck together," explained Furusawa. "The support network started at the top, as Gotoh-san was so approachable and always listened to us," she recalled, "but it must have been so hard for herself being the first one."

Both Gotoh and Furusawa attest that the prevailing view in the 1980s was that women in the workplace were inferior to men, even those holding the same college degree and passing the same national exam. The gender-based division of roles was so strong that almost all the adult women that the male bureaucrats knew were housewives, over whom they harbored an unwarranted sense of superiority.

"I guess the incumbent men felt that women colleagues like us were so foreign," mused Furusawa. "They were inconvenienced because suddenly they were unable to enjoy blokey banter in our presence." Younger career bureaucrats today would find it hard to believe—since 2015, 30% is the required minimum for female recruits per cohort. (See Figure 12.2.)

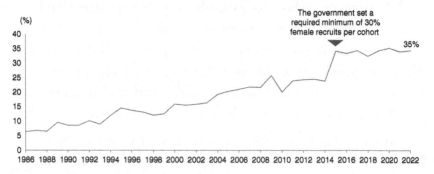

Figure 12.2   Proportion of women recruited to be career civil servants in Japan from the national civil service recruitment examination (Comprehensive Service) (%)

Note: Minimum intake quota of 30% set in 2015 pushed up women recruits into Kasumigaseki.
Created by the author based on: Cabinet Secretariat. (2022). 女性国家公務員の登用状況のフォローアップ (Translation: Follow-up on the status of promotion of female civil servants). https://www.cas.go.jp/jp/gaiyou/jimu/jinjikyoku/files/20220601_followup.pdf (accessed 4 June 2023); Gender Equality Bureau Cabinet Office. (2020). White paper on gender equality 2020. https://www.gender.go.jp/about_danjo/whitepaper/r02/zentai/html/zuhyo/zuhyo01-01-03.html (accessed 4 June 2023).

The in-your-face gender-based discrimination delivered a detri-
mental blow to working women at the time—imprinted in Gotoh's
mind was the impression that no one expected much out of her, a
sense of worthlessness that took her nearly two decades to shake off.

"Things slowly improved, allowing me to breathe again," is how
Gotoh described the late 1990s. Albeit intermittently, with a two- to
three-year cycle, more and more women graduates were trickling in,
diluting the male homogeneity at the Ministry of Transport. As her
seniority rose, Gotoh started meeting people outside Kasumigaseki,
the nerve center in Tokyo where government offices are. "The outside
world saved me from spiraling down into the narrow organizational
silo of the Ministry," she said. A supportive boss reassured Gotoh that
she never needed 10 out of 10 people to like her—he appreciated her
regardless.

Turning Point: Japan Coast Guard

Despite the helpful colleagues, the sense of worthlessness continued
to nag at her. When her next assignment was announced as an international crisis management officer for the Japan Coast Guard (JCG)
after her request to be transferred to Paris had been turned down,
she felt discouraged—"I thought this could be my last post with the
Ministry, after which I'd resign."

In normal times, the crisis management officer leads risk preven-
tion and handles maritime crimes, such as piracy, in collaboration
with overseas JCG equivalents. However, during a crisis, the role of
crisis management officer becomes prominent because they represent
the JCG to other government organizations, including the Cabinet
Office and Ministry of Foreign Affairs, as well as to external media.

Even though her confidence was at a low point going into the
assignment, the JCG experience turned out to be transformational.
First, a few months into her assignment, in December 2001, a mega

event shook Japan: an incident involving a spy ship in the southwestern waters of Kyushu, near Amami-Oshima, an island between Okinawa and Kyushu. During this so-called Battle of Amami-Oshima, an armed North Korean vessel confronted the JCG, which ended in the vessel self-destructing and sinking after the JCG fired in self-defense. The authorities later identified the vessel as a spy craft.

Following standard procedure, the JCG commandant made the critical decision to shoot. The sensation lasted for days in Japan. As crisis management officer, Gotoh was in the thick of it, consolidating intelligence, liaising with the government, and reviewing all media communications.

Salvaging the vessel proved challenging both technically and politically. Negotiation with other government departments as well as China—as the vessel sank in China's Exclusive Economic Zone—ensued, which Gotoh's team was responsible for. "The commandant was determined to expose the criminal act of North Korea, and we patiently took all the steps [toward the extraction]," Gotoh told me. With its weapons and criminal evidence inside intact, the vessel was finally lifted out of the water in September 2002, nine months after the incident.

In the highly tense aftermath of the attack, she found the team on the ground genuinely supportive of her. "The men in the JCG shared a strong sense of justice and wholeheartedly trusted me with my decisions," she recounted. "With my boss, the JCG commandant, appropriately guard-railing my decisions, I was in full command."

Furusawa describes Gotoh's leadership style as the opposite of top-down and macho: "Gotoh-san would encourage staff [members] and always be on their side." The JCG team responded well to her leadership; "the trust was palpable," described Gotoh. Though symbolically feminine, her style was never weak. The incident, Japan's first discharge of weapons on a foreign vessel in 48 years, revealed the state of underground malfeasance by North Korea and shocked the nation.

"On any given day, the unexpected can happen to any of us," emphasized Gotoh, "and through the experience you gain confidence with a bonus of lifelong friends." So unexpected it was that most lifers at JCG could spend their entire career without facing such a national crisis. When she earned the trust of the guardsmen at JCG through her ground-up leadership style, she found that her gender had ceased to be relevant.

"It is rational at JCG where you confront life-or-death situations," said Furusawa, who would come to occupy the same JCG post as Gotoh, as she drily explained the work culture to me. "In the face of crisis, it is only your grit as a leader that matters," and she theorized that the closer to life-and-death situations an organization is, the less gender bias can survive at the workplace.

Gotoh took away a new sense of accomplishment, a taste of teamwork, and a boost in morale from the JCG assignment. Mid-40s, she was finally out of the dark tunnel, and "I started having a positive outlook."

Boomerang: New York to Yamagata

As if to compensate for her rejected transfer to Paris, the Ministry gave Gotoh a post as director of the Japan National Tourism Organization in New York City in 2004. The life of a mid-level career bureaucrat tends to be a succession of two- to three-year assignments, which Gotoh had no objection to; "I have no trouble going where people need me."

Japan was an even rarer destination than today for Western travelers in the early 2000s, well before Japan's inbound tourism surge under the second Abe administration from 2012. "I believed that, rather than taking a blanket approach, Japan should promote many of its unique draws, from arts to nature, to the educated niche audience who understood them," Gotoh explained.

To this end, the bureau she led had American travel journalists and food writers report on the underappreciated gems of Japanese culture. On top of that, Gotoh resorted to guerrilla tactics. "If I come across a downtown gallery featuring Japanese pottery in its window, say, I'd just go in and ask if they would be interested in organizing an exhibition together to promote Japan with us, the Japan National Tourism Organization." Gotoh recalled fondly, "strolling the streets of New York, I was always looking around" for such opportunities.

How effective this casual walk-in approach could be in New York was an eye-opener. "In Japan, especially in the public sector, you would always take steps of formal introduction," Gotoh illustrated, "but in New York I found that you could skip that and still have a reasonable shot of at least reaching the person in charge." The cultural difference also manifested itself in the project execution; in stark contrast to the meticulous construction of top-down budget and plans that Japanese project sponsors expected, the American approach delegated authority to the team on the ground who could think while they ran.

Her stimulating New York days ended abruptly after 16 months. Back at the Ministry in Tokyo, the governor of Yamagata Prefecture, a region in Northeastern Japan with which she had no direct link to, was asking if Gotoh could be one of his two deputy governors, a position governors have the authority to appoint. The lack of gender diversity in politics was starting to be highlighted in Japan, prompting some governor candidates in the 2000s to assign female deputy governors in their election campaigns. Career bureaucrat women, who understood administration and management, were prime candidates.

Did she have a choice to say no, to opt to stay in New York? It would not have been entirely impossible, although "transfers for civil servants are not up to us as individuals," Furusawa explained, "even though in Gotoh-san's case the New York assignment was cut very

short." Gotoh, who had some sympathy for Yamagata because her
paternal ancestors hailed from the prefecture, reasoned that "maybe
[my going to Yamagata] was my late father's wish from heaven."

Compared to New York, Yamagata, where she would spend the
next three years, wound the clock back decades in terms of the professional environment. "It was as if the staff in prefectural government
had never seen a woman in a senior position before," she marveled.
"And the governor, who had pleaded for my assignment, hinted
that I should keep a low profile—I was only deputy governor to be
a symbol."

Frustrated, she spent sleepless nights in the first months. "All day
long, all I did was give speeches at ceremonies and meetings," she
recalled, "and people were shocked if I ever spoke in my own words,
off-script." It took her a while for her to gather herself—if her role
was not defined for her, it was up to her to define it herself.

Gotoh decided that her mission as an outsider deputy governor was to catalyze change. Gotoh invigorated local communities
by breaking silos, both within Yamagata and outside, by organizing
forums for industries through the lens of tourism and hosting networks for local women. "Perhaps invisible to Tokyo, people in the
regions have so much growth potential," Gotoh said, "but if you
remain in a silo, the incumbent force can crush you. You'd need to
offer them a trigger to think outside the box."

Eventually, Gotoh also found a new meaning in her formal
speeches. "Visibility of a woman at the top of the prefectural government encourages fellow women that they can do it, too." One
person was left unhappy, however: the governor. "He was supposedly
annoyed that I outshone him," she sighed. "Why did it have to be a
zero-sum game? I had no intention to run for governor. I could be
commending his leadership if he had let me be. He could have leveraged me rather than try to silence me."

Private Sector: JR Kyushu

Returning to the Ministry in Tokyo after Yamagata, Gotoh assumed several senior positions including director for the Policy Research Institute for MLIT. In 2014, when she was 56, JR Kyushu, one of the seven regional Japan Railway (JR) companies formed out of National Railway's break-up and privatization in 1987, beckoned her. Senior bureaucrats retiring before age 60 is common. The destination is often private sector companies looking for senior talent with intimate knowledge of administration and regulation.

It was Gotoh's second encounter with Kyushu, having previously spent a short stint in 1997 at the Kyushu District Transportation Bureau, which "felt like fate to return to Kyushu after a big loop [of New York, Yamagata, and Tokyo]. Through my close friends working there, JR Kyushu had always impressed me as an upbeat challenger," she recalled.

Having retired from the Ministry, she returned to Kyushu as a board member at JR Kyushu and to lead the Travel Services business, which sells travel packages. Not only was Travel Services far from being glamorous within a railway company, but the unprofitable division also needed a turnaround. "The staff believed that cheaper was better and often sold themselves short," recalled Gotoh, "but there are many upsell opportunities if you can match the customer's need to the value of your offerings."

Gotoh sought to shore up communication skills at the sales counter by giving the staff members, mostly female, opportunities to study the packages and by rehearsing customer–sales clerk conversations. Under her leadership, their first customer relationship management (CRM) system was introduced to improve on personalized marketing—"I had this incredible woman from JTB, the largest travel agency in Japan, seconded to us [to work on CRM]."

Soon, the staff members started feeling love from customers; "customers who enjoyed the recommended travel package would write thank-you letters and drop in with souvenirs," according to Gotoh.

The unprofitability of Travel Services was just cut to a quarter when the Kumamoto Earthquake hit in 2016 and temporarily damaged the outlook on Kyushu tourism, from which Travel Services eventually managed to pull itself out of.

Gotoh also suffered a personal misfortune around the time—in 2017 she was diagnosed with early-stage breast cancer. When information on the internet only confused her, she turned to her colleagues. "The breast cancer survivors among the female staff [members] were very helpful," she emphasized. "They shared their real-life diaries going through the [cancer] experience, which was so much more helpful than the internet."

Gotoh commuted to the hospital and would eventually beat the cancer. "Now I want to give back what I received from these colleagues, who even launched an internal hotline for breast cancer," she said. "I vowed to learn from them, which is why I am talking very openly about my own cancer experience."

After JR Kyushu's initial public offering in 2016, Gotoh was appointed chief financial officer of the newly public company in 2017. However, after two years, the deteriorating condition of her aging mother compelled Gotoh to resign from her CFO role in 2019 and return to Tokyo. The lopsided supply and demand of senior professional women like Gotoh meant that opportunities were and remain abundant; since 2019, she has sat on the board of DENSO and Shiseido as a nonexecutive director.

"I Just Want to Be Useful"

Izumi Kuwano, the second-generation owner-operator of Tamanoyu, one of the most established Japanese inns in the spa resort town of Yufuin, Oita Prefecture in Kyushu, has known Gotoh since 1997. "In the local business community, no one remembers the national bureaucrat [who rotates through a revolving door of local assignments]," she affirmed, "but Gotoh-san was different."

First, Gotoh made a lasting impact in every post she occupied because she focused on developing people. Her effort produced batches of long-term followers from Yamagata to Kyushu. "Everywhere she went, she took care of staff [members], and especially the women," Kuwano said. "Gotoh-san knew how important it was to improve the working environment for women, especially in the outer regions so that they did not have to experience the difficulties that she had fought through as a woman."

Second, Gotoh keeps her contacts activated—"I dwell on the relationships," she laughed. Using her rich Rolodex, she crosspollinates—for example, Gotoh invited Kuwano and her fellow Yufuin business leaders to Yamagata, where she served as deputy governor, to exchange views on tourism with the local Yamagata community—"Gotoh-san made sure to connect Yamagata with the outside network."

Last, Gotoh's vision for tourism, a recurrent theme in the various chapters of her career at the Ministry of Transport, resonates with a progressive resort town such as Yufuin, Kuwano said. Gotoh believes that successful tourism needs to integrate with a thriving local community. From Kyushu to Yamagata, she sought to support local communities to build and promote their unique value from her role in the administration.

The past three decades witnessed an evolution of tourism in Japan—the pivot from group- to individual-based travel for Japanese in the 1990s, the rise of inbound tourism in the 2010s, followed by over-tourism and the post-COVID pivot toward sustainable tourism. "It's as if the times are finally catching up with Gotoh-san," Kuwano attested.

But what about the parochialism of the countryside, I wondered. Wouldn't sexism be worse in Kyushu than in Tokyo? In fact, the red-blooded Kyushu culture is known to be macho. "In 1997, the local business community initially organized a protest against the fact that the Ministry had dared to send a female general manager. They felt slighted by Tokyo," chuckled Gotoh. However, "after one to two months of working together, they apologized," she explained. The episode did not surprise Kuwano. "Countryside people are rather simple after all," she explained. "Once convinced of Gotoh-san's sincerity, they would happily take her side, woman or not."

When I asked her what motivates her to keep going, Gotoh promptly answered that she "wants to be useful to people." In her 20s and 30s, she was doubtful if she was—as "the first woman" at the Ministry, she felt there were few expectations for her performance. However, gaining confidence by the mid-career JCG post and through her vocation of supporting tourism, she started having the sense that she was indeed helping others. From there, there was no turning back from the positive momentum—and the people she met over the different phases of her long career constitute a rich personal asset that she continues to cultivate.

Gotoh never married and has no children. "I was never especially lucky in that department," she said breezily, "but I have a close-knit extended family with my two sisters, nephews and nieces." In truth, being married to a career bureaucrat whose life is disrupted by moves every few years is full-time work on its own, for which very few men would have volunteered in the 1980s or 1990s. Back then, the choice of a full-time career or a family was presented as binary for educated women. "In my case, staying single was a consequence of inaction rather than the result of making an explicit choice not to marry," Gotoh reflected.

Furusawa, six years junior to Gotoh at the Ministry of Transport, had a child. It was not an easy experience—when Furusawa consulted the HR department at the Ministry in 1994 before giving birth, she was told "no one would take a woman after childcare leave." She had to return to work right after her maternity leave. "My milk stopped in two days," she winced, "I managed to cope with support from my in-laws." Today, taking childcare leave of about one year is the norm for civil servants with 100% of women opting to take leave.

A memorable instance for Furusawa in the 1990s was at an after-work party with the higher-ups in the Ministry of Finance (MoF), for whom the four or five women from the Ministry of Transport, including Furusawa and Gotoh, were grudgingly mobilized to entertain. When the senior MoF men, perhaps out of concern over the dwindling cohort of future taxpayers, started reprimanding women without children, Gotoh calmly explained how it was a personal choice—"how she deftly handled the awkward situation was impressive," remembered Furusawa.

"Why did we put up with all that [sexism]?" Furusawa shook her head. The position of career women in 1980s Japan was so nascent that their role in the workplace was only understood as an extension of their role in the home—women poured tea and cleaned. As irrational as it was, it was so baked into the mindset that no one thought about it twice. Women may also have played along, rationalizing that, rather than ruffling the feathers, it was wise to keep their heads down. Many women may have given up on a meaningful career in that way.

Today, under investors' pressure to improve governance, the Japanese government and the private sector is desperate to increase the number of senior women professionals. The oft heard gripe, however, is that the talent pool is too small and that the few who qualify, as does Gotoh, are inundated with board positions. But who can blame the women in Gotoh's generation who, despite their educational pedigree, dropped out early or mid-career from the main stage of the workforce, having had their wings broken by the gender-based aggression at the workplace?

The saving grace of the Ministry is that at least opportunities were equally given to men and women. By contrast, in the private sector, women were often promoted at a much slower speed than equivalent men, a practice still observed in some mid- to small-sized companies today. These opportunities, including the turning point of her posting at the JCG, became Gotoh's career lifesavers; as a survivor, she grabbed them and redefined her femininity as a strength.

Japanese Businesswomen Need More Than a Place at the Table

This column was originally published in Nikkei Asia *on March 27, 2023, and has been modified for the purpose of this book. The information contained in this article is correct at the time of publishing in* Nikkei Asia.

Over the past decade, waves of corporate governance reform have relentlessly pressured the Japanese business world to increase the ratio of women in senior corporate leadership roles.

As of last year, women held 9.1% of the board seats and senior corporate and auditing positions at Japanese listed companies, up from 1.6% in 2012, according to figures compiled by the Gender Equality Bureau Cabinet Office.[5]

Although the upward curve is generally encouraging as a sign of greater gender diversity at work, Japan's two corporate camps both merit a closer look: the majority that satisfies itself with a "diversity of optics," treating women in senior roles as window dressing to satisfy compliance requirements, and the minority that embraces a "diversity of substance," leveraging women's perspectives to improve the workings of management.

The diversity of optics, although marginally beneficial for motivating the next generation of young women—you must see women in management to believe it is possible—treats females as ornamental and thus does little to improve the quality of management.

Only by empowering smart and vocal women can gender diversity contribute to better senior-level conversations. Unfortunately, there are still many cases of companies that aim for nothing higher than optical diversity.

When my friend in a senior corporate position was asked if she could recommend a few female candidates to join the board of her top client as nonexecutive directors, she was delighted. Carefully combing through her Rolodex, she put together an impressive short-list, confident that it would not disappoint her client.

But it did. Weeks later, when she followed up on her referrals, the client's chief executive admitted that none of those interviewed quite matched what his management was looking for. Careful prying by my friend revealed the truth: "These ladies are all too fired up," the CEO said.

Too motivated, these would-be women directors did not fit the bill for the client. In the end, the company was looking for no more than the window-dressing form of gender diversity. But that CEO is not alone in appreciating diversity only at an optical level.

Women, because of their minority status in business, can bring fresh dimensions to an otherwise homogenous group of businessmen. Less encumbered by the mainstream expectations placed on their male counterparts, I have seen many women in professional positions experience career detours, including years spent overseas or pursuing interests outside of work.

When such differences are interpreted as alarming foreignness worthy of exclusion to maintain conventional harmony, we lose the benefit of diversity of substance.

Ironically, men also lose out by refusing to embrace a diversity of substance.

A former deputy prefectural governor, now in her 60s, recently told me how the male governor she served under was uncomfortable with her rising visibility.

"It was abundantly clear that I was never going to run for the governor's office and threaten his position," she mused. "If he let me be, I would be openly praising him for his generous leadership, which could only be positive for him."

But the governor's zero-sum mentality—believing that any positive limelight she enjoyed would be his loss—clouded his vision. He simply wanted her to be present "as a symbol."

It is tempting to belittle this narrow-mindedness as petty insecurity. But the outcome of such subconscious zero-sum calculation is not to be underestimated.

In South Korea, there has been a violent backlash against feminism from some young men who equate women's advancement with a loss of their perceived entitlement.[6] In the Western world, a similar mindset can play out racially in the form of xenophobia toward immigrants.

The urge to neutralize minorities who stick out is innate and strong, so much so that I have seen men, competitive with one another by default, suddenly band together just to sabotage a smart and vocal woman. This is why we must design conscious organizational countermeasures.

At the workplace, formal mentorships for junior and mid-ranking women are a well-known recipe for promoting gender diversity. Although a good match can work wonders, too often mentorships can take on the character of obligatory sessions based on an employer's arbitrary assignment, much like an additional mandatory diversity training meeting.

My best mentor was an invisible hand. Someone higher in the organization who takes a genuine interest in guiding a younger woman's career can shield her from hostility or jealousy at the workplace or at least help her to strategize better. A stealth mentoring program, where matches are not publicized, could be a way to experiment with institutionalizing such a mechanism.

For any woman who has swum against the tide for too long, my advice is to look for an exit and try new waters before you are washed ashore. The prime time of one's career is too short to put up with an environment that underappreciates one's worth. Otherwise, self-doubt can eventually result in a career death spiral.

Fortunately, there are as many, if not more, men who embrace the diversity of substance as those who do not. The trick is to find an environment with a majority who do.

The old business adage "You cannot manage what you cannot measure" can partly explain the overemphasis on a diversity of appearances. Numerical yardsticks, such as the number of women in managerial positions or on a company's board, are certainly useful for measuring gender equity outcomes.

But we must remember that even more meaningful is a diversity of substance, which can be a true enabler of quality discussions and innovation. Blasting past the numbers game, we must appreciate the different perspectives offered by minorities, such as women in business in the case of Japan.

Even with a healthy ratio of women on a board as nonexecutive directors, a thin pipeline of senior in-house female executives should sound an alarm bell for investors and management alike to investigate further. It is time we got past obsessing over diversity just in appearance and take an honest look at ourselves through the lens of diversity of substance.

Employers Should Encourage Risk-Taking to Beat Impostor Syndrome

This column was originally published in Nikkei Asia *on April 30, 2023, and has been modified for the purpose of this book. The information contained in this article is correct at the time of publishing in* Nikkei Asia.

Anthony Bourdain, the celebrity chef famed for his unpretentious culinary travels and witty writing, told an interviewer in 2016, "I feel like I've stolen a car—a really nice car—and I keep looking into the rearview mirror for flashing lights."[7]

The haunting remark, in the context of his suicide two years later, hints at how he likely suffered from impostor syndrome, a common belief among successful people that they will one day be found fraudulent as not being as talented as others assume.

Impostor syndrome was originally identified and studied by the psychologists Pauline Rose Clance and Suzanne Imes in a 1978 research paper on high-achieving women titled, "The Impostor Phenomenon in High-Achieving Women: Dynamics and Therapeutic Intervention."[8]

The condition is now widely recognized as affecting men, too, albeit to a lesser degree. Meanwhile, high-profile contemporary women, ranging from former US first lady Michelle Obama to Sheryl Sandberg, the ex-chief operating officer of Meta, have notably confessed to suffering from it.

It is not just high-profile Western celebrities. Some young bright professionals around me in Tokyo also fall prey to the condition.

In the context of Japan, which honors humility, high self-expectations can breed a subliminal fear of appearing arrogant, further complicating the damage from impostor syndrome. We are in the double bind of being called out for either hubris or for faking it. Japanese women experience this more severely because the culture here particularly extols humility for women.

Individuals can take measures to calibrate self-expectations. With the right support, we can tame, if not altogether banish, impostor syndrome and achieve better inner peace with ourselves.

Randy Capocasale, an engagement manager at EY Strategy and Consulting who previously served as a US Army captain, told me about his serious brush with impostor syndrome as a fresh lieutenant.

"I tried to do things perfectly, but this mindset definitely prevented me from being as decisive or willing to take risks as I should have been," he said. It was not until his second year in the army when he was deployed for combat to Afghanistan that the penny dropped.

"Training is often a guide, but the situation was constantly changing. Everyone had to adapt and make quick decisions as they went along," he said. Only then did he realize that he could lead better by lowering his own bar and that "making his best attempt without hesitation was most of the battle."

The moral of the story is that hands-on practice trumps textbook studies in beating impostor syndrome. Although you may scrape your knees, using your best judgment in the moment lets you "learn to trust yourself," Capocasale said.

Generally, women tend to have a harder time lowering the bar of self-expectation than men do. As Ginka Toegel, a professor at Swiss business school IMD who specializes in leadership development for female executives, told me recently, "Women are unsatisfied with anything less than 100 out of 100, whereas men consider 70 out of 100 to be really good."

Why the difference? According to research studies, the answer may lie in the gendered development of the brain. Some aspects of girls' brains develop earlier than boys' on average.[9] This can favor girls academically.

Indeed, some studies have found that overall, girls achieve better grades than boys.[10] Consequently, compared to boys their age, girls become more used to having a near-perfect score. On the flip side, they remain unimmunized to failures.

Perfect little girls can grow into women fearful of failure as, ironically, the advantage of early development hurts women disproportionately in later phases of life. This can result in women being disadvantaged for promotion. A 2018 LinkedIn study found that women apply for 20% fewer jobs than men and are 16% less likely to apply after viewing a job posting, suggesting that women often hold themselves back unless they check every box.[11]

The early development gap between genders notwithstanding, risk aversion is becoming more common among both young men and women in the developed world, including in Japan. Fewer children per family means more parental attention spent per child. So-called helicopter parents are vigilant about removing foreseeable obstacles from their child's path.

Growing up in this kind of environment, a child, regardless of gender, can fail to develop a full sense of risk-taking. Notably, last year's annual survey of fresh university-graduate hires by Recruit Management Solutions, a Japanese company providing talent development and consulting services, showed that fewer respondents than ever saw being "challenged without the fear of failure" as a priority in their new job.[12]

Employers, partly out of respect for individual choice and partly due to compliance pressure, hesitate to give such young people tough assignments. When playing safe becomes the prevailing guideline for both sides, opportunities for such an employee to test their judgment in the moment become scarce, depriving them of an exercise that can help close the expectation gap between their selves and the world.

On a societal level, the fear of failure is hurtful because it fuels more cases of impostor syndrome and dials down the spirit of entrepreneurialism. We all lose out collectively with less risk-taking, resulting in less innovation over time.

Change, therefore, is needed all around. Although individuals must actively calibrate their unreasonably high self-expectations, a helpful workplace encourages staff members of both genders to fail and learn through stretch assignments.

Conventionally, men often get ahead despite early career failures, which they boast about later as battle scars. They thrive on the philosophy that what does not kill you makes you stronger.

Women, however, typically play it safe for fear of failure. Employers must recognize this gendered trait and be extra careful to challenge women before they slip away from tough assignments. Should they fail, let them learn. When they are back on their feet, why not celebrate these women as we would with men?

Today, impostor syndrome is exacerbated through the fallacy of composition: individuals holding high self-expectations and the system around them—parents, schools, and workplaces—sensitively respecting them out of good intentions. Though it may not progress to the extent of leading to suicidal thoughts as in Bourdain's case, impostor syndrome can weigh heavily on talented individuals' minds and clip their wings before they can fly.

We must recognize that impostor syndrome is a societal malaise, not a holier-than-thou signaling ploy for the already successful. Coming back to a basics-of-life lesson is the best cure: we can grow personally only by being thrown out of our comfort zone and giving it our best shot.

References

1. National Personnel Authority. (2022). 2022 年度国家公務員採用総合職試験 (春) の合格者発表 (Translation: Announcement of successful candidates for National Civil Service Recruitment Comprehensive Service Examination in Spring 2022). https://www.jinji.go.jp/kisya/2206/2022sougousaigou.html (accessed 15 June 2023).

2. Shiseido. (2023). Financial highlights / data. https://corp.shiseido.com/en/ir/library/highlight.html (accessed 15 June 2023).

3. DENSO. (2022). Finance and performance data. https://www.denso.com/global/en/about-us/investors/financial/ (accessed 15 June 2023).

4. Ministry of Education, Culture, Sports, Science, and Technology. (1970, 1980). Basic School Survey. https://www.mext.go.jp/b_menu/toukei/chousa01/kihon/1267995.htm (accessed 15 June 2023).

5. Gender Equality Bureau Cabinet Office. (2022). 上場企業の女性役員数の推移 (Translation: Number of female directors at listed companies). https://www.gender.go.jp/research/weekly_data/05.html (accessed 19 June 2023).

6. *Nikkei Asia*. (2022). South Korean feminism will survive today's reactionary backlash. https://asia.nikkei.com/Opinion/South-Korean-feminism-will-survive-today-s-reactionary-backlash (accessed 19 June 2023).

7. *CNBC*. (2018). How succeeding later in life shaped Anthony Bourdain: "I feel like I've stolen a car." https://www.cnbc.com/2018/06/11/how-succeeding-later-in-life-shaped-anthony-bourdain.html (accessed 19 June 2023).

8. Clance, P. R., & Imes, S. A. (1978). The imposter phenomenon in high achieving women: Dynamics and therapeutic intervention. *Psychotherapy: Theory, Research & Practice, 15*(3), 241–247. https://doi.org/10.1037/h0086006

9. Lim, S., Han, C. E., Uhlhaas, P. J., & Kaiser, M. (2015). Preferential detachment during human brain development: Age- and sex-specific structural connectivity in diffusion tensor imaging (DTI) Data. *Cerebral Cortex, 25*(6), 1477–1489. https://doi.org/10.1093/cercor/bht333

10. O'Dea, R. E., Lagisz, M., Jennions, M. D., & Nakagawa, S. (2018). Gender differences in individual variation in academic grades fail to fit expected patterns for STEM. *Nature Communications, 9*, 3777. https://doi.org/10.1038/s41467-018-06292-0

11. LinkedIn. (2019). New report: Women apply to fewer jobs than men, but are more likely to get hired. https://www.linkedin.com/business/talent/blog/talent-acquisition/how-women-find-jobs-gender-report (accessed 19 June 2023).

12. Recruit Management Solutions. (2022). 新入社員意識調査 2022 (Translation: New graduate recruits attitude survey 2022). https://www.recruit-ms.co.jp/press/pressrelease/detail/0000000377/ (accessed 19 June 2023).

ACKNOWLEDGMENTS

The 12 protagonists featured in this book deserve the primary credit for the book. I thank them particularly for their honesty—it can be hard to reassess your life in front of an interviewer. As one protagonist put it, they inadvertently "opened a box kept close for long." I thank Ayako Sonoda, Chikako Matsumoto, Makiko Nakamori, Mami Kataoka, Masae Yamanaka, Masami Katakura, Miyuki Suzuki, Noriko Osumi, Ryoko Nagata, Yasuko Gotoh, Yuki Shingu, and Yumi Narushima for their courage and for generously spending time with me.

I would like to particularly thank Ryoko Nagata, who appeared in the first *Japan Times* article under "Women at Work." Not only did she agree to be our first guinea pig but she also generously introduced me to three other protagonists from her personal network: Noriko Osumi, Yumi Narushima, and Masae Yamanaka.

Sculpting their profiles would have been impossible without the insights of those surrounding the protagonists. I was fortunate to speak with many people whom the women identified as being influential in their career. I appreciate them all taking time out of their busy schedules to revisit their relationship with the protagonists and to share their thoughts with me.

My colleagues at EY work as a wonderful team, supporting me in my writing endeavors. I am indebted to my fellow partner in the Perth office, Vincent Smith, who recruited me into EY in the first place, for encouraging my writing from the day I joined the firm. Thank you for your thoughtful feedback and for believing in the power of writing.

Randy Capocasale, an EY senior manager based in Tokyo, is my original co-conspirator in concocting the idea for the *Japan Times* "Women at Work" series, which forms the basis of this book. Randy also kindly and patiently edits my drafts.

Miri Yasuda, another EY consultant based in Tokyo, painstakingly proofreads and fact-checks all my articles with hawk-like attention to details. Her grace and professionalism impress every protagonist and interviewee she interacts with.

Sharon YX Shen, an EY consultant based in Shanghai, gives thoughtful feedback to everything I write. Her constant moral support is invaluable.

I would like to also express my sincere gratitude to Jonathan Mak, Simon Chau, and Daiki Hayashi for providing background research, fact-checking, interview assistance, and most of all, for keeping me honest and motivated. Without you, I would never have finished this book.

The EY corporate team, including brand, marketing, and communications (BMC), have always provided support in the background for editing. My special thanks to Peter Wesp, Hideharu Fujimori, Ed Kuiters, Kyoko Wada, and Harumi Saito. Megumi Umeda, responsible for diversity and inclusion at EY Japan, provided her support from the early days for the book project.

This book is largely based on my contributions to two media platforms, the "Women at Work" series featuring 12 women for the *Japan Times* and opinion columns for *Nikkei Asia*. I am grateful for the support of the editors at these institutions; Jordan Allen and Takashi Yokota at *Japan Times*, and Stefan Wagstyl, Josh Spero, Jason Koutsoukis, and Zach Coleman at *Nikkei Asia*.

Professor Ginka Toegel from IMD, where I attended a strategy and leadership course in 2014, never hesitated to share her insights at my request, which enriched a number of these articles.

Writing these personal stories about the 12 protagonists made me reflect on my own career as well, the majority of which I have spent as a management consultant. I have the great fortune of having had many mentors over the years. A few senior partner colleagues at my previous employer, A.T. Kearney, particularly come to my mind for encouraging me to write even though it fell out of the scope of consulting: Otto Schulz, Mark van Weegen, and John Kurtz. Without their support, I would have abandoned writing long ago.

These stories particularly resonated with me when the women reminisced about the strong influence of their mothers, who taught them to be independent. I am too grateful for my parents, who instilled in me during my early childhood the importance of hard work. Writing requires patience, and in my case a constant balancing act with my other duties as an EY partner.

When my spirit was low, my close friends and family were cheerleaders for my writing, which kept me going. It is my hope that this book will be a small token of appreciation for your love and support.

The views reflected in this book are the views of the author and do not necessarily reflect the views of the global EY organization or its member firms.

INDEX